KW-481-339

MICRO-MUSIC

LIVERPOOL INSTITUTE
OF HIGHER EDUCATION
LIBRARY
WOOLTON ROAD,
LIVERPOOL, L16 8ND

Also available in the Papermac Computer Library:

Women and Computing: the Golden Opportunity
by Rose Deakin

How to Buy Software: the Master Guide to Picking the Right Program
by Alfred Glossbrenner

Logo on the Sinclair Spectrum
by Graham Field

Maximize your QL
by Susan Curran and Ray Curnow

MICRO-MUSIC FOR THE FOR THE COMMODORE 64 AND BBC COMPUTER

GARY HERMAN

MACMILLAN

LIVERPOOL INSTITUTE
OF HIGHER EDUCATION
THE MARKLAND LIBRARY
Accession No. 94691
Class No. 789.9
HER
Catal. C.Ult 31/10/85 S.M.

Copyright © Gary Herman 1985

All rights reserved. No reproduction, copy or transmission of this publication may be made
without written permission. No paragraph of this publication may be reproduced, copied or
transmitted save with written permission or in accordance with the provisions of the Copyright
Act 1956 (as amended). Any person who does any unauthorized act in relation to this publication
may be liable to criminal prosecution and civil claims for damages.

Series consultant: Ray Hammond

First published 1985 by
PAPERMAC
a division of Macmillan Publishers Limited
4 Little Essex Street London WC2R 3LF
and Basingstoke

Associated companies in Auckland, Delhi, Dublin, Gaborone, Hamburg, Harare, Hong Kong,
Johannesburg, Kuala Lumpur, Lagos, Manzini, Melbourne, Mexico City, Nairobi, New York,
Singapore and Tokyo

Typeset by Bookworm Typesetting
Printed in Great Britain by The Pitman Press, Bath

British Library Cataloguing in Publication Data

Herman, Gary
    Micro-music for the Commodore 64
    and BBC computer.
    1. Music—Data processing   2. Microcomputers
    I. Title
    780'.28'5404 MT723

ISBN 0-333-37675-7

Contents

Introduction

This book is meant for those people with some programming skill and little or no experience of music or acoustics. I would be more than happy if musicians also found it useful, because the interaction between them and computers can be immensely fruitful.

Contrary to popular opinion, the computer is neither a major threat to human values nor the saviour of civilization. It is a tool, an instrument in every sense of the word – quite miraculous because of its versatility, but neither better nor worse than any versatile creature, animate or inanimate.

Some uses to which computers are put are menacing, others are boring, but several enrich our lives. Musical use is one of these last – not because the computer will make the musician's work easier, a proposition as difficult to defend as the idea that computers will herald the age of the so-called paperless office (anybody who has seen inside even a small computer installation knows they eat paper). No, computer music is potentially enriching because – in the guise of the home micro – it brings a contemporary art within the reach of a whole new group of people, who may find in computer composition and performance what they have failed to find in the violin or the piano: a means of expression.

I have attempted to make this book both practical and easy. The programs are all written in BASIC; they are there to illustrate the text, and to provide practical examples and material with which to experiment. There are also some programs that I hope will simply delight.

The book concentrates on two computers, the BBC model B and the Commodore 64. At the time of writing, these were the only machines that combined musical capabilities with widespread popularity. The scene, as ever, is changing rapidly, with peripherals, software, MSX and MIDI daily growing in number or influence.

Since the book deals with many of the fundamentals of sound synthesis and musical composition, I hope it will remain useful to people for some time to come. Unfortunately, various dialects of BASIC tend to differ markedly in areas like sound and graphics; it would have been ridiculous to try to cover every approach to sound generation available. I have tried not to duplicate programs too much for the BBC and Commodore, hoping rather that owners of one machine might be inspired to translate programs into their BASIC. In any case, not every program has a direct equivalent – but the ideas are universal. I have tried to deal with them in general terms. I can only hope the reader finds them useful.

I should like to thank Nick Holmes for providing me with the program included in Appendix 1, in which he reserves all rights. I should also like to mention the work of Jim Butterfield, Bruce Bayley, Peter Gerrard, Ian Waugh, Jim McGregor and Alan Watt, which I found stimulating. As noted throughout the book, no program is so good it can't be improved upon. Please improve on mine.

Finally, I'd like to thank all my friends – too numerous to mention – for not letting this book preoccupy them as much as it did me. And I'd like to dedicate it to my mother, bless her.

1

Sound, music and computers

Pythagoras discovered the simple numerical relations of what we call musical intervals. A tuned string will sound the octave if its length is halved. Similarly, if the length is reduced to three-quarters we obtain a fourth, if to two-thirds a fifth. A fourth and a fifth together make one octave, that is $\frac{4}{3} \times \frac{3}{2} = \frac{2}{1}$. Thus these intervals correspond to the ratios in the harmonic progression $2:\frac{4}{3}:1$. It has been suggested that the three intervals of the tuned string were compared to the three ways of life [trade, soldiery and philosophy − G.H.]. While this must remain speculation, it is certainly true that the tuned string henceforth plays a central part in Greek philosophical thought. The notion of harmony, in the sense of balance, the adjustment and combination of opposites like high and low, through proper tuning, the conception of the mean or middle path in ethics, and the doctrine of the four temperaments, all these go back in the end to Pythagoras' discovery. . . . It is very likely that the discoveries in music led to the notion that all things are numbers. Thus to understand the world around us, we must find the number in things.

Bertrand Russell, *Wisdom of the West*

Although best remembered for the theorem that bears his name, Pythagoras' single most important contribution to humanity has surely been this unifying notion of mathematical harmony. It underlies all of our (western) science and most of our art. The idea that proportion and order are at the heart of all things, that qualities are but the perceptible face of quantities, is so deeply ingrained in us that it comes to the mind almost as an instinct. All the more curious, then, that the computer – the most eminent of mathematical instruments – should have gained a popular reputation as an enemy of the arts and a dehumanizing monster: a thing of dry calculation, of bills and payrolls and inventories.

Since almost the earliest days of computing, the monsters have been used to investigate and produce music. Precisely because music and mathematics are so intimately connected, the computer readily became an instrument of musical analysts and musicians themselves. And because a computer's ability to manipulate numbers is in theory unlimited, it is in theory the most versatile and unrestrained of all musical instruments – capable of mimicking and surpassing an entire orchestra in complexity, or a single flute in purity.

Those who condemn the computer as science's vilest champion in an imagined battle between science and art are usually those who know the least of science and the least of art. To understand how a computer can make music, it is necessary first of all to know what music is. All of us know what numbers are – even when we don't understand them. But music . . . well, all of us are bath-tub singers and music listeners. We understand music (or some of it); but do we know what it is?

First of all, music is sound – a phenomenon we experience as physical vibrations, most often through the medium of our ears. But not all vibrations are sound and not all sound is music. To be sound, a physical vibration has to be heard (or, at least, hearable). It must not be too fast or too slow; it must not be too small a vibration and it must be transmitted or transmittable to the ear through some medium. For the most part, the medium is air, which picks up the vibrations of a sound source and transmits them by itself vibrating. Other media work as well as, if not better than, air – water and bone being among the most familiar.

A curious property of sound is that vibrations which are not themselves audible often have effects on audible sounds. Discrimination in hearing changes from one species to another, from one member of one species to another, and from one member of a species at a certain age to the same member at a different age. Dogs, for example, can hear faster vibrations than human beings; while the older you are, the worse your hearing is.

All the same, certain conventional limits have been set on audibility. *Frequency* is the word used to describe the speed of a vibration. It is measured in units called Hertz (shortened to Hz). One Hertz is one complete vibration every second. A complete vibration can be considered a movement in one direction followed by an equal movement in the opposite direction. Almost all vibrations consist of such cycles of movement repeated over and over. One cycle per second (c.p.s.) is the same as one Hertz. It is conventionally considered that vibrations with frequencies outside the range

20 Hz to 20,000 Hz (or 20 KHz) are inaudible to human beings. The limits of human hearing are 20 Hz to 20 KHz.

The size of a vibration is called its *amplitude*. This can be thought of as the amount of energy in the vibration (although the relationship between amplitude and energy is more complex than that suggests). If a vibration is within the range of audible frequencies, then there is a close connection between its amplitude and the loudness of the sound it produces. (Low and high frequency sounds generally appear to be quieter than middle-range frequency sounds of the same amplitude.)

Loudness is a perceived characteristic of sound and is not simply proportional to amplitude. It seems to be a feature of human hearing that it discriminates on the basis of logarithmic change. For loudness to double, amplitude must increase almost sixfold. The range of audible amplitudes is enormous; the loudest sound discernible without pain has an amplitude a million times greater than that of the quietest sound humans can hear. In order to deal with this amplitude range, the decibel (or dB) is used. The quietest sound discernible is given the conventional value 0 dB. An increase of 3 dB represents a doubling of sound power (measured in watts). An increase of 6 dB represents a doubling of the amplitude of a sound. The maximum amplitude is conventionally considered to be 120 dB; 1 dB represents the smallest difference in amplitude that a human being can detect; 0 dB is very, very quiet, while 120 dB is very, very loud.

Having determined what constitutes a sound, we have yet to decide which sounds are musical.

The nature of music

Musicologists may argue for ever about the definition of their chosen subject of study. The only easy answers to the question 'What is music?' are the wrong ones: music is what musicians produce; music is anything written by Beethoven or the Beatles; music is Mantovani or Marvin Gaye.

At one extreme of the debate is an argument that music is any sound somebody wants to hear, be it bird-song, breaking glass or Boy George. At the other extreme is the argument that music is a sequence of regular sounds obeying strict rules of melody, rhythm, harmony and counterpoint – often predictably so. The first definition is too loose to be of any practical use to those wishing to make music, and the second definition is too restrictive to allow innovation, creativity or even the Blues (which broke the rules).

For most practical purposes, music has to have some regularity, but regularity alone is not enough. In some situations a buzz-saw may be considered musical; usually it is not. A single note played with no variation is extremely regular, but it tends towards tedium rather than music.

The introduction of regularity as a criterion begs the questions of how much regularity, what sort of regularity and in what context. We take it for granted that the sounds readers intend to produce on their computers will be wanted and musical from that point of view, even if they extend no further than elaborations on *zap, bang, pling!* Regularity is a question of the processes and characteristics that structure sound in order to achieve a desired end: a sound which dies away rapidly; a sound which makes people who hear it want to get up and dance; a sound which surprises, startles, consoles or comforts.

The computer offers unparalleled control over musical processes and characteristics, once we understand how structure can be represented in terms of number. Stand-alone microcomputers are still limited as performing or composing instruments, especially when compared to high-speed, high-capacity mainframes. But micros have the advantage of widespread availability. They show the way and, more than that, allow everybody with an elementary grasp of numbers and a little programming skill to become a composer and performer. They make music easy.

Electricity in music
Those who argue that the computer and the music it produces are 'artificial' overlook the plain fact that every musical instrument – since people first fashioned a primitive trumpet from a ram's horn – has been artificial. Even the art of singing has been learned from manufactured instruments. 'Natural' music may exist as bird-song and in some hidden corners of the world, but the rest is artificial. The essential differences between the sackbutt and the synthesizer lie in the quality of the artifices, the context of each instrument's use and the technology and culture which produced it.

Every new technology creates new opportunities. Art, as the repository of the creative and challenging, often grasps these opportunities from the sheer excitement of novelty. For music, the first big change since the arrival of the symphony orchestra came with the introduction of electricity into the concert halls.

There have been two broad, and not entirely independent, trends in the development of 'electric' music from the beginning of the twentieth century. The first used electricity to improve or adjust the sounds of existing music. This trend saw the introduction of microphones, amplifiers, electric guitars, tape recorders, hi-fi, rock'n'roll and, ultimately, the whole panoply of the modern recording industry.

The second trend used electricity as a means of tearing music apart and rebuilding it – from scratch, if possible. Well before the outbreak of World War II, there were a number of new instruments in existence, intended to create sound never before heard, to synthesize familiar sounds from basic 'raw materials', or to do both.

Instruments like the teleharmonium, the trautonium and the theremin met with some success as objects of curiosity for music listeners and as vehicles for experimentation by avante-garde composers. Even primitive electrical sound generation allowed a high degree of control over musical parameters – combined, in many cases, with an almost other-worldly purity of tone. The combination was attractive to musicians influenced by the pervasive early-twentieth-century mood of formalism and modernism. However, these early instruments were too primitive to survive much beyond the span of curiosity and experimentation – although the eerie tones of the theremin, especially, may be familiar from science fiction and suspense movies of the fifties and early sixties.

The theremin illustrates many of the problems with the new electric instruments. Its tones took the form of a continuous whistle produced by the player positioning his or her hand at varying distances from the instrument. The instrument utilized the capacitive effect of the hand (as do some contemporary touch switches) but although the sound produced was rather like that made by a musical saw, the theremin (along with many other instruments of its time) was too unlike any conventional instrument to be readily acceptable to musicians. The most successful early 'synthesizers' were more conventional looking keyboard instruments, particularly the famous Hammond organ.

Rapid developments in electronics during and just after World War II allowed the development of more audacious machines than the musical curiosities of an earlier generation. With real-time performance dominated by successful and relatively simple amplification techniques, the burden of sound synthesis fell to scientists and composers with the time and motivation to research the field and develop their ideas.

The scientists became involved because the financial interests of the telecommunications industry were well served by an investigation of signal-processing techniques. It was also said that some record and radio companies had the quaint notion of entirely automating music production, thus ridding themselves of the necessity to pay living musicians.

The work on sound synthesis was concerned to study what happened when sound was converted into electrical signals and back again into sound, as on a telephone line or during a radio transmission. A number of machines were constructed in order to identify and manipulate the significant characteristics of a sound. Among these was the first digital sound instrument, the Vocoder.

The Vocoder is still in use today as a device for creating effects using voice and music. Its origins lay in the telephone scramblers of World War II; it worked, essentially, by transforming voices into digital pulses for transmission over telephone lines. Although machines like the Vocoder had a powerful and lasting impact on sound synthesis, the big step forward didn't really come until RCA introduced the Mark II Electronic Music Synthesizer in the early fifties.

This machine used computer techniques developed in the forties. Punched paper tape (like a pianola roll) fed it all the information necessary to synthesize a sound, coded in binary form and read by metal brushes making contact through the holes. The EMS was immensely flexible and capable of fine resolution of sound parameters (8 bit micros, as a rule, can operate only with a resolution of one part in 256, while the RCA machine, having no data bus, had a theoretically infinitesimal resolution). Its main drawbacks were its operating speed and power consumption (it was a valve machine), the limited number of channels which had to be repeatedly programmed to build up complex sounds, and the tedious programming procedures.

For leisurely analysis and synthesis of sound, the EMS was invaluable. It demonstrated the theoretical advantages of using programmable machines to synthesize sound. But if RCA intended to use the machine for the commercial production of music, as has been suggested, they were disappointed.

Another approach to programmed sound synthesis was successfully tried some years later. English composer Daphne Oram's 'Oramic' graphic synthesizer extended the principle of movie soundtrack operation. The device was programmed by drawing masks on to perforated film strips, which were drawn across banks of photocells. The system responded to digital information – encoded as strategically placed single dots determining, for example, frequency – and to analogue information – encoded as an opaque shape moving across some photocells and determining, say, note duration. Individual parameters could easily be altered on the Oramic, and the system was fast to program and easy to use. However, its hybrid nature and the use of hand-drawn masks ensured that the Oramic was more acceptable as a teaching machine than as an instrument for composition and performance.

In any case, big digital computers were coming into their own. Just around the corner lurked Robert Moog with his synthesizer.

The synthesizer
The earliest Moog synthesizers were completely analogue devices, played in real-time using a standard piano-type keyboard. The particular key struck determined the frequency of the synthesizer's output tone. Other parameters were controlled by use of potentiometers or through a patching system. The Moog was one of the first electronic devices to make full use of silicon-based components (transistors, in the first instance). Silicon components allowed the manufacture of circuits which could be easily and reliably controlled by inputting a specific range of voltages. Voltage control enabled inventors like Moog to link up oscillators, amplifiers and filters in virtually any desired combination so that any one could be used either to control, or to provide a signal input to, another. A voltage controlled oscillator (VCO), for example, could be controlled by setting an appropriate potentiometer; it, in turn, could provide a signal to a voltage controlled amplifier (VCA) or be used as the source of a control voltage for the VCA. In this latter case, the VCO's output could be used to introduce a vibrato in the VCA stage. The system was

modular, flexible and almost noise-free. All the same, the first Moogs were monophonic instruments, capable of playing only one note at a time. For that reason they were commonly used as studio instruments; complex pieces were built up by tape multi-tracking (recording a number of synchronized monophonic sequences on separate tape tracks).

Perhaps the best-known early Moog performance was Walter (later, Wendy) Carlos's 1969 LP, *Switched-On Bach* – although the Monkees had featured Moog synthesizer on their albums two years before. Carlos's record reproduced some familiar pieces by J. S. Bach played entirely on Moog. The record was hugely popular and demonstrated that synthesized music need not stray too far from commonly accepted notions of what music was.

By the time record buyers were beginning to hear about synthesizers, digital synthesis using computers was well established in laboratories and among composers. During the sixties, the musical use of computers evolved along three parallel but connected paths. At the beginning of the decade, a great deal of work was done in developing music composition systems and direct synthesis techniques. Sometime later, the computer made its entrance as a device for controlling external synthesizers and discrete digital or analogue synthesis modules.

Among the best-known music composition systems was Hiller and Baker's MUSICOMP, introduced in 1963. Like other composition systems, MUSI-COMP is effectively a program to aid and, to a degree, automate the arduous process of writing original scores. Lajean Hiller, MUSICOMP's co-author, worked closely with the avant-garde composer John Cage. The earliest successful direct synthesis system to be implemented on a computer was Max Matthews and Joan Miller's MUSIC IV, developed at Bell Laboratories a little after MUSICOMP. In 1968, Matthews and Miller – along with two others – produced an improved version, the famous MUSIC V.

Largely because of the high cost of computer time in the sixties, early direct synthesis techniques were not completely direct; the penultimate stage of synthesis fed a digital output to a tape.

Direct synthesis works on the principle that any sound can be represented as a graph of amplitude (or, crudely, volume) against time. A simple vibration can then be shown (as it would be on an oscilloscope) as a simple shape repeating in a train. The whole train is a soundwave; the shape is a waveform; and one waveform is one cycle. When a sound is converted into an electrical signal – by use of a microphone, say, or a record-player cartridge – amplitude is transformed into voltage. It is possible to sample the signal voltage and store the results as data in a digital computer. If enough samples are taken quickly enough, the original signal can be reconstituted by outputting the data *in the order in which it was stored* to a fairly simple device called a digital-to-analogue converter (or DAC). The DAC converts numbers into voltages, and the resulting sequence of voltages (if graphed) reproduces the shape of the original soundwave. The voltages can then be used to drive a loudspeaker, and the original sound will be heard.

Direct synthesis simply omits the first couple of stages in this process. Instead of sampling an existing sound, data is produced by a series of calculations. Such data then represents the shape of a wholly imaginary soundwave, which can be realized by a DAC with an audio output. Completely new sounds, as well as any familiar one, can be produced. MUSIC IV and MUSIC V stored their data on magnetic tape. It was necessary only to play the tape through a DAC to produce the synthesized sound.

Direct synthesis is a slow process even for a mainframe. There is usually a great deal of number-crunching to be done. But it is the most versatile method of sound synthesis possible. A hybrid form, deriving from the use of minicomputers to control external synthesizers, can approach this versatility on a micro.

MUSYS, installed by Peter Zinovieff in a recording studio in London in the early seventies, was one of the first hybrid types of digital sound synthesizers. It combined compositional software, some direct synthesis techniques and control of external electronic musical instruments and audio devices. In a highly simplified form, this sort of system has been embodied in many contemporary microcomputers. What made such a technological stride possible was the development of the microprocessor and of single-chip sound synthesizers through the seventies and early eighties.

The BBC uses a Texas Instruments 76489 synthesizer chip, while the Commodore uses a Mostek 6581 Sound Interface Device (SID). Both are extremely powerful (particularly the SID) – if not early Moogs, then at least electronic organs in tiny dual-in-line packages. Like some of the other topics touched on in this chapter, they will be taken up again (see Appendix 3). Combined with the BASIC sound commands implemented in the BBC and Commodore, these chips – under microprocessor control – form the basis of respectable music systems, equally at home as compositional aids, real-time instruments and the hearts of elaborate sound synthesizers.

2

Repetition and regularity

The simplest form of computer tone generation, as typified by the BEEP command on the Sinclair Spectrum, involves directly switching a transducer from a register or ordinary memory location. The transducer might be a piezo-electric buzzer (as on the Spectrum), a loudspeaker (as on the Lynx) or – stretching the definition of 'transducer' a little – the sound circuitry of your television (as on the Aquarius).

The process typically involves setting up a delay loop and a counter. The delay loop controls the rate at which pulses are sent to the transducer, so controlling the eventual frequency of the note produced. A 2 byte delay loop allows a range of 65,535 frequencies. The delay loop waits to send a pulse to the transducer for a period determined by the 2 byte number. Each time a pulse is sent the counter is decremented by one until it reaches zero, when the process stops. In this way the counter effectively times the sound.

This is not the place to go into the fine details of BEEP commands. At present, it is important to note only that even this crude form of music production is far from simple. It involves a surprisingly complicated relationship between two of the fundamental parameters of all sound: frequency and duration. The key concept which unites both these parameters is *time*.

Every sound is an event, i.e. every sound takes time. Since musical sounds display, by our definition at least, a degree of regularity, they can be thought of as defining their own time. The units are not seconds or minutes, but the cycle of each single vibration. A musical sound, then, is merely the audible record of its own passage.

Conventionally, however, we set a standard by which we can judge something of the quality of a sound. That standard is clock-time; using it, we can measure the duration of a single vibration. This measurement, in seconds (in practice, usually milliseconds), is called the period of the soundwave. The inverse of the period of a wave is its fequency; if you multiply period in seconds by frequency in Hertz, the result is 1.

Apart from the period, there is another measurement of duration important in music: the length of a note. A single note is the simplest piece of music possible. If you divide the duration of a note (D) by its period, the result is the number of cycles in the note. You would get the same result by *multiplying* duration by frequency.

Here is a program, for the BBC model B, to perform frequency and duration calculations simply (the principle can be adapted quite easily for the Commodore since the calculations are so simple).

```
    10 REM FREQUENCY/PERIOD/DURATION CALCULATO
R,BBC,G.HERMAN 1984
    20 CLS:PRINT"PLEASE INDICATE WHICH PARAMET
ERS YOU WILL ENTER"
    30 INPUT"FREQUENCY(1) OR PERIOD(2)";A
    40 IF A<1 OR A>2 THEN 20
    50 INPUT"NUMBER OF CYCLES(1) OR DURATION(2
)";B
    60 IF B<1 OR B>2 THEN 20
    70 IF A=1 THEN A$="FREQUENCY":B$="PERIOD":
C$="SECOND":X$="HERTZ"
    80 IF A=2 THEN A$="PERIOD":B$="FREQUENCY":
C$="HERTZ":X$="SECONDS"
    90 IF B=1 THEN D$="NUMBER":G$="DURATION":F
$="SECOND"
    100 IF B=2 THEN D$="DURATION":G$="NUMBER":F
$="CYCLE"
    110 I=0:CLS
    120 PRINT"ENTER ";A$:INPUTC:D=1/C:PROCDEC:I
FH=1THEN120
    130 PRINT:PRINT"ENTER ";D$:INPUTE
    140 IF A=B THEN D=E/C ELSE D=E*C
    150 A$=D$:B$=G$:C$=F$:C=E:X$="":I=1
    160 PROCDEC:IFH=1THEN130
```

```
  170 PROCAGAIN
  180 DEFPROCDEC
  190 H=0
  200 IFC>999999THENPRINT"TOO LARGE":H=1:ENDP
ROC
  210 S$="S"
  220 IF D<0 THEN D=-D
  230 IF D=1 THEN S$="":T$=""
  240 IF D<1 THEN S$="":T$="OF A "
  250 IF I=1 THEN T$=""
  260 E$=STR$(D)
  270 IF INSTR(E$,"E")=0THENU$="":GOTO340
  280 IF RIGHT$(E$,1)="1"THENU$="TENTHS  "
  290 IF RIGHT$(E$,1)="2"THENU$="HUNDREDTHS"
  300 IF RIGHT$(E$,1)="3"THENU$="THOUSANDTHS
"
  310 IF RIGHT$(E$,1)="4"THENU$="TEN-THOUSAND
THS "
  320 IF RIGHT$(E$,1)="5"THENU$="HUNDRED-THOU
SANDTHS "
  330 IF RIGHT$(E$,1)="6"THENU$="MILLIONTHS"

  340 PRINTA$C;X$'B$"="LEFT$(E$,INSTR(E$,"E")
-1)" "U$T$C$S$
  350 ENDPROC
  360 DEFPROCAGAIN
  370 PRINT:INPUT"AGAIN (Y/N)";AN$
  380 IF LEFT$(AN$,1)="Y"THEN RUN ELSE END
  390 ENDPROC
```

PROGRAM 2.1

A note can be any chosen length – from one period to an indefinite amount of time. A crude musical piece can be constructed just by running a number of different notes together. Such a piece can be completely specified by a series of number pairs (if we assume volume to be constant and therefore irrelevant); each pair effectively represents *two* durations: period and note duration. Hence the use of two registers in BEEP commands and the like.

The BBC micro's ENVELOPE command includes a feature allowing you to string three notes together in one command. Without going into details, here is a program to do that.

```
    10 ENVELOPE1,100,0,16,12,1,1,1,127,0,0,-12
6,126,126
    20 SOUND1,1,53,60
```
PROGRAM 2.2

The BBC Model B command assumes a first note and then tells the
computer what changes to make to it in order to arrive at the two next notes.
Unfortunately there is no simple way of doing this on the Commodore 64.
Any routine would just have to play three successive notes in the ordinary
way.

By inserting the programs in loops, a sequence of notes can be repeated.
While the notes have the specified durations, the result is sometimes known
as an arpeggio. Rock and jazz fans may prefer to describe it as a riff. The effect
of shortening the notes is obvious and provides a good demonstration that
note duration as well as period or frequency has a dramatic effect on the
quality of a musical sound. If the notes are very brief and the frequency
changes are small, the effect begins to resemble the phenomenon known as
vibrato (of which more later). This short program for the BBC allows you to
experiment with note sequences.

```
    2 CLS
    5 INPUT"PITCH NUMBERS 1,2 AND 3: "A,B,C

    6 INPUT "TEMPO (0-127)"T
    7 INPUT "DURATION (0 TO 255)"D
   10 ENVELOPE1,T,0,B-A,C-B,1,1,1,127,0,0,-12
6,126,126
    20 SOUND1,1,53,D
```
PROGRAM 2.3

One of the most powerful tools at the musician's disposal is the rest. A rest
is simply a period of silence between notes. It can be thought of as a note of
zero frequency and, like any other note, it can have a duration. A rest can be
thought of as a note whose length is much less than its period. Here is a
program for the BBC (which is much faster than the Commodore) that allows
you to specify duration and period for three notes. Try experimenting by
setting period greater than, equal to or less than note duration.

```
   20 REM NOTE USE OF ARRAYS TO STORE NOTE DA
TA
   30 REM AND THE FORMULA FOR OBTAINING BBC P
ITCH NUMBER FROM A FREQUENCY (LINE 160)
   40 REM THIS FORMULA IS ACCURATE WITHIN LIM
ITS, BUT YOU SHOULD BE CAREFUL WITH THE PARAM
ETERS
   50 REM ESPECIALLY SINCE THE PERIODS YOU SH
OULD SPECIFY MUST BE MORE THAN 1/20TH SECOND
FOR THE DEMONSTRATION TO WORK
   60 REM WHICH MEANS YOU ARE LOOKING AT FREQ
UENCIES BELOW THAT WHICH THE BBC CAN HANDLE
   70 REM IN FACT, THE LONGEST PERIOD THE BBC
 CAN COPE WITH IS ABOUT 8 OR 9 THOUSANDTHS OF
 SECOND
   80 REM YOU CAN JUST ABOUT OBSERVE HOW THE
MUSICAL QUALITY OF SUCH A NOTE DISAPPEARS AS
DURATION APPROACHES PERIOD
   90 MODE0
  100 DIM D(3),R(3),F(3),P(3),DD(3)
  110 FOR X=1 TO 3
  120 PRINT"ENTER DURATION AND PERIOD "X'" IN
 SECONDS (MAX. 12 SECONDS DURATION)"
  130 INPUT D(X),R(X)
  140 F(X)=1/R(X)
  150 DD(X)=D(X)*20
  160 P(X)=4*(LOG(F(X)/124))/(LOG(1.0596444))

  170 NEXT
  180 CLS
  190 PRINT "PERIOD                 FREQUENCY  PIT
CH-NO  ACTUAL DURATION (SECONDS)"
  200 FOR X=1 TO 3
  210 Y=4+2*X
  220 P=SGN(INT(P(X)))*INT(P(X))MOD256
  230 PRINTTAB(0,Y)R(X)TAB(14,Y)F(X)TAB(25,Y)
P;TAB(40,Y)D(X)
  240 NEXT
  250 REM: ADD A LOOP HERE TO SEE THE EFFECT:
FOR Z=1 TO 1000
  260 FOR X=1 TO 3
  270 SOUND X,-15,P(X),DD(X)
  280 NEXT
```

```
290 REM: NEXT (SEE LINE 250)
300 INPUT"AGAIN (Y/N)";AN$
310 IF LEFT$(AN$,1)="Y"THEN110
320 END
```
PROGRAM 2.4

Sine and pulse waves
So far all this assumes that musical vibrations are very regular and very repetitive. In fact, the ideas can be generalized, but the simplest form of micro music does tend to conform to our assumption. Most books tell you that the simplest kind of sound is produced by a sine wave. In musical and mechanical terms, that is correct. The sine wave is probably the most common waveform in the world. You see it in ripples and in stretched strings; it is simply related to all forms of regular circular and spring-like motion.

Musically the sine wave produces a tone of unsurpassed purity. In a very important sense it has proved to be the most fundamental of all waveforms producing the most fundamental of all sounds. You may, however, spend years making music on your computer without ever seeing or hearing a sine wave. From the point of view of the computer, the simplest and most fundamental wave of all is the pulse wave and, in particular, its symmetrical variant, the square wave.

(As we have said, the raw material of electronic music is electric current. This fact is useful because it allows us directly to examine the form of soundwaves using an oscilloscope. More than that, the processes by which computers produce sound involve such direct parallels that we can talk about the soundwaves as though they were waves of electric current, introducing few if any mistakes or misunderstandings. From now on we shall, for the most part, slip between descriptions of soundwaves and electric waves with no comment. The typical graphs of soundwaves represent changes in amplitude or volume level with time, while the corresponding graph of an electric wave – as seen, for example, on an oscilloscope display – is a record of changes in voltage with time.)

By definition, a pulse wave has a 'rectangular' graph. A pulse is produced whenever a voltage changes from one steady or 'plateau' level to another and back again. If the initial change is a rise, we call the pulse 'positive going'. If it is a fall, the pulse is 'negative going'. No pulse is ever precisely rectangular, although high-speed digital circuitry can produce very close approximations to the ideal. However, pulse waves are assumed to be precisely rectangular, produced by instantaneous switching between voltage levels.

All the information on a computer takes the ultimate form of electronic signals – series of pulses or pulse waves shifted around the computer's circuits and operating as instructions or data. A high voltage is conventionally represented in numerical terms by the binary digit '1', while a low voltage is the binary digit '0'. Basic computer theory shows us that 'high/low' and '1/0' can also be interpreted as 'on/off'. A pulse is produced every time a switch is turned on and off (positive going) or off and on (negative going). A pulse wave is produced by a train of such pulses. One complete cycle of a pulse wave, its period, covers the moment something is switched on, the whole time it stays on, the moment it is switched off and the whole time it stays off *until just before* turning on again.

Because pulses have only two voltage states (or, in sound terms, amplitude levels), they are unique among waveforms. In particular there are a theoretically infinite number of pulse waves of the same frequency, because the ratio of on-time to off-time for any given period can take any value from 0 (permanently off) to 1 (permanently on or, simply, a direct current).

This ratio is known as the mark/space ratio of a pulse wave. The mark or on-time is also known as the pulse width – for obvious reasons – and the pulse width as a percentage of the wave's period is known as the duty cycle of that wave. Duty cycles and mark/space ratios give us the same information in different form.

As an example, imagine a pulse wave with a frequency of 100 Hz. Its period is one-hundredth of a second. To produce it something would have to be turned on and off one hundred times in every second, and a one-second burst of this wave will contain one hundred complete pulses. If the pulse is high for one-thousandth of a second (i.e. the pulse width is one-thousandth of a second), then the mark/space ratio is 1:9 and the duty cycle is 10%.

From now on we'll assume that all pulse waves have a duty cycle of 50% (a 1:1 mark/space ratio), unless otherwise stated. This sort of pulse wave, which is high and low for equal amounts of time, is called a square wave.

Duty cycle and tempo
Here the Commodore begins to come into its own. To begin this section, here is a program to work out duty cycles for that computer and to hear the results of different values.

```
1 REM "PULSE WIDTH RECKONER",1984,C-64
2 REM "PULSE WIDTH SWEEP USING CHANNEL 1 FREQUEN
CY"
3 REM THIS PROGRAM MAY BE USED TO CALCULATE PULS
E WIDTH BYTES
4 REM TO HEAR THEIR EFFECT AND TO HEAR A SWEEP T
HROUGH DIFFERENT VALUES
```

```
5 REM - WHICH IS A MODULATION.
6 REM YOU CAN ALSO HEAR THE EFFECT OF ADDING HAR
MONICS AND OTHER FREQUENCIES
7 REM BY PLAYING NOTES ON THREE CHANNELS WITH AN
 APPROPRIATE SUSTAIN.
8 REM THE INITIAL ADSR VALUES ALLOW THIS
10 A=40:R=40
100 POKE54296,15:POKE54276,0:POKE54283,0:POKE542
90,0
110 GOSUB 600
120 INPUT "HOW MANY CHANNELS (1 TO 3):";CH
130 IF CH<1 OR CH>3 THEN 110
140 FOR X=1 TO CH
150 PRINT "CHANNEL ";X
160 INPUT "FREQUENCY: ";FR
170 INPUT "DUTY CYCLE (AS %): ";DC
180 IF DC<0 OR DC>100 THEN 170
190 GOSUB 500
200 PRINT"----------------------------------------
"
210 NEXT
220 FOR X=1 TO 3000:NEXT
230 POKE54276,0:POKE54283,0:POKE54290,0
235 INPUT "PULSE WIDTH MODULATION (Y/N)";E$
236 IF E$="Y" THEN GOSUB 700
240 INPUT"AGAIN (Y/N): ";A$
250 IF A$="Y" THEN 270
260 END
270 INPUT"CHECK   ENVELOPE (Y/N): ";B$
280 IF B$="Y" THEN GOSUB 600
290 GOTO 120
400 PRINT "CH. FREQ.  % CYCLE.  HIGH BYTE.LOW BY
TE"
410 V=54272+7*(X-1)
420 POKEV,LF(X):POKEV+1,HF(X):POKEV+2,LP(X):POKE
V+3,HP(X)
430 POKE V+5,A: POKE V+6,R: POKE V+4,65
440 PRINT X;;FR,DC,HP(X),LP(X)
450 RETURN
460 END
500 F=(INT(FR/0.0596))/256:HF(X)=INT(F):LF(X)=IN
T(256*(F-HF(X)))
510 P=(INT(4095*DC/100)):HP(X)=INT(P/256):LP(X)=
```

```
     INT(P-256*HP(X))
515  IF X=1 THEN GR=FR
520  GOSUB 400
530  RETURN
600  REM ADSR
605  PRINT CHR$(147)
610  PRINT"ATTACK/DECAY ";A;" SUSTAIN/RELEASE ";R
620  INPUT"CHANGE (Y/N): ";C$
630  IF C$="N" THEN RETURN
640  INPUT"ATTACK/DECAY (O TO 255)";A
650  INPUT"SUSTAIN/RELEASE (O TO 255)";R
660  IF R<O OR R>255 THEN 600
670  GOTO 605
700  PRINT CHR$(147)
710  PRINT "PULSE WIDTH SWEEP ON CH.1 FREQUENCY"
715  X=1:FR=GR
718  INPUT "STEP (1 TO 100, DEFAULT 10)";Q
719  IF Q<1 OR Q>100 THEN Q=10
720  FOR DC=0 TO 100 STEPQ: GOSUB 510: FOR P=1 TO
     200: NEXT: NEXT
725  RETURN
```

PROGRAM 2.5

This is very useful since the 6581 chip used by the Commodore 64 to produce sound allows you to change the duty cycle of a pulse wave. Unfortunately the BBC Model B's chip – the 76489 has no such facility, producing more or less constant-width pulse waves. However, here is a program for the BBC Model B which produces pulse waves by switching the computer's internal cassette motor relay on and off. The MOTOR0 and MOTOR1 commands do this job, which is normally undertaken automatically during LOAD and SAVE operations. In these programs you can alter the amount of time for which the motor relay stays on and the amount of time for which it is off simply by inserting appropriate values in the FOR . . . NEXT loops. The programs ask you for these values and then play your note.

```
  5 CLS
 10 INPUT DURATION%,FREQUENCY%
 20 FOR X%=1 TO DURATION%
```

```
30 *MOTOR 1
40 FOR Y%=1 TO FREQUENCY%
50 NEXT
60 *MOTOR 0
70 NEXT
```
PROGRAM 2.6

Using a program of this sort as the foundation, a complete and interesting piece of music may be built up by specifying note duration for a sequence of different notes as well as period and duty cycle. This program plays a short piece for you. The sound is rather like that of a hammer-clavier.

```
20 REM 'MUSIC' PRODUCED BY
30 REM DATA FOR CYCLES AND
40 REM DURATION. THE PROGRAM
50 REM GIVES A ROUGH GUIDE TO
60 REM FREQUENCY & DURATION
70 REM ALTHOUGH THEY'RE NOT
80 REM RELIABLE.
90 REM NOTE THAT THE
100 REM RELATIONSHIP BETWEEN
110 REM FREQUENCY,CYCLES &
120 REM NOTE DURATION IS VERY
130 REM COMPLEX.
140 CLS
150 READ CYCLES%,DURATION%
155 IF DURATION%=0 THEN 170
160 PRINT TAB(0,10)"APPROX FREQUENCY="INT(1
800/(2*DURATION%))
170 PRINT TAB(0,12)"NOTE DURATION="(CYCLES%
*DURATION%*2/1800)
175 IF CYCLES%=0 THEN FOR Y%=0 TO 2*DURATIO
N%:NEXT:GOTO 150
180 FOR X%=1 TO CYCLES%
190 *MOTOR 1
200 FOR Y%=0 TO DURATION%
210 NEXT
220 *MOTOR 0
230 FOR Y%=0 TO DURATION%
```

```
240 NEXT
250 NEXT
260 GOTO 150
270 DATA 100,10,200,5,100,10
280 DATA 20,20,50,10,100,15
290 DATA 60,25,40,10,60,15,50,25
300 DATA 60,2,30,5,500,2
305 DATA 0,300: REM REST
306 DATA 300,0
310 DATA 30,5,40,5,45,5
320 DATA 40,10,60,20,50,10
330 DATA 50,10,40,20,50,50
340 DATA 100,30,200,5,200,10
```
PROGRAM 2.7

Finally, another duration variable may be brought into play – the tempo, which represents the speed of the piece, but influences all the other relevant durations in a global fashion. This program allows you to judge the effect of tempo using the simple system of the last few programs to experiment with. It also accepts duty cycle input, although the variations are not very noticeable. The lesson is simply that all aspects of musical time interact dynamically. Musical performance and composition are as delicate a business as clockwork.

```
 20 REM (WITH DUTY CYCLE INPUT)
 30 REM (WITH TEMPO INPUT)
 40 REM NOTE THAT VARIABLES
 50 REM HAVE A CRUDE EFFECT
 60 REM ON THE SOUND
 70 REM INCIDENTALLY, THERE
 80 REM IS NO REAL TUNE
 90 REM IN THESE PROGRAMS
100 REM ALTHOUGH A TUNE
110 REM WOULD OBVIOULSY
120 REM BE POSSIBLE TO
130 REM TO CONSTRUCT
140
150 CLS
```

```
160 INPUT "TEMPO"T
170 INPUT "DUTY CYCLE AS %"DC%
180 READ CYCLES%,DURATION%
190 IF DURATION%=0 THEN 210
200 PRINT TAB(0,10)"APPROX FREQUENCY="INT(1
800/(2*DURATION%))
210 PRINT TAB(0,12)"NOTE DURATION="(CYCLES%
*DURATION%*2/1800)
220 IF CYCLES%=0 THEN CLS:FOR Y%=0 TO 2*DUR
ATION%:NEXT:GOTO 180
230 FOR X%=1 TO CYCLES%/T
240 *MOTOR 1
250 FOR Y%=0 TO T*DURATION%*(DC%/100)
260 NEXT
270 *MOTOR 0
280 FOR Y%=0 TO T*DURATION%*(1-DC%/100)
290 NEXT
300 NEXT
310 GOTO 180
320 DATA 100,10,200,5,100,10
330 DATA 20,20,50,10,100,15
340 DATA 60,25,40,10,60,15,50,25
350 DATA 60,2,30,5,500,2
360 DATA 0,300: REM REST
370 DATA 300,0
380 DATA 30,5,40,5,45,5
390 DATA 40,10,60,20,50,10
400 DATA 50,10,40,20,50,50
410 DATA 100,30,200,5,200,10
```
PROGRAM 2.8

Note duration

The BBC Model B and Commodore 64 computers use BASIC instructions to specify frequency. The machine code routines, or PSG hardware, that handles tone generation bypass the problems connected with the effect of period on note duration. Note duration is treated as independent of frequency. This is not the case with every micro. Some require you to specify a period or frequency and the number of cycles in the required tone. For a given number of cycles, however, the duration of a note will be shorter the higher the frequency. Programming a real piece of music demands a series of calculations in order to work out the absolute duration of each note.

Remember that every micro uses a 'clock' to time all its operations, and that these clocks – themselves pulse wave generators operating at very high and constant frequencies – often operate at different speeds with different machines. To produce a standard A-above-middle-C, for example, the computer must generate 440 cycles in every second. Since clock speeds vary from around 1 MHz (one MegaHertz or one million cycles a second) to around 4 MHz, note production involves a division by a constant specific to each clock speed. The hardware used to produce the note is a shift register, commonly used for the purposes of binary division in calculators and household digital clocks.

The easiest way to avoid these problems is to employ a system which triggers a note at a specific frequency of indefinite duration. The note will be turned off only when the computer receives an instruction to do so. In practice, many micros offer such a facility. Note duration, then, is a matter of inserting a delay between the command to turn on the note and the command to turn it off. This can be thought of as a sort of second-order pulsing system; it involves the use of circuits (or software) specifically designed to be triggered into indefinite oscillation.

In programs 2.6 to 2.8, we used FOR . . . NEXT loops to generate delays between first-order pulsing operations. Such programs can be embedded in a further FOR . . . NEXT loop whose job is to determine note duration.

As programs 2.7 and 2.8 demonstrate, an effective method of setting frequency and duration is through DATA statements. Other parameters – for example, duty cycles – could be input in the same fashion. Once that has been done, multipliers (such as the tempo variable T in program 2.8) could be used to alter any group of values overall, thus allowing us to perform a piece with different note frequencies or durations. We could even change these in the course of performance. However, while a global change of note duration affects tempo, a global change of frequency affects what is called the key of the piece. Key changes are known as transpositions. If the changes are localized, or if they are produced by rapidly changing the value of the multiplier itself, then they are often known as modulations. The programs below are simple adaptations of program 2.6, which produce a frequency modulation effect known as a glide, a sweep from one frequency to another. By changing line 80, for example, to A%=2−A% FREQUENCY%=FREQUENCY%−10*A%+10, the frequency will switch between two values, giving a 'vibrato' effect.

On the Commodore such features are built into the 6581 chip, and we will come to them later.

```
 5 CLS
10 INPUT DURATION%,FREQUENCY%
20 FOR X%=1 TO DURATION%
30 *MOTOR 1
40 FOR Y%=FREQUENCY% TO 0 STEP-1
50 NEXT
60 *MOTOR 0
70 NEXT
80 FREQUENCY%=FREQUENCY%-100
90 GOTO 20
```
PROGRAM 2.9


```
 2 REM DIFFERENT SOUND QUALITY
 3 REM IS RESULT OF SWITCHING
 4 REM MOTOR 0 AND MOTOR 1
 5 REM ROUND, THUS CHANGING
 6 REM MARK-SPACE RATIO
 9 CLS
10 INPUT CYCLES%,FREQUENCY%
20 FOR X%=1 TO CYCLES%
30 *MOTOR 0
40 FOR Y%=FREQUENCY% TO 0 STEP-1
50 NEXT
60 *MOTOR 1
70 NEXT
80 FREQUENCY%=FREQUENCY%-10
90 GOTO 20
```
PROGRAM 2.10

Going back to duration itself, the two programs below show how the BBC Model B and the Commodore 64 use FOR . . . NEXT loops to determine how long a note lasts. On the BBC Model B, a count of about 1800 represents a second. On the Commodore 64 a count of about 1000 represents a second. The SOUND statement in the BBC Model B program uses –1 as the built-in note duration. This means that the note will last indefinitely. A second SOUND statement is required to turn the note off. In the Commodore 64 program we simply switch on the sound with a POKE 54276,33 instruction and switch it off by POKEing the same location with a zero.

```
20 POKE 54296,15:REM VOLUME
30 POKE 54277,0:POKE 54278,240:REM ADSR
40 POKE 54272,37:POKE 54273,17:REM NOTE FREQU
ENCY
50 POKE 54276,32+1:REM SAWTOOTH AND GATE ON
60 FOR P=1 TO 1000:NEXT:REM DURATION LOOP
70 POKE 54276,0:REM NOTE OFF
```
PROGRAM 2.11


```
10 REM BBC DURATION LOOP
20 SOUND 1,-15,53,-1: REM TURNS ON NOTE OF IN
DEFINITE LENGTH
30 FOR P=1 TO 1800:NEXT: REM NOTE DURATION
40 SOUND 17,0,0,0: REM NOTE OFF
50 REM NOTE THE 17 IN LINE 40 WHICH TURNS A N
OTE OFF IMMEDIATELY
```
PROGRAM 2.12

3

Sound fundamentals

Part 1: Waveforms

Given a particular waveform, we can completely specify a musical tone by three parameters: frequency, amplitude and duration. As we have seen, frequency and duration are related by the equation:

FREQUENCY * DURATION = NUMBER OF CYCLES

Each cycle of a regular sound will have a particular period, given by 1/*Frequency*. The period is the time taken for one cycle to occur; if sound waves travel at a particular speed (or velocity), then we can work out how far a sound will travel in the course of one cycle, since (as your school maths should have taught you) DISTANCE = SPEED * TIME.

This figure is called the *wavelength* (although usually referred to by the Greek letter *lambda*, λ , we shall use a capital L). The wavelength can be thought of as the distance between two peaks of a wave.

Sound does have a velocity, which varies according to the medium it travels in. In air this velocity is about 760 m.p.h. (or 340 metres a second), the so-called 'speed of sound' or, in aircraft technology, Mach 1. We can write:

L=V(speed of sound)/F(frequency).

Or:

L=V*PERIOD.

If you think of a wave as being produced by a vertically vibrating particle, then wavelength can be thought of as the *horizontal* distance travelled by the particle during the time it takes for the particle to move from one peak to the next peak. This can be confusing since the *vertical* distance from peak to trough, A, is described as a peak-to-peak value.

This vertical distance is the wave's *amplitude*. We have seen how amplitude is related to loudness and how our perception of loudness is logarithmic in nature. Amplitude and loudness are also related to frequency, but these relationships are extraordinarily complex, since they are really about how the ear operates, and the ear is an extremely delicate and sophisticated machine. The subject becomes even more complicated when we consider not only the behaviour of our ears, but also the behaviour of musical instruments in the real world.

Our ears increase in sensitivity with frequency up to about 2 to 2.5 KHz and then decrease as frequency gets higher. Loudness, in general, increases with the logarithm of energy, but at the low and high ends of the audible spectrum the response curves change markedly. The threshold of audibility (which measures the quietest sound we can hear) increases, while the threshold of feeling (which measures the loudest sound we can hear without pain) decreases. The entire range of hearable sounds therefore decreases at low and high frequencies. The range is greatest at around 1 KHz, a figure conventionally taken as the frequency of standard audio tones.

In a sense, our ears are 'tuned' to a frequency of about 1 KHz. Tones of this frequency are used in many of the most important tests on electronic audio equipment, notably as standards against which the frequency response of amplifiers, loudspeakers and the like are measured. The 1 KHz tone is also the standard against which the frequency response of the ear is measured. Subjective tests using a 1 KHz standard give a particularly impressive idea of how loudness and frequency interact. The effect is most marked at low frequencies whose apparent loudness increases dramatically for sounds with amplitudes of around 30 dB (about equivalent to the power generated by the ordinary speech of one person). For this reason, many audio amplifiers include a 'loudness' switch to boost bass response at low output levels: at low amplitudes, bass frequencies seem to be unnaturally quiet only because they rapidly drop off from their 'natural' high values.

Musical instruments also display a variety of non-linear effects when you come to consider the relationship between frequency and amplitude. Most of these are complex enough to take up whole treatises on their own. One, however, can be dealt with here, partly because its consideration is vital to an understanding of the complexities of music synthesis and partly because one of our computers (the Commodore 64) allows the effect to be directly synthesized. The effect is known as *resonance*.

Resonance
Acoustic musical instruments can be described as general physical systems
that amplify a primary vibration. The primary vibration may be caused by a
reed, a string, a diaphragm, the passage of air across a small aperture or even
the player's mouth. Secondary vibrations occur in sounding-boards, sound
boxes or columns of air. Like all natural vibrations, those associated with
musical instruments die away more or less rapidly; we say that the vibrations
are heavily damped if they die away quickly, or lightly damped if they die
away slowly.

With plucked, bowed and hammered instruments (guitar, violin and piano,
for example), the primary vibrations are provided by the strings. These in turn
are tightly coupled to a sounding-board or sound box (usually by means of a
bridge), which is forced to vibrate at the same frequency as the string. The
amplitude of this forced vibration is small compared to the amplitude of the
string's vibrations; but, since large bodies of air are in contact with the
secondary vibrator, the total energy expended by the forced vibration is quite
large.

Just as the string itself always vibrates at a certain frequency determined by
its length, thickness, density and the tension in it, so the whole system which
constitutes the instrument will, if allowed, vibrate at a frequency fixed by
appropriate physical characteristics. The frequency associated with the system
is called the natural frequency of that system. When the natural frequency
and the primary frequency coincide, the phenomenon of resonance occurs.

One parlour-game display of resonance is the trick of making cut glass ring
by rubbing its edge with a damp finger. The resulting whistle is caused by
sympathetic vibrations at the natural frequency of the glass, and this can be
altered by, for example, filling the glass with more or less water. The effect has
been successfully exploited in a number of twentieth-century instruments,
among them the haunting 'ondes martineau', an electronic instrument
developed in the 1930s. Resonance is also used in many brass and
woodwind instruments, where a column of air of variable length forms a
system with a range of natural frequencies; the length is varied by use of
valves or some form of stopping.

Resonance is not usually acceptable in stringed instruments. If it does
occur, it usually takes the form of an unwelcome ringing. This is because
stringed instruments are lightly damped systems and therefore resonate at
precise frequencies – a feature that can be made use of in tuning a stringed
instrument because of the way a vibrating string will cause another string to
vibrate at almost precisely the same natural frequency. The exceptions to this
rule are mostly oriental stringed instruments (like the sitar or the bazouki) and
some early instruments like the dulcimer, which use certain strings as
sympathetic resonators to give a distinctive ringing tone. In some instruments
– the piano, for example, – great care is taken to ensure that resonance does

not occur by ensuring that the natural frequency of the sounding-board is very high.

However, resonance is crucial to other instruments, and these are generally the ones with heavy damping (woodwinds and brass, for example). The heavy damping ensures that resonant frequencies are not very accurately pointed, so that the resulting sounds are not sharply defined around one frequency. Resonance acts to boost the amplitude of a tone at the resonant frequency. A frequency spectrum diagram would show the effect – it's basically a graph.

Along the horizontal axis we see the range of audible frequencies from 0 Hz up to 20 KHz, and along the vertical axis we see amplitude. The peaks are resonant frequencies. On either side of the peaks are marked the 3 dB roll-off points – that is, those frequencies at which *power* output is reduced by a half from the peak (which is equivalent to a decrease of a factor of about 1.4 in *amplitude*). Such spectra give us two important measurements: the difference between the upper roll-off point (FU) and the lower roll-off point (FL) is known as the bandwidth of the resonator; and the ratio of central frequency (FC) to bandwidth (FC/(FU-FL)) is called Q or the quality factor.

A sharp resonator, such as a tuned string, will have a low bandwidth and, more importantly, a high Q; whereas a less sharp resonator will have a high bandwidth or a low Q. Q is often referred to as a measure of the slope of curve around the resonant frequency on a spectrum diagram: a rapid rise being equivalent to a high Q.

Resonance is important because it is one of the key spices which go to make up musically interesting sounds. A resonator can be thought of as resembling a tuned electronic circuit. When you tune in a station on your radio or TV you are doing no more than changing the natural frequency of an electronic circuit to match that of the radio waves it is intended to pick up. A tuned circuit discriminates: it responds well to some frequencies (which ones depends on the central frequency and the bandwidth), and badly or not at all to others. The same sort of thing happens in a filter, which can boost or cut a certain range of frequencies, thus giving control over the tone of a sound.

Most filters in common use are analogue, cheaply constructed from one or two capacitors and resistors. Circuits can be found in any electronics textbook, or ready-made filters bought cheaply. One could be added to the output of your BBC computer to give a degree of control over the sound not afforded by the machine itself. The SID chip on the Commodore 64 includes a software accessible programmable filter, with resonance control, which will do the job for you. Such filtering is a complicated area whose finer points need not detain us; but SID allows you to do it, and it works.

Here are two small programs that allow you to see the effect of filtering and resonance on just one channel. The first gives an unadorned rendition of a well-known theme tune.

```
10 REM CBMTUNE1 (CLOSE ENCOUNTERS)
15 REM NB ALL NOTES SAME LENGTH EXCEPT FOR LAST
ONE WHICH USES DIFFERENT DELAY
20 POKE 54296,15:POKE 54277,64: POKE 54278,128
30 READ A,B
40 FOR P=1 TO 400: NEXT
50 IF A=0 THEN 90
60 POKE 54273,A: POKE 54272,B
70 POKE 54276,17
80 GOTO 30
90 FOR P=1 TO 800: NEXT: POKE 54276,16
100 DATA 19,63,21,154,17,37,8,147,12,216,0,0
110 REM THANKS TO PETER GERRARD FOR THE TUNE....
.!
```
PROGRAM 3.1

```
10 REM C-64 FILTER WAH AND RESONANCE
12 PRINT CHR$(147):REM CLEAR SCREEN
15 REM LOW PASS+MAX VOL:ADSR:LOW BYTE OF CUT-
OFF FREQUENCY
20 POKE 54296,31:POKE 54277,64: POKE 54278,12
8:POKE 54293,0
22 REM LOOP THROUGH RESONANCE VALUES
25 FOR R=0 TO 240 STEP 16:POKE 54295,1+R
28 PRINT CHR$(19);TAB(10);"RESONANCE";R
30 READ A,B
50 IF A=0 THEN 90
55 REM LOAD FREQ BYTES OF NOTES
60 POKE 54273,A: POKE 54272,B
65 REM TURN ON TRIANGLE WAVE
70 POKE 54276,33
72 REM FREQUENCY SWEEP
75 FOR F=0 TO 255 STEP 5:POKE 54294,F:NEXT
80 GOTO 30
85 REM LONG NOTE AND TURN OFF TRIANGLE
90 FOR P=1 TO 800: NEXT: POKE 54276,0
92 REM RESET DATA POINTER AND MOVE TO NEXT RE
SONANCE VALUE
95 RESTORE:NEXT
100 DATA 19,63,21,154,17,37,8,147,12,216,0,0
```
PROGRAM 3.2

As you can see, the commands are complicated, since you have to set the filter cut-off frequency (that's our central frequency), direct the oscillator whose output is to be filtered, select the type of filter and set resonance. The registers that do these things are all listed in Appendix 3; here we merely describe the significant action of the filter.

Firstly, the synthesis of natural resonance requires a spectrum output that peaks at the resonant frequency. With acoustic instruments, resonance is an additive phenomenon (that is, vibration is heaped upon vibration), but the commonest techniques for synthesizing (among them SID's) are subtractive (that is, frequencies on either side of the resonant frequency are filtered out, leaving a perceived 'hump' in the spectrum). In other words, we use a tuned circuit or digital equivalent as a filter. The particular kind of filter we use to synthesize naturally occurring resonance is called a band-pass filter for obvious reasons. Other filter types will be dealt with later, but there is nothing in principle to stop you adding resonance to them for some interesting, non-naturalistic effects.

While acoustic instruments have more or less fixed resonant characteristics, we need not obey any similar constraints. Anyone familiar with contemporary music will be well acquainted with a form of dynamic resonance known as 'wah-wah'. Try this program to see how it's done.

```
10  REM C-64 WAH EFFECT
15  FORX=54272T054396:POKEX,0:NEXT
16  REM NOTE USE OF LOW PASS FILTER BELOW
20  POKE54278,128:POKE54296,31:POKE54295,1
25  FOR RPT=1 TO 40
30  POKE54276,33:READ A,B
40  IF A=0 THEN 90
42  POKE54273,A:POKE54272,B
45  FOR F=0 TO 255 STEP 3*RPT
50  POKE54294,F
76  NEXT
80  GOTO 30
90  RESTORE:NEXT:POKE54276,0
100 DATA 19,63,21,154,17,37,8,147,12,216,0,0
```
PROGRAM 3.3

The trick is to sweep the centre frequency up and down the spectrum to give a wailing, almost human effect. The reason why it is almost human is that a great deal of human speech depends on resonance. Voiced sounds – the ones formed by using your mouth as a sound box (try saying the vowels) – are particularly characterized by 'formants', a series of resonant frequencies determined by the physical shape taken up by your mouth and vocal tract when the sounds are made. An interesting experiment is to use all three SID oscillators to produce individually controllable formants of the same frequency.

Oscillators

In the previous section we saw how different frequencies are associated with different amplitudes and different loudnesses in common sounds and music. We briefly introduced the idea of filters, tuned circuits and resonance. It is interesting that the idea of a natural frequency is really what musical instruments are all about. They are, in effect, systems formed from tunable physical subsystems each with their own natural frequencies. Computer music is generated by similar electronic subsystems with natural frequencies of their own – tuned circuits, acting not as filters or resonators but as freely running *oscillators*.

An oscillator is just a circuit that is continuously changing state in a regular and repetitive way; oscillators are among the fundamental building blocks of electronics, found in everything from radios and quartz watches to tape recorders and computers.

Oscillation exists all around you. The ebb and flow of the sea's tides are an oscillation produced by the waxing and waning of the sun and moon's gravitational influence and the rotation of the earth. Anything with a spring in it is an oscillator, more or less heavily damped; the tensing and relaxing of a spring are a model for the phenomenon. We can think of the cycles of nature as oscillations of a very low frequency; some people have even argued that the universe, now expanding and now contracting, is an oscillator with an unbelievably minute frequency.

At the heart of any computer is a very accurate oscillator producing clock pulses at a frequency of anything upwards of 1 MHz, which hold the whole thing together and keep it operating in synchrony. This clock provides us with the raw material for music making: how does it do this?

Briefly, the clock generator in a micro is a form of an oscillator whose frequency is governed by the natural frequency of a piece of quartz crystal. Under the influence of electric current the quartz will vibrate at a very high rate with a no lesser degree of accuracy. These vibrations are then used to turn electronic switches on and off; this produces sharply defined square waves at a regular frequency, which can be divided down to the required frequency to manage the rest of the computer's circuitry, and even to produce audible sounds at a frequency 100 or more times lower. The computer itself can be used to give an idea of how it does this.

The programs below are all built around a model for a simple form of oscillator similar to the quartz type – one that is common in all manner of digital circuitry. It is called an *astable multivibrator*; in essence it works like this: two switches (which could be electromechanical relays, transistors or logic gates) are wired up together so that a current flowing out of one will switch the other one on and itself off. With a suitable delay built into the system (any oscillator requires such a delay), the two switches will go on turning on and off to their heart's content at a rate determined only by the circuit delay itself. The delay governs the natural frequency of the circuit.

The programs have a delay built in due to the time it takes for a computer to perform any task. All but the first have extra delay programmed in, which can be altered to give different frequencies at the 'output'. The programs have all been written for the Commodore 64, but use such elementary BASIC that they can be simply rewritten (if necessary) for any other micro. They model a simple astable, a more sophisticated astable which responds not to a changed state but to a changing state (called 'edge detection'), a divider circuit which allows us to derive low frequencies from high ones and a number of different counters which demonstrate how different waveforms can be derived from a simple square wave by digital techniques alone.

```
10 REM ASTABLE LISTING
20 IF X=1 THEN X=0
30 PRINT X
40 IF X=0 THEN X=1
50 PRINT X
60 GOTO 20
```
PROGRAM 3.4

This almost trivial program uses just one variable to represent the state of an oscillator; $X=1$ means the oscillator is on, and $X=0$ means it is off. The result is a never-ending list of 0s and 1s down the screen, appearing at a rate determined by the timing of the computer alone.

```
1 REM ASTABLE WITH EDGE DETECTION
2 REM C-64. NOTE DELAY & INITIAL X,Y
3 REM ALTER THESE TO OBSERVE EFFECT
10 X=0:Y=1:PRINT CHR$(147)
20 IF X=1 THEN FL=1
30 IF Y=1 THEN GL=1
40 IF X=1 THEN X=0
50 IF Y=1 THEN Y=0
60 IF X=0 AND FL=1 THEN Y=1
70 IF Y=0 AND GL=1 THEN X=1
80 PRINT CHR$(19);" Q:","-Q:"
```

```
90 PRINT X,Y
100 FOR P=1 TO 100:NEXT
110 FL=0
120 GOTO 20
```
PROGRAM 3.5

Here we model a more sophisticated oscillator, with X and Y standing for the outputs from two linked 'switches'. The outputs are written to the screen as Q and –Q, since, as you can see, one is always the reverse of the other. Line 100 also includes a delay to slow down the changes; this may be considered the equivalent of a capacitor and resistor network in a real astable. The change of state in this model (as in practical astables) is governed not just by the existing state of the outputs, 'fed back' as it were to their opposite inputs, but also on the state of 'flags', FL and GL. These can be considered to model the way a real electronic circuit responds to a change of state (it detects the 'edges' of waveforms as they go high or low). Each flag is set by X and Y going high. X and Y and the flag FL reset themselves, which mimics another aspect of a capacitative link in a real circuit – that the capacitors discharge themselves to earth. The 'circuit' must take a particular state when it is 'switched on', therefore we set X and Y in line 10 to specific and possible values.

```
1 REM ASTABLE WITH EDGE DETECTION
2 REM C-64. NOTE DELAY & INITIAL X,Y
3 REM ALTER THESE TO OBSERVE EFFECT
4 REM WITH SOUND OUTPUT
5 POKE 54296,15
6 POKE 54272,0:POKE 54273,255
10 X=0:Y=1:PRINT CHR$(147)
20 IF X=1 THEN FL=1
30 IF Y=1 THEN GL=1
40 IF X=1 THEN X=0
50 IF Y=1 THEN Y=0
60 IF X=0 AND FL=1 THEN Y=1
70 IF Y=0 AND GL=1 THEN X=1
80 PRINT CHR$(19);" Q:","-Q:"
90 PRINT X,Y
95 POKE 54276,X*129
100 FOR P=1 TO 100:NEXT
110 FL=0
120 GOTO 20
```
PROGRAM 3.6

The next program merely adds sound output (a blip) whenever X goes high. If we could speed it up, these blips would merge into a note of definite frequency (as with the MOTOR O/1 programs of Chapter 2).

```
1 REM ASTABLE FEEDING BISTABLES
2 REM C-64. NOTE DELAY & INITIAL X,Y
3 REM ALTER THESE TO OBSERVE EFFECT
4 REM WITH SOUND OUTPUT
5 REM BISTABLES ACT AS DIVIDERS
6 REM CONNECTED TO CUMULATIVE COUNTERS
7 REM HARMONICS AND ATTENUATION POSSIBLE
8 POKE 54296,15
9 POKE 54272,0:POKE 54273,255
10 X=0:Y=1:PRINT CHR$(147)
15 L=-1:M=-1:N=-1:K=-1
20 IF X=1 THEN FL=1
30 IF Y=1 THEN GL=1
40 IF X=1 THEN X=0
50 IF Y=1 THEN Y=0
60 IF X=0 AND FL=1 THEN Y=1
70 IF Y=0 AND GL=1 THEN X=1
75 L=L+1
80 PRINT CHR$(19);" Q:","-Q:","COUNT:"
90 PRINT X,Y,L
95 POKE 54276,X*129
98 IF X=1 THEN GOSUB 200
100 FOR P=1 TO 400:NEXT
110 FL=0
120 GOTO 20
200 S=1-S:M=M+1
210 PRINT " S=(Q/2):"
220 PRINT S,,M
230 IF S=1 THEN GOSUB 300
250 RETURN
300 R=1-R:N=N+1
310 PRINT " R=(Q/4):"
320 PRINT R,,N
330 IF R=1 THEN GOSUB 400
350 RETURN
400 T=1-T:K=K+1
410 PRINT " T=(Q/8):"
420 PRINT T,,K
450 RETURN
```
PROGRAM 3.7

This program models frequency division by setting up a series of subroutines in lines 200-250, 300-350 and 400-450. The output of each routine (S, R and T) holds its value until the routine before it, and eventually the oscillator output, goes high. Electronic circuits that do this are called bistables, latches or, sometimes, counters; because they are stable in each possible state (unlike the oscillator itself), they are said to latch themselves into a fixed state and they can therefore be used to count the pulses coming in by registering each time they latch. The program uses these subroutines to output a cumulative count. As you can see, a chain of such counters can be used to divide the frequency of an input signal by any given multiple of two. Since each musical octave (a complete range of notes as in the conventional *do, re, mi, fa, so, la, ti, do*) represents a doubling of frequency as you go up the scale from one *do* (or C) to the next, we can produce all the octaves we need from one 'top octave' by using a chain of bistable dividers like this.

```
1 REM ASTABLE FEEDING BISTABLES
2 REM C-64. NOTE DELAY & INITIAL X,Y
3 REM ALTER THESE TO OBSERVE EFFECT
4 REM WITH SOUND OUTPUT
5 REM BISTABLES ACT AS DIVIDERS
6 REM CONNECTED TO CUMULATIVE COUNTERS
7 REM WITH RESET ON EIGHTH BIT
8 POKE 54296,15
9 POKE 54272,0:POKE 54273,255
10 X=0:Y=1:PRINT CHR$(147)
15 L=-1:M=-1:N=-1:K=-1
20 IF X=1 THEN FL=1
30 IF Y=1 THEN GL=1
40 IF X=1 THEN X=0
50 IF Y=1 THEN Y=0
60 IF X=0 AND FL=1 THEN Y=1
70 IF Y=0 AND GL=1 THEN X=1
75 L=L+1
80 PRINT CHR$(19);" Q:","-Q:","COUNT:"
90 PRINT X,Y,L
95 POKE 54276,X*129
96 IF L>=7 THEN L=-1:M=L:K=L:N=L
98 IF X=1 THEN GOSUB 200
100 FOR P=1 TO 100:NEXT
110 FL=0
120 GOTO 20
200 S=1-S:M=M+1
```

```
210 PRINT " S=(Q/2):"
220 PRINT S,,M
230 IF S=1 THEN GOSUB 300
250 RETURN
300 R=1-R:N=N+1
310 PRINT " R=(Q/4):"
320 PRINT R,,N
330 IF R=1 THEN GOSUB 400
350 RETURN
400 T=1-T:K=K+1
410 PRINT " T=(Q/8):"
420 PRINT T,,K
450 RETURN
```
PROGRAM 3.8

This program resets the cumulative counter with every eighth pulse, thus producing a cycle of values: 0, 1, 2, 3, 4, 5, 6, 7 . . . 0, 1, 2, 3, 4, 5, 6, 7 and so on. The program is included because it demonstrates how a ramp wave can be generated by a simple square wave feeding into a series of resettable bistables. While the outputs of successive counters rise to only half the peak value of the counter before them, the rate at which they recycle is always the same. Thus we can use astables and bistables both to produce a range of frequencies by use of appropriate delays and divisions, and also to produce waveforms at a range of amplitudes but all with the same frequency. This enables the computer to adjust the 'volume' of its output; but, as with resonance, the process is essentially subtractive. Instead of amplifying a small input into larger outputs, digital circuits are best suited to 'attenuate' a large input into a range of smaller outputs almost invariably in steps of 3 dB – that is, taking a standard signal and producing outputs 0 dB, 3 dB, 6 dB, 9 dB and so on (usually up to 27 dB) less than the input. Each 3 dB step down represents a halving of the output power.

```
1 REM TRIANGLE WAVE GENERATOR   C-64
2 REM LISTING 3.8. COUNTS UP AND DOWN
3 REM INSTEAD OF RESETTING ON THE
4 REM EIGHTH PULSE, THUS PRODUCING
5 REM GRADUAL RISE AND FALL WHICH CAN
6 REM BE USED TO PRODUCE TRIANGLE WAVE
7 REM FROM A SQUARE WAVE INPUT.
8 POKE 54296,15
9 POKE 54272,0:POKE 54273,255
10 X=0:Y=1:PRINT CHR$(147)
```

```
15 SN=-1
20 IF X=1 THEN FL=1
30 IF Y=1 THEN GL=1
40 IF X=1 THEN X=0
50 IF Y=1 THEN Y=0
60 IF X=0 AND FL=1 THEN Y=1
70 IF Y=0 AND GL=1 THEN X=1
80 PRINT CHR$(19);" Q:","-Q:","COUNT:"
90 PRINT X,Y,L
95 POKE 54276,128+X
96 IF X=1 THEN GOSUB 200
98 IF L>=7 OR L=0 THEN SN=-1*SN
99 L=L+SN
100 FOR P=1 TO 1000:NEXT
110 FL=0
120 GOTO 20
200 S=1-S
210 PRINT " S=(Q/2):"
220 PRINT S,,M: REM NOTE HOW M,N,K
222 REM PRODUCE STEPPED VALUES
224 IF L>=7 OR L=0 THEN 230
225 M=M+SN
230 IF S=1 THEN GOSUB 300
250 RETURN
300 R=1-R
310 PRINT " R=(Q/4):"
320 PRINT R,,N
324 IF M=3 OR M=0 THEN 330
325 N=N+SN
330 IF R=1 THEN GOSUB 400
350 RETURN
400 T=1-T
410 PRINT " T=(Q/8):"
420 PRINT T,,K
450 RETURN
```
PROGRAM 3.9

To round off this section, here is a program that uses 'up-down' counters – again, common electronic circuits – to produce a triangle rather than a ramp 'waveform'. Doing this digitally invariably involves producing a wave either half the frequency of the equivalent ramp wave or half the amplitude. To maintain amplitude, the wave must start counting down from the peak level at the point where a ramp wave would restart its cycle; or, to maintain frequency, the triangle wave must start counting down from the point at which a ramp wave would have reached half its peak level.

Programmable sound generators

The programs above were all much too slow to be used to produce music. The principles can be employed in machine code programs to output control and signal voltages on any suitable port. But both the BBC and the Commodore micros contain dedicated circuits which do most of the donkey-work for us. These circuits, the so-called programmable sound generators (PSGs), use all the principles dealt with above to produce a wide range of musical tones. Appendix 3 gives a detailed breakdown of the insides of the BBC's Texas Instruments PSG and Commodore's Mostek PSG (the 76489 and 6581, to give them their official names). The detailed operations of PSGs are important, but for the moment it's enough to know the general outlines.

PSGs are essentially addressable networks of oscillators and counters used to produce a number of sounds at a variety of frequencies and levels of attenuation. In the case of the 6581 SID, there are also facilities for producing a number of waveforms and for filtering. SID is even more versatile than that, but we'll leave it at that for the moment. To operate a PSG, it must first be enabled and addressed. You must turn it on and switch it into whatever mode you require. Then, either after a specific number of clock cycles or on receipt of an acknowledge signal from the chip, the PSG requires data to set whatever register it is you have addressed.

Typically the computer's clock provides the PSG's fundamental oscillation. A number of registers accept data, which then determines what frequency is produced by the PSG, how much attenuation to give each tone and so on. The relevant circuits are set, and the tone emerges. All this takes time, a specific number of clock cycles; in order to speed things up addresses and data are introduced to the PSG as signals on a parallel bus – in other words, as bytes.

One major difference between the 76489 and SID is that Mostek's chip sits in the system memory, and communication with its registers is done using the computer's address and data bus. The 76489 only employs the data bus, interpreting some data as addresses and some as data proper. In theory this should make SID faster than the 76489. In practice, however, SID is considerably more complex than its cousin and consequently requires more manipulation. The end result on the BBC Model B and the Commodore 64, which also takes into account the frequency of each micro's clock and the speed of its software, is that each chip does some things quite rapidly and others quite slowly: horses for courses.

We have seen in broad outline how the hardware works. Much of the quality of a computer as a musical machine will be determined by the quality of its software. Both the BBC and Commodore micros use BASIC commands to perform all the necessary addressing and data transfer tasks; machine code could be used, but the advantages are not great for the inventive BASIC programmer.

It would be difficult to find a programming area that better demonstrates the diversity available in one computer language than sound commands. In effect, the Commodore 64 has no sound commands at all. Instead it relies exclusively on POKEs to the appropriate locations. The locations are all in system memory in the input/output block (locations 53248 to 57343 inclusive or D000 to DFFF in hex; this block can be referred to as page D). There are twenty-nine locations in all from 54272 (register 0) to 54300 (register 28 or 1C hex). The first twenty-five registers are write-only, and PEEKing them will not work; the last four registers are read-only, so you cannot POKE values into them. These last four registers are used to supply control voltages to the other registers – a feature partly available on the BBC Model B through use of the analogue-to-digital converter. The Commodore's sound registers 25 and 26 are designed to read the voltage level available from two potentiometers, and are accessible through the Commodore's joystick ports, where they are meant to be connected up to games paddles. They could be used to control any appropriate SID registers.

The BBC's A-D port includes four channels designed to be connected to potentiometers. These are meant for use with two twin-potentiometer joysticks; again, through the appropriate linking software they could be used to control sound output. The relevant values on the BBC are returned by the variable ADVAL(X), where X is 1, 2, 3 or 4 and indicates A-D channels 0, 1, 2 and 3. A reference voltage of 1.8 is taken from the A-D port (pin 11 or 14) to one end of the pot. The other is taken to ground and the slider to the A-D input. On the 64, PEEK(54297) returns the value on potentiometer A (PEEK(54298) for pot B). A 5 volt reference is available from pin 7 on the game controller ports. This should be connected to one end of the pot and the slider taken to the A-D input. There is an on-board buffer on the 64 for the analogue signals.

The BBC's A-D converter returns values between 0 and 65535, while the Commodore's equivalent, SID, registers return values between 0 and 255. In either case, the values returned need to be scaled to a suitable range to control the desired effect.

```
110 REM C-64 A TO D
120 REM NOTE THAT PEEKS ARE NOT ASSIGNED TO A
VARIABLE
130 REM THIS SAVES TIME AND ENSURES THAT UPDA
TES ARE ACCURATE
```

```
140 REM IN THIS EXAMPLE, POTA IS USED FOR FIN
E FREQUENCY CONTROL
150 REM AND POTB FOR VOLUME CONTROL
160 REM THESE COMMANDS SHOULD BE INCLUDED IN
A MAIN PROGRAM LOOP
170 REM IN ORDER TO MAINTAIN A CONSTANT UPDAT
E
180 POKE 54296,(PEEK(54298))/17: REM VOLUME
190 POKE 54273,34: REM HIGH BYTE OF C-5
200 POKE 54272,PEEK(54297): REM LOW BYTE OF F
REQUENCY
210 REM ADSR AND WAVEFORM POKES SHOULD COME H
ERE
```
PROGRAM 3.10

```
10 REM BBC A TO D
20 REM THE TWO SOUND STATEMENTS ACCEPT VALUES
 FROM A-D CHANNELS 0 AND 1
30 REM CONTROLLING VOLUME AND FREQUENCY RESPE
CTIVELY
40 REM ONCE AGAIN, THESE STATEMENTS WOULD APP
EAR IN SIMILAR FORM
50 REM WITHIN A CENTRAL PLAY LOOP
100 SOUND 1,-ADVAL(1)/4096,53,10
110 SOUND 2,-15,ADVAL(2)/256,10
```
PROGRAM 3.11

Learning to handle the Commodore sound facilities from BASIC is a matter of practice. Appendices 2 and 3 will help, but the 64, in particular, requires a great deal of juggling with numbers. It is useful to keep a subroutine available that can be combined with any program you require to give registers and values mnemonic variable names. This program does just that, and also clears the SID registers. It should be loaded first and have the substantive program written round it.

```
10 PRINT CHR$(147):GOSUB 1000: REM INITIALISE
999 REM REGVAR
1000 S=54272
1010 FOR X=1 TO 3
1020 CH=7*(X-1)
1030 FL(X)=S+CH:FH(X)=FL(X)+1:PL(X)=FH(X)+1:PH(X
)=PL(X)+1:WF(X)=PH(X)+1
```

```
1040 AD(X)=WF(X)+1:SR(X)=AD(X)+1
1050 NEXT
1060 HC=SR(3)+1:LC=HC+1:RF=LC+1:MV=RF+1:PX=MV+1:
PY=PX+1:O3=PY+1:E3=O3+1
1070 FOR X=O TO 24: POKE S+X,O: NEXT
1080 RETURN
```
PROGRAM 3.12

The BBC programmer has a similar problem, especially when confronted by the ENVELOPE command, with its fourteen parameters. A similar subroutine or procedure could be written for that machine.

The BBC's BASIC commands make at least some effort in the direction of everyday language. SOUND is used to control the output of the machine and controls four parameters: channel, volume, frequency and duration. It is really more complicated than that, but we'll leave it at the basics for now. ENVELOPE can, if required, be called by the SOUND command (by setting the volume parameter to a positive number between 1 and 15) and it controls two aspects of the 76489's sound output. First, it allows modification of the note frequency specified by the SOUND command (the so-called 'pitch envelope') and, second, it allows attenuation of the output (the so-called 'amplitude envelope'). It complicates matters by also allowing a degree of independent control over note duration; for, unlike the Commodore, the duration of notes must be specified in BBC code – they do not, as a rule, just continue to play until told to stop.

Part 2: Time and Tuning

Note duration
Appendix 2 gives a complete introduction to the BASIC sound commands on the BBC and Commodore micros, with programming examples dealing particularly with the duration parameters. Note duration is perhaps the most important of all the fundamental musical parameters. Although duration seems a trivial parameter, more information is included in it than in any other fundamental note parameter: waveform, amplitude or frequency. A crude but effective demonstration of this involves trying to deduce a specific tune from a sequence of sounds in which just one parameter varies. If the parameter is anything other than duration, the task is effectively impossible. But a trained ear can often recognize a tune from just a sequence of similar sounds with varying durations. A one-line program is the simplest way of producing a sound on the BBC micro.

```
10 SOUND 1,-15,137,20
```
PROGRAM 3.13

L. I. M. E.
THE MARKLAND LIBRARY
STAND PARK RD., LIVERPOOL, L16 9JD

In this example the numbers following the SOUND command specify that
channel 1 is to be played at maximum amplitude, producing a note of
frequency 440 Hz (the standard A-above-middle-C) for a duration of one
second (the figure 20 determining a duration of 20 * 0.5 seconds).

A Commodore program to do the same job looks considerably more
complicated. While the BBC allows you to produce a continuous tone
without using ENVELOPE, it is wise to put the equivalent commands in a
Commodore program, because the Commodore always uses the envelope
registers and will, in consequence, give you an envelope that depends on
values you will not know (though they are usually zero). The other major
differences are these: to use a pulse wave (as the BBC does) you need to set a
specific pulse width, you need to set a waveform and you need two separate
commands to specify the frequency of the eventual tone. The simplest 64
sound programs will look something like this:

```
10 REM C-64 SIMPLEST SOUND PROGRAM
15 POKE 54276,0: REM CLEAR CONTROL REGISTER
16 REM IT IS SOMETIMES NECESSARY TO PRELUDE A
 SOUND COMMAND BY A COMPREHENSIVE
17 REM CLEAR-OUT, EG. 'FOR X=0 TO 24:POKE 542
72+X,0:NEXT'
20 POKE 54296,15:REM VOLUME
30 POKE 54277,0:POKE 54278,240:REM SOUND ENVE
LOPE
40 POKE 54272,37:POKE 54273,17:REM LOW AND HI
GH FREQUENCY BYTES
50 POKE 54276,17:REM TRIANGLE WAVEFORM AND NO
TE ON
60 FOR P=1 TO 1000:NEXT: REM NOTE DURATION (A
TTACK, DECAY AND SUSTAIN PHASES)
70 POKE 54276,0:REM NOTE OFF
```
PROGRAM 3.14

The duration of this note is governed not by a single parameter but by a
delay loop (FOR . . . NEXT in this case). This determines the amount of time
the note plays at its sustain level, of which more in the next chapter.
Meanwhile try setting this loop to different values to see the effect.

There are a number of points to make as guides to good programming
practice on both the BBC Model B and the Commodore 64. First, when using
the ENVELOPE command on the BBC it is vital that the program deals with
ENVELOPE parameters before it comes to the associated SOUND command. This means that ENVELOPE should be declared (like dimensioning an

array) before it is called by SOUND. It is useful to set out all your envelopes in a procedure that is itself called at the beginning of a program. If the envelope uses variables, these can then be safely changed anywhere in the program.

Remember with the Commodore that in most cases only a very few of the possible note parameters will need to be changed continuously in a piece of music. Typically these will be the frequency parameters and the state of the waveform output. The waveform registers are used to turn notes on, and off. To hear a note, the overall volume register must be set – which can be done anywhere in the program before the first note is heard; if necessary, the setting can be revised later in the program. The envelopes should also be set before notes are turned on. To hear notes, then, a separate routine can be written including POKEs to the frequency registers and then POKEs to the waveform registers. The waveform registers must contain a 1 on bit 0 (the gate bit) to start the note. Resetting this bit to 0 then turns the note off (in practice, the bit is 0 if the register contains any even number). To move from one note to another, it is generally wise to POKE the relevant waveform register with zero or an even number; doing this will usually turn off an apparently unstoppable note. It is also useful to set all waveform registers to 0 at the beginning of a program in order to avoid a common programmer's error, which manifests itself as a lack of any sound output due to 'locking up' the waveform registers. This happens when bit 3 of a register is set to 1. The positioning of commands in your programs is often crucial, because it governs whether notes will be heard at all and also, to a large extent, the speed at which the programs run.

Pitch

So far we've dealt with one major musical parameter exclusively in terms of frequency. Music, however, makes far more extensive use of the concept of pitch, which is sufficiently different from frequency to require some explanation. Frequency is an absolute measurement, which specifies the number of cycles that occur in one second of a particular sound. Pitch, on the other hand, is a relative phenomenon – not even, strictly speaking, a measurement, because its determination is in practice subjective.

The existence of pitch depends on a sound having a determinable frequency. There are some musical sounds that have no determinable frequency or a frequency only partially determinable. These last are called 'unpitched' and 'semi-pitched' tones respectively and are typified by the 'white noise' feature available on both the BBC and Commodore micros, and the so-called 'periodic' noise featured on the BBC. Pitch is an attribute of regularity or (as it is usually described) periodicity. White noise is purely random, while 'periodic' noise contains random and periodic elements.

The difference between pitched, semi-pitched and unpitched tones can be readily seen on an oscilloscope. The pitched tones can be clearly divided into repeating cycles, while no such cycles are detectable in unpitched tones. The semi-pitched tones, not surprisingly, seem to be composed of both repeating and non-repeating elements. Two familiar examples of semi-pitched tones are a ringing bell and the whistling wind. 'Pure' white noise sounds like unobstructed wind or sea.

A PSG produces semi-pitched and unpitched tones by means of the same sort of digital pseudo-random number generator your computer utilizes in the BASIC operator RND. This is known as a shift-register sequence generator and it takes a binary number as input (the seed) and produces an apparently random sequence that starts repeating if you stay with it long enough.

By passing the output of the shift register through a suitable filter a sound resembling white noise can be produced. This is not genuinely randomized noise, but is like a decimal which recurs only after a long sequence of digits. If you take a small subsequence of the decimal, it will *look* random. Such a subsequence may be allowed to repeat rapidly – which, in terms of sound, produces a semi-pitched tone. The longer the subsequence, the more like white noise the corresponding sound.

If you look at an oscilloscope display of, say, the sound produced by an acoustic musical instrument, it doesn't necessarily seem to be regular. Even regular tones (like those associated with square waves) don't sound much like the pure tone produced by the classic sine wave. The eighteenth-century French mathematician Joseph Fourier showed that any typical waveform (technically, single-valued, continuous periodic waveforms of finite amplitude) can be considered to be the sum of an infinite number of simple sine waves whose amplitudes and periods all have a simple arithmetic relationship to the amplitude and frequency of the original compound waveform. The amplitude of a particular component can be considered, in particular cases, to be zero; if we describe the original waveform as a function of time we can write:

$$F(T) = A(1)*sin(W*T) + A(2)*sin(2*W*T) + A(3)*sin(3*W*T) + ...$$

where F(T) gives the values of the compound amplitude to be plotted against time, T, on a graph; the first term is known as the fundamental; W is 2*pi*FREQUENCY; and A(N) is the amplitude of the Nth component wave.

Though seeming very complicated, this is an immensely powerful result. In music all the terms after the fundamental represent the so-called 'harmonics' of a wave. Since soundwaves are not audible above 20 KHz, we usually don't bother with very high harmonics, but it is a consequence of Fourier's theorem that square waves, for example, contain all and only the odd harmonics of the fundamental, while certain sawtooth waves contain all the odd and even harmonics. Odd harmonics are waves described by the A(N)*sin(N*W*T) terms in the Fourier expansion when N is an odd number, and similarly for even harmonics. The expression N*W*T means that the frequency of the harmonics is N times the frequency of the fundamental. In simple waves like the square and sawtooth, the amplitude of harmonics decreases by the same proportion as the frequency increases.

For most practical purposes, we need consider only six or so harmonics. A simple example of how the theorem works (using only two harmonics) is demonstrated in the following program for the BBC Model B, which may be simply adapted for other computers. (The sound is not accurate, since the BBC does not use sine waves, but the effect is useful.)

```
1REM"Simple Fourier"
10REM***Original program by Ian Waugh***
15REM***amplitude and frequency interact**
*
16REM***the higher the frequency the lower
the amplitude***
17REM***since at higher frequencies the gr
aph has less time to reach maximum amplitude*
**
20MODE4
25DIMAmp%(3),H%(3)
30VDU28,0,4,39,0
40VDU24,0;0;1279;850;
60INPUT"How many harmonics(0 to 2)"Harmoni
c%
62IFHarmonic%=0THEN80
65INPUT" all(1),even(2),odd(3)"H%
70ON H% GOTO72,74,75
72H%(1)=2:H%(2)=3:GOTO80
74H%(1)=2:H%(2)=4:GOTO80
75H%(1)=3:H%(2)=5:GOTO80
80H%(0)=1
85INPUT"Frequency(1-10)"Freq%
90FORX%=0TOHarmonic%:PRINT"Amplitude ";X%+
1:INPUT" 0 to 20 "Amp%(X%)
100NEXT
110PROCWAVE
120PRINT"f0 enters another wave"'"f1 clears
screen"'"f2 finishes"
140 IFINKEY(-33)THEN60
150 IFINKEY(-114)CLG
160 IFINKEY(-115)MODE7:END
170 GOTO140
```

```
180 DEF PROCWAVE
182PROCSound
185Coordy%=0
190 VDU29,0;450;
200 MOVE0,0
210 FORTime%=0 TO 1279 STEP 10
220 FORX%=0TOHarmonic%
230 Coordy%=Coordy%+Amp%(X%)*SIN(RAD(Freq%*
H%(X%)*Time%))
240 NEXT
250 DRAWTime%,Coordy%
260 NEXT
265FORX%=1TO3:SOUND16+X%,0,0,0:NEXT
270 ENDPROC
280DEF PROCSound
290 FORX%=0TOHarmonic%
300 SOUNDX%+1,-Amp%(X%)/2,24*Freq%*H%(X%),-
1
310NEXT
320ENDPROC
```
PROGRAM 3.15

The harmonic content of a wave is best shown by use of a spectrum diagram, which gives an immediate picture of the harmonics present in the wave and their relative amplitudes. It should be clear from such a diagram that, for example, a filter may be used to alter the harmonic content of any waveform (see the discussion above).

The harmonic content of a waveform defines what is known as its timbre or, sometimes, colouration (by comparison with the spectra of lightwaves). Timbre is a major feature of our perception of sound and of the character of particular musical instruments. Once again, synthesis conventionally approaches the matter of timbre from a subtractive point of view, while acoustically speaking timbre is an additive phenomenon. Synthesizers, analogue and digital, usually produce one or more waveforms that are rich in harmonics (square, sawtooth and triangle) and then filter out unwanted harmonics to create new timbres. Acoustic instruments, however, produce timbre effectively by adding various sine waves together.

The subject of harmonics brings us back to pitch, for even harmonics can be thought of as the fundamental *plus* a number of octaves, and the octave is the fundamental unit of pitch. When we hear a sequence of pitched tones we hear them primarily as notes rather than frequencies. Each note has a specific frequency, but what counts most for music is the relationship between the notes, which is called the *interval*.

The notes are conventionally called by alphabeticl names – C, C# (C-sharp, to all intents and purposes is the same as D-Flat), D, D#, E, F, F#, G, G#, A, A# and B. The interval between one C and the next is called an octave, and it is divided into twelve equal smaller intervals, known as semitones.

There are two competing systems of octave intervals (called 'systems of tuning'), both designed to ensure that the intervals between semitones sound equal. The systems are laid out in Appendix 4. The commonest system uses an 'equally tempered scale', which specifies that the ratio of frequencies of successive semitones will be the 12th root of 2, roughly 1.05946. The equally tempered scale was introduced to allow simple transposition of musical pieces from one key to another. A piece of music may be thought of as a sequence of notes starting, say, C-E-G . . . and ending, say, . . . G-B-C. Note intervals are more important than the precise notes themselves, so the same 'tune' can be played with totally different notes – starting, say, D-F#-A . . . and ending . . . A-C-D. The original piece of music is said to belong to a particular key, characterized, at least in part, by the notes used in it. The new piece, in which every note has been shifted by two semitones, is said to have been transposed to a new key. Equal temperament was developed to make sure such transpositions worked, because earlier tuning systems didn't work on the basis of equal intervals between each semitone.

The classic non-tempered scale uses the system of 'just' tuning, in which the intervals that matter are those associated with simple note sequences. These sequences are essentially those produced when a vibrating string is divided into simple proportions. The best-known is perhaps the C-major scale, which contains just the notes playable on the white keys of a piano (C, D, E, F, G, A and B – or *do, re, mi, fa, so, la, ti*).

Just tuning ensures that the Pythagorean proportions deriving from vibrating strings still apply. For example, the third note in the C-major scale is E, and the ratio of frequencies of E to C in this scale – derived from vibrating strings – is 5:4. Similarly the fifth interval is associated with a ratio of 3:2. A chord of C-major (the tonic of the C-major scale) is produced by playing C, E and G together; with just tuning the intervals and chords are particularly harmonious. Although it is mathematically elegant and musically pleasing, just tuning doesn't allow you to transpose a piece from, say, C to D on the same instrument – because the note D as played in the key of C will have a different frequency from the note D as played in the key of D. This was the problem equally tempered scales were introduced to solve.

Pitch, then, is the human sense of musical intervals. Roughly speaking, it is related to frequency exponentially. For example, the standard frequency of A (440 Hz) produces lower and higher notes of A by halving and doubling the frequency: 110 Hz, 220 Hz, 440 Hz, 880 Hz, 1760 Hz and so on. Going from 110 Hz to 220 Hz is the same change in pitch (on both equally tempered and just scales) as going from 880 Hz to 1760 Hz. The absolute difference in frequency, however, is, respectively, 110 Hz and 880 Hz. A frequency change of 110 Hz at a bass frequency represents a pitch change of one octave. At high enough frequencies, such a change in frequency may be all but unnoticeable.

Pitch is important, because computers themselves work at the level of frequency. It is up to software (both low and high level) to help us produce intelligible pitches and notes. Theoretically any tuning system we choose is available on a computer, including microtonal systems that use minimum intervals of less than a semitone. In practice, efficient musical use of the computer means that tuning systems have, from time to time, to be brought into play.

The BBC's sound generator produces waves of frequencies given by the formula:

$$F = N/(32*n)$$

where N is the frequency of the clock used to control the chip, n is the decimal equivalent of a 10 bit number written to the chip and F is the resulting frequency in Hertz.

There are 1024 possible frequency values, a range of some ten octaves (since 1024 is 2 to the power 10). The BBC itself spans half the possible octave range, allowing 256 frequency values (input as pitch parameters in the SOUND statement ranging from 0 to 255). Examination shows that the frequencies may not exactly match any tuning. Almost certainly the note produced by any given pitch parameter will deviate from the value claimed for it in the user's guide.

The user manual says that the lowest note produced by the machine is B-below-B-below-middle-C (produced by a pitch parameter of 1) and that a pitch parameter of 53 produces a middle-C. It also says that a unit increase in pitch parameters produces a rise in pitch of one-quarter of one semitone (i.e. a rise of a semitone is equivalent to increasing the pitch parameter by 4). For most casual users this is accurate and convenient enough, allowing a degree of microtonality or, if you prefer, a degree of fine tuning and a convenient way of programming a chosen octave by adding multiples of 4 to a base figure. It also should allow easy transposition.

Unfortunately the tuning is not reliable, presumably because of the software, and it becomes less reliable the higher you go in pitch. The range of frequency is from about 124 Hz to about 5 KHz – rather too trebly for most serious synthesis. The lowest tone (with a pitch parameter of 0) is fairly close to B-below-B-below-middle-C on a just tuned scale. On the more useful equally tempered scale, middle-C would be produced by a pitch parameter of between 51 and 52. Moreover the accuracy of the microtones leaves something to be desired.

That said, the tuning system gains in ease of use what it loses in accuracy Slight out-of-tuneness can even add interest to a piece of music. But if you want your BBC to play along with other instruments, you would be advised to tune them to the computer rather than rely on what the BBC manual says.

The following program uses the pitch parameter to produce a musical glide (a more or less smooth transition from one note to another). As you can see, the idea that one semitone equals a difference of 4 in the pitch parameter, and that one octave is consequently equivalent to a difference of 48, makes programming quite easy. All the other BBC programs using pitch parameters in this book set a variable called BASE, which is effectively the root note of the octave. Notes are then described by pitch parameters in the form BASE + N or, more useful if you want to store the notes in an array, in the form BASE + 4*N (where N can be used as the argument for array variables). Transposition is also simplified by this approach since, for example, adding 4 to every pitch parameter in a piece should simply take the whole piece up one semitone, while adding 48 would take it up an octave. The most annoying feature of this is a result of the BBC's modulo arithmetic feature, which means that should you specify a pitch parameter of, say, 261 (which would be an E) what you get is a note that corresponds to 261 − 256, or 5 (which will give you what the manual says is a C).

```
1REM BBC GLIDE
5 REM SMOOTH GLIDE IS GIVEN BY SETTING DURATI
ON TO -1 (INDEFINITE)
7 REM AND CHANNEL TO 1+16 (FOR INSTANT FLUSH)
8 REM PROGRAM COULD BE SLOWED BY SETTING DURA
TION TO POSITIVE VALUE BELOW 255
9 REM OR BY ADDING A DELAY LOOP AT, SAY, LINE
 25
10 FOR F=0 TO 48
20 SOUND 17,-15,53+F,-1
30 NEXT
```
PROGRAM 3.16

(Try adding STEP 4 to line 10, to get a glide in semitone steps.)

For simplicity's sake, we will from now on accept the official version of the tuning on the BBC, but bear in mind its deficiencies.

The Commodore uses a much more elaborate system than the BBC. As a result it is more tiresome but much more accurate. Once again, a word of warning: the Commodore user guide does not necessarily give you a reliable indication of frequencies. It is worth experimenting if you want your computer to harmonize with other instruments. Program 3.17 will convert frequency into Commodore parameters and vice versa; as such, it may provide a useful subroutine to do that job in larger programs. Program 3.18 does the same job using note names as inputs rather than frequency. It is useful for transcribing written music into DATA statment. It also plays the note entered.

```
1 REM COMPLETE FREQUENCY RECKONER, G.HERMAN, 198
4
10 PRINT CHR$(147)
12 POKE54276,0
15 INPUT "PLAY MODE (Y/N):";D$
18 PRINT CHR$(147)
20 INPUT"FREQ > BYTES (1) OR BYTES > FREQ (2)";N
30 IF N<1 OR N>2 THEN 20
40 ON N GOSUB 100,200
42 IF D$="Y" THEN GOSUB 500
45 PRINT:PRINT
46 INPUT "TABULATE SUBSEQUENT VALUES(Y/N)";B$
48 IF B$="Y" THEN GOSUB 300
49 FOR X=1 TO 1000:NEXT:POKE54276,0
50 INPUT "ANOTHER (Y/N)";A$
60 IF A$="Y" THEN 10
70 END
100 PRINT CHR$(147)
110 INPUT"FREQUENCY IN HERTZ:";FR
120 PRINT:PRINT
130 PRINT TAB(15);"HIGH BYTE";SPC(3);"LOW BYTE"
140 H=INT(FR/0.0596):F=H/256:HF=INT(F):L=F-HF:LF
=INT(256*L)
150 PRINT FR,,HF,LF
180 RETURN
200 PRINT CHR$(147)
210 INPUT"BYTES (HIGH FIRST):";HF,LF
220 PRINT:PRINT
230 PRINT TAB(10);"FREQUENCY EQUIVALENT"
240 FR=INT((HF*256+LF)*0.05961)
250 PRINT FR,,HF,LF
260 RETURN
300 IF N=1 THEN 400
305 INPUT "BY LOW OR HIGH BYTE (L/H):";C$
306 IF (C$="L")+(C$="H")=0 THEN 305
307 INPUT "STEP (1 TO 100):";S
```

```
308 IF S<0 OR S>100 THEN 307
310 INPUT "HOW MANY VALUES(0-20)";X
320 IF X<0 OR X>20 THEN 310
322 IF C$="L" THEN Q=LF
323 IF C$="H" THEN Q=HF
324 PRINT CHR$(147):PRINT"FREQUENCY      HIGH BYT
E      LOW BYTE "
325 FOR P=0 TO X*S STEP S
328 IF Q>=256 THEN HF=HF+1:Q=Q-256
330 IF C$="L" THEN LF=Q
331 IF C$="H" THEN HF=Q
333 GOSUB 240
334 IF D$="Y" THEN GOSUB 500
335 Q=Q+S
355 NEXT
360 RETURN
400 INPUT "HOW MANY VALUES(0-20)";X
410 INPUT "STEP (1 TO 100):";S
420 IF X<0 OR X>20 THEN 410
425 PRINT CHR$(147):PRINT"FREQUENCY      HIGH BYT
E      LOW BYTE "
430 FOR P=0 TO X*S STEP S
440 GOSUB 140
445 IF D$="Y" THEN GOSUB 500
450 FR=FR+S
460 NEXT
470 RETURN
500 POKE 54296,15
510 POKE 54272,LF: POKE 54273,HF: POKE 54277,24:
POKE 54278,136:POKE 54276,17
520 RETURN
600 REM NOTE SLIGHT DISCREPANCIES IN VALUES - US
E TRIAL AND ERROR
700 REM WHEN FITTING VALUES IN TO AN ACTUAL PROG
RAM
800 REM SOME INTERESTING EFFECTS CAN BE ACHIEVED
900 REM BY SELECTING APPROPRIATE VALUES IN PLAY
MODE
```

PROGRAM 3.17

```
1 REM "PITCH RECKONER "
2 REM BY G.HERMAN,1984
3 REM FOR THE C-64
```

```
5 DIM F(12),N(12),HB(12),LB(12)
10 N$="C.C£D.D£E.F.F£G.G£A.A£B."
15 PRINT CHR$(147)
16 PRINT "----------X TO EXIT TO SYSTEM---------
-"
17 PRINT "ENTER NOTE-FOLLOWED BY HASH FOR SHARP"
18 PRINT "OR ANY KEY FOR NATURAL"
19 PRINT "FOLLOWED BY OCTAVE (O-7, DEFAULT 4)"
20 PRINT"========================================
"
21 PRINT"                  H/L BYTES..DATA NO..FREQ"
22 PRINT "NOTE: ";
23 GETA$:IF A$="" THEN 23
24 IF A$="X" THEN POKE 54283,0:END
25 PRINT A$;
26 GETB$:IF B$="" THEN 26
27 IF B$<>"£" THEN B$="."
29 PRINT B$;
30 GETC$:IF C$="" THEN 30
31 IF VAL(C$)<0 OR VAL(C$)>7 THEN C$="4"
32 IF (A$="B" OR A$="E") AND (B$="£") THEN PRINT
 " NO £ FOR THIS NOTE":GOTO 22
34 PRINT C$;
36 IF A$+B$+C$="B.7" THEN PRINT" TOP NOTE A£7":
GOTO 22
38 QP=0
39 FOR Z=1 TO LEN(N$)
40 IF MID$(N$,Z,1)=A$ THEN QP=1
50 NEXT
55 IF QP<>1 THEN PRINT" ERROR":GOTO22
60 A$=A$+B$
70 GOSUB 1000
190 PRINT TAB(15);HB(FL);"-";LB(FL);TAB(25);N(FL
);"-";F(FL)
195 GOSUB 300
200 RESTORE
210 GOTO 22
220 END
300 POKE 54296,15:POKE 54279,LB(FL):POKE54280,HB
(FL)
310 POKE 54284,40:POKE 54285,40:POKE54283,17
320 FOR P=1 TO 100: NEXT
330 RETURN
```

```
1000 REM*****************************************
**************************
1010 A$=LEFT$(A$,2)
1015 L=LEN(A$):FL=0
1020 FOR X=1 TO LEN(N$) STEP 2
1030 IF MID$(N$,X,L)=A$ THEN FL=(X+1)/2
1035 IF FL=(X+1)/2 THEN X=X+1
1040 NEXT
1050 IF FL<1 THEN 1000
1060 OC=VAL(C$)
1080 FOR Y=1 TO 12: READ F(Y): F(Y)=INT((F(Y)/10
00)*2^((OC-4)))
1090 N(Y)=INT(F(Y)/0.0596044433)
1100 HB(Y)=INT(N(Y)/256):LB(Y)=N(Y)-HB(Y)*256
1110 NEXT
1200 RETURN
10000 DATA 261624,277200,293656,311124,329648,34
9228
10010 DATA 370040,392040,415316,440000,466136,49
3856
10020 REM NOTE THAT THESE CALCULATIONS ARE BASED
ON STANDARD FREQUENCIES
10030 REM AND ON THE 64'S DECLARED CONSTANTS. CH
ANGES IN DATA OR THE VALUE IN
10040 REM LINE 1090 WILL GIVE DIFFERENT RESULTS,
WHICH MAY BE USEFUL FOR TUNING
10050 REM TO OTHER INSTRUMENTS.
```
PROGRAM 3.18

The Commodore sound chip produces frequencies according to the formula:

$$F=(n*N)/16777216$$

where n is the decimal equivalent of a 16 bit number written to the chip, N is the clock frequency used to control the chip and F is the resulting frequency in Hertz.

Given the Commodore's standard 1 MHz clock, this formula reduces to:

$$F=n*0.059604645$$

This long decimal number may be familiar from the approximate 12th root of 2 that we dealt with before. Indeed, SID is cleverly arranged to provide accurate equally tempered tuning. The resolution of the chip is practically infinite, there being 65,536 possible frequencies attainable over a range of some eight octaves. The lowest possible frequency is 0, while the highest is approximately equal to 3900 Hz, or around A# three octaves above A#-above-middle-C.

A frequency or pitch parameter is entered by POKEing the relevant locations (54272, 54273; or 54279, 54280; or 54286, 54287) with a low frequency byte and a high frequency byte respectively. The formulae used above show that calculating the relevant bytes from frequency information, and making adjustments for inaccurate tuning to individual notes, can be done quite simply. The optimum method for entering musical information is perhaps to work out a satisfactory tuning over two octaves and then use that as data to calculate values for any other notes or octaves you require. An example is shown in the program below, with the relevant DATA statement REMmed.

```
89 REM C-64 NOTE CALCULATION SUBROUTINE
90 REM SUBROUTINE TO CALCULATE HIGH AND LOW F
REQUENCY BYTES GIVEN A TABLE
91 REM OF 'DOUBLE BYTE' FREQUENCY NUMBERS (SE
E LINE 1000).
92 REM THESE NUMBERS REPRESENT FREQUENCIES OF
 THE NOTES IN THE LOWEST AUDIBLE
93 REM OCTAVE ON THE C-64.  LINE 210 WORKS OU
T THE APPROPRIATE NUMBER FOR
94 REM HIGHER OCTAVES (OCTAVE NUMBER IS HELD
IN VARIABLE 'O'), STARTING WITH C.
95 REM LINE 220 CONVERTS THIS NUMBER INTO EQU
IVALENT HIGH AND LOW BYTES TO BE
96 REM POKED INTO THE 64'S FREQUENCY REGISTER
S.
97 REM A SIMILAR SYSTEM, BUT USING ABSOLUTE F
REQUENCIES IN HERTZ, IS USED IN
98 REM THE PITCH RECKONER PROGRAM IN THIS BOO
K.
99 :
100 DIM F(12),H(8,12),L(8,12),N(8,12)
200 FOR X=1 TO 12:READ F(X)
210 N(O,X)=F(X)*2^O
220 H(O,X)=INT(N(O,X)/256):L(O,X)=N(O,X)-256*
H(O,X):NEXT
1000 DATA 268,285,301,318,335,352,385,402,419
,452,486,503
```

PROGRAM 3.19

Finally, the use of two frequency registers in the Commodore allows some interesting effects. While the low byte can be adjusted for fine tuning or effectively continuous glides (known as glissandi as opposed to the jerkier glides, which are known as portamenti), adjusting the high byte results in gross frequency sweeps, which, properly used, can be very effective.

```
10 REM C-64 GLIDE
20 POKE 54296,15:POKE 54277,36:POKE 54278,175
30 INPUT"STARTING FREQUENCY, HIGH AND LOW BYTES"
;H1,L1
40 INPUT"END FREQUENCY, HIGH AND LOW BYTES";H2,L
2
45 Q=H1:IF H1>H2 THEN Q=H2
50 Z=(256*(H2-H1)+(L2-L1))
55 POKE 54276,0
58 POKE 54276,17
60 FOR X=0 TO Z*SGN(Z) STEP Q
65 POKE 54273,H1:POKE 54272,L1
70 L1=L1+Q:IF L1>=256 THEN H1=H1+1:L1=L1-256
80 NEXT
90 POKE 54276,0
```
PROGRAM 3.20

Similar tricks can be played on the BBC using the ENVELOPE command, but we'll come to that later.

4

Controlling amplitude

Your computer can be programmed to play a simple piece of music without further ado. All that is required is a single routine to play a note into which pitch and duration data are entered using a READ . . . DATA instruction. The routine need be no more complicated than the one-line BBC program of the last chapter (or its Commodore equivalent). Pitch and duration are read into the appropriate variables (in our example for the 64, there are not even any duratation data since all notes apart from the last are the same length) and are thus assigned to the sound routine.

The programs are almost disarmingly simple, yet they can form the heart of far more versatile and elaborate musical programs. Their simplicity arises from the fact that only two of the vast range of musical parameters are dealt with: frequency and duration.

```
 1 REM BBC-GREENSLEEVES, BASIC VERSION
 2 REM NOTE PLACING OF DATA
10 DATA 165,5,177,10,185,5,193,10,197,10,1
93,5
20 DATA 185,5,173,5,157,20,165,5,173,5
30 DATA 177,5,165,5,165,5,165,5,161,5,165,
5
40 DATA 173,10,161,5,145,34
```

```
   50 DATA 165,5,177,10,185,5,193,10,197,10,1
93,5
   60 DATA 185,5,173,5,157,20,165,5,173,5
   70 DATA 165,2,161,3,153,3,161,3,165,60
  100 FOR X%=1 TO 36:READ FREQ%,DUR%:SOUND 1,
-10,FREQ%,DUR%:NEXT
  200 END
```
PROGRAM 4.1

```
10 REM C-64 TUNE WITH DURATION
20 POKE 54296,15:POKE 54277,9: POKE 54278,33
25 REM READ FREQ BYTES AND DURATION
30 READ A,B,C
50 IF A=0 THEN END
60 POKE 54273,A: POKE 54272,B
70 POKE 54276,17
71 REM '20' CAN BE SUBSTITUTED FOR, TO CHANGE
   TEMPO
72 FOR P=1 TO 20*C:NEXT
75 POKE 54276,0
77 REM DELAY BETWEEN NOTES
80 GOTO 30
100 DATA 19,63,20,21,154,20,17,37,30,8,147,15
,12,216,40,0,0,0
```
PROGRAM 4.2

Adding just one extra variable enormously enhances the effect. For example, we could allow volume to change locally by adding a third DATA item and associated variable, which would be assigned to the volume parameter of the BBC's SOUND command or the master volume register (location 54296) on the Commodore. This would give emphasis (or accent) to parts of the 'composition'. In general such deviations from an established norm as represented can be described as *modulations* – in this case, amplitude modulation.

We could draw a graph of an amplitude modulation, indicating time along the horizontal axis and amplitude along the vertical. The shape of this graph would represent an *envelope*, so-called because the amplitude modulation envelopes, in a sense, the notes that form the music. What we can do for a sequence of notes, we can also do for a single note. This is the more commonly used sense of the word 'envelope', in which we vary the amplitude of one note according to the shape of the envelope.

The obvious way to construct a note envelope in a program is to make the amplitude parameter a variable that changes while pitch stays constant. In the examples below, this is done by using a FOR . . . NEXT loop in which the loop counter variable is converted into an amplitude parameter.

```
1 REM BBC 4.3
2 REM TRY CHANGING DURATION FIGURE IN SOU
ND STATEMENT FOR EFFECT
10 FOR X%=15 TO 0 STEP -1
20 SOUND 1,-X%,53,1
30 NEXT
```
PROGRAM 4.3

```
1 REM BBC 4.3 (VARIANT)
2 REM BY USING THE FLUSH CONTROL (SOUND 1
7...) WE GET A RAPID SEQUENCE OF VERY
3 REM BRIEF TONES, SO X% COUNTS DOWN FROM
750 AND HAS TO BE DIVIDED BY 50
4 REM TO STAY WITHIN THE BBC'S VOLUME RAN
GE
5 REM TRY IT WITH X%=15 TO 0!
10 FOR X%=750 TO 0 STEP -1
20 SOUND 17,-X%/50,53,1
30 NEXT
```
PROGRAM 4.3A

```
5 REM C-64 ENVELOPE USING FOR...NEXT LOOP
10 S=54272:L=S:H=S+1:W=S+4:A=S+5:R=S+6:V=S+24
20 Y=15:F=34:E=240:Q=33:X=10
30 FOR P=0 TO 24:POKE S+P,0:NEXT
40 POKE R,E:POKE H,F:POKE W,Q
50 REM CHANGE 'P' AND 'Y' VALUES FOR DIFFEREN
T ENVELOPES
60 FOR P=1 TO 40:POKE V,Y:Y=Y/1.06:NEXT
70 POKE W,0
```
PROGRAM 4.4

This approach needs to be handled with care on the Commodore, since that computer requires its built-in envelope feature to be used. On the BBC you can ignore the ENVELOPE command altogether. With the 64, it is important to set parameters that will, as far as possible, suppress the influence of the built-in envelope, but we will deal with this at greater length later.

You can easily tell the difference between the notes produced without modulation and those produced using it. The modulation makes the note sound more interesting; it seems to have a shape, growing and dying away just like the notes produced by most familiar instruments. All notes have an amplitude envelope, even if that envelope would look more like a box shape if drawn – straight sides, flat top – than an interesting sequence of slopes. The 'built-in' envelope used in program 4.4 is such a box shape. It resembles the cross-section of a plateau, rising steeply to a constant amplitude and falling off just as steeply when the note ends. The notes modulated by the FOR . . . NEXT loops above rise just as steeply and then fall away gradually to zero amplitude. This isn't the only kind of envelope you could apply to a note using a FOR . . . NEXT loop. One approach would be to set amplitude values as the elements of an array and then use the control variable of the loop to index the array. I include two variants of this approach (both for the BBC) one of which, although longer, gives a smoother sounding result.

```
  1 REM BBC
 10 DIM AMP%(15)
 20 FOR X%=1 TO 15
 30 READ AMP%(X%)
 40 SOUND 1,-AMP%(X%),53,1
 50 NEXT
 60 END: REM 'RESTORE:GOTO 20' TO REPEAT
 70 DATA 2,15,14,12,10,10,9,9,8,8,8,7,6,4,2
```
PROGRAM 4.5

```
  1 REM BBC
 10 DIM AMP%(15)
 20 FOR X%=1 TO 15
 30 READ AMP%(X%)
 32 NEXT
 35 FOR X%=1 TO 15
 40 SOUND 1,-AMP%(X%),53,1
 50 NEXT
 60 RESTORE:GOTO35
 70 DATA 2,15,14,12,10,10,9,9,8,8,8,7,6,4,2
```
PROGRAM 4.5A

(The examples use BBC BASIC but could be adapted for the 64, as an exercise.)

Using arrays to define amplitude envelopes allows you to achieve some weird effects – notes whose volume suddenly changes, or rises or falls in jerky steps, or falls to zero in the middle of the note. But these do not often sound *right*.

The sounds made by acoustic instruments – indeed, all naturally occurring sounds – display envelopes of one broad type: the sound rises to a peak and decays to zero, sometimes holding at a 'plateau' level for a while but always making smooth transitions. Sound synthesis has arrived at a convention for describing this sort of envelope. It is called the attack-decay-sustain-release (or ADSR) envelope.

ADSR envelopes see an individual sound as divided into a maximum of four phases: the attack phase during which the sound rises to a peak level, the decay phase during which it declines, the sustain phase during which the note holds at plateau amplitude and the release phase during which it drops to zero. Computer synthesis of ADSR envelopes inevitably simplifies the phenomenon of amplitude modulation. Each musical instrument has a distinctive envelope, which the ADSR envelope attempts to mimic. The attempt is often successful, even though it relies exclusively on the grossest similarities between the natural and the synthesized envelopes.

Typically, stringed instruments have a fairly sharp attack and a gradual decay/release. Brass and woodwinds have a noticeably gentler attack and a slightly sharper decay/release; sustain is also common with brass and woodwind and with bowed but not plucked or struck strings. The pipe organ has a gradual attack and a sharp decay/release; it also often features a considerable degree of sustain. Percussive instruments (including the piano) have sharp attack, giving the percussive effect, and comparatively gentle decay and release (sharpen decay to get a crisper or 'plinkier' effect).

It is always worth experimenting with ADSR parameters, if only because the results are sometimes surprising. Small changes in parameters can often have a substantial effect, while it is equally likely that a large change will have little apparent effect at all. For example, if sustain is set at its highest possible level (by POKEing 240 into the 64's sustain register or setting the BBC 'decay target level' to 126), then the decay setting will have no effect, since with maximum sustain there will be no decay but only release.

Many of the programs in this book allow you to change envelope parameters in run-time. It is worth keeping a notebook to write down particularly successful or pleasing groups of parameters for future reference.

ADSR in practice

There is no substitute for experimenting with ADSR envelope parameters. To give you some idea of what's going on when you do, we'll take a brief look at how our two computers use them.

On the BBC, the amplitude envelope is specified by the last six parameters of the ENVELOPE command. Details of the timings involved are given in Appendix 2. The six parameters are:

(i)   attack step;
(ii)   decay step;

(iii)   sustain step;
(iv)   release step;
(v)   peak amplitude (at end of the attack phase);
(vi)   plateau amplitude (at end of the decay phase).

Unlike the Commodore, the BBC's envelope parameters specify the maximum amplitude of the note; the normal amplitude parameter (in the SOUND command) is given over to calling the ENVELOPE command. The BBC ENVELOPE command also specifies parameters in terms of the relevant change in amplitude that will occur during the phase − only the last two specify levels of amplitude. Since the 76489 chip allows only sixteen levels of attenuation to be specified (from 0 to -28 dB in steps of -2 dB), there are only sixteen possible step or amplitude values specifiable for each phase of the amplitude envelope. The BBC allows step parameters in the range 0 to 127, and peak and plateau amplitude can be any value up to 126. However, these values are divided into bands so that each amplitude level can be specified by any one of eight parameters: 0-7, 8-15, 16-23, 24-31, 32-39, 40-47, 48-55, 56-63, 64-71, 72-79, 80-87, 88-95, 96-103, 104-111, 112-119, 120-127. It is not clear why the maximum peak and plateau levels are set at 126: it seems likely this is because the machine code routine that handles the ENVELOPE command may not recognize a peak value of 127 where a step parameter has also been 127.

The values seem complicated, especially when it comes to working out their signs (positive or negative). As with other BBC commands, the operating system ensures that any value that goes over or under an acceptable limit is brought in range again by an appropriate addition or subtraction. Each phase works in the same way: the specified value is merely added to the previous value (with zero as the very first value) until peak, plateau or zero levels are reached. In order to produce a fall in amplitude, therefore, you must specify a negative step value. Positive step values always produce a rise, and zero values produce no change. Finally, remember that the release phase of an envelope is entered only after the note has been turned off (usually at the end of its specified duration). The step parameter in the release phase then determines the rate at which the note dies away to silence. (I haven't followed the BBC manual's system of abbreviations for the parameters, usually because it makes more sense to give them less ambiguous 'names'. These can be observed in any of the relevant programs.)

The Commodore also uses an ADSR system and, once again, the timings are listed in Appendix 2. The major difference is that the Commodore's attack, decay and release parameters specify rates rather than amplitude steps. Each value is entered as a nybble (half a byte); so once again there are sixteen possible values for each phase. Only the sustain value is interpreted as a level. There are sixteen possible levels, the sustain nybble (values between

0 and 240 in multiples of 16 POKEd into the relevant SR register) specifying the fraction of peak level that will constitute the plateau level: thus 0 means a zero sustain level, while 240 means the note will sustain at maximum amplitude. As far as A, D and R values are concerned, the lower the value the faster the phase takes place. Thus the sharpest attack is set by a value of 0 and, for example, the gentlest decay is set by a value of 15. POKEing the relevant AD register with 15 will then give a sharp attack followed by a gentle decay. POKEing the register with 240, on the other hand, will give the gentlest attack and the sharpest decay, since 240 equals 240 + 0 or, as a byte-long binary number, 11110000.

As with the BBC, the release phase takes place only when a note is terminated, and it determines how long it will take for the note to die out from its sustain level to zero. If the sustain level is zero, the release parameter will have no effect. When a sustain level is set, it is usual to add a delay loop to the program to specify the length of the sustain phase. When the delay is over (or if the note is turned off by resetting the gate bit to 0 in the relevant waveform register) the release phase takes over and the note dies away. The release phase can take as long as twenty-four seconds; you should therefore pay some attention to the value programmed as release parameter.

You'll realize by now that the 64 does not include a peak amplitude parameter in its envelope specification. This is because peak level is set by the overall volume control register (location 54296). The level has sixteen values which, unlike the BBC, are linearly scaled. The 76489 chip's use of twenty-eight dB levels ensures that you can set volume to decrease through linear parameters, for example, and the result will be a logarithmic decline. This is a more natural system, taking the ear's logarithmic variation in sensitivity into account. If you want to achieve the same sort of logarithmic change with the Commodore's 6581 SID chip, it will be necessary to program the volume register with exponentially varying values. Thus if POKE 54296, VOL is included within a FOR . . . NEXT loop in order to simulate decay, VOL should be specified as in the following program.

```
5 REM C-64 NATURAL DECAY
10 S=54272:L=S:H=S+1:W=S+4:A=S+5:R=S+6:V=S+24
20 Y=30:F=34:E=240:Q=33:X=10
30 FOR P=0 TO 24:POKE S+P,0:NEXT
40 POKE R,E:POKE H,F:POKE W,Q
60 FOR P=1 TO60:POKEV,Y-3.3*LOG(P):NEXT
70 POKE W,0
```
PROGRAM 4.6

Commonly, you merely set the volume at a suitable level and leave it there, using the envelope registers as the only means of varying amplitude.

Tremolo

We could superimpose an amplitude envelope on a continuous note repeatedly. In analogue synthesizers the commonest way of doing this is to use a low frequency oscillator (LFO) to control the amplitude of the ordinary tone-generation oscillator. The LFO will typically have a frequency range between about 0.1 and 30 Hz (that's between one cycle every ten seconds and thirty cycles every second), and its output will be a standard waveform. The effect of superimposing such a low frequency wave on to an audio frequency wave will be to produce a tone of continuously varying volume.

At the right frequency and degree of modulation the LFO wave can be used to provide a single ADSR-type envelope. This is sometimes done on analogue synthesizers. More commonly the LFO is used to produce an effect known as tremolo.

Tremolo sounds like a wavering in a tone, often confused with the slight, rapid, repetitive variations in the frequency known as vibrato. Of the two, tremolo is easier to produce on a computer but must be handled carefully if the effect is to remain musical. Adding tremolo is one fairly simple way of 'livening up' the normally dry tones produced by the sort of simple digital techniques available on small micros. It also allows one particularly interesting special effect, by using noise as the modulated sound. Some useful rhythmic effects can be achieved this way; try it out using the following programs.

This program for the BBC Model B gives an effective tremolo, and may be converted into a form suitable for inclusion in a larger program. As shown, it is essentially a demonstration, allowing you to hear the effect of various rates and depths of tremolo. You can obtain anything from a slowly rising and falling envelope, through a pleasant mandolin-type sound, to a weird sort of stuttering. The first listing uses a sine wave as the modulating waveform. It is followed by a simpler program in which amplitude switches between two values – effectively, a square-wave modulation.

```
1 REM BBC TREMOLO EFFECT
2 REM ANY VALUES WORK BUT
3 REM BEST RESULTS WITH RATE OF 100-200
4 REM AND DEPTH OF 1-5
5 REM TRY 53,2,200 AS VALUES
10 CLS
20 INPUT"PITCH VALUE"'"TREMOLO DEPTH"'"TRE
MOLO RATE"';PV%,DP%,RT%
30 FOR Y%=1TO2 STEP0
40 FOR X%=0TO359 STEPRT%
```

```
50  V%=DP%*COS(X%)+7
60  SOUND 1,-V%,PV%,1
70   NEXTX%,Y%
```
PROGRAM 4.7

```
 1  REM BBC
 5  INPUT"DEPTH,RATE"DEPTH%,RATE%
10  FOR X%=1 TO 100
20  V%=-15-DEPTH%*(INT(X%/2)=X%/2)
30  SOUND 1,V%,53,RATE%
40  NEXT
```
PROGRAM 4.8

Another way of producing tremolo on the BBC is to use a loop to repeatedly call a short ADSR envelope or to switch between envelopes. (The '17' in the sound statements is necessary to restart the envelope on every cycle. Had the statements just included a channel number without adding 16 to activate the 'flush' feature in the BBC's sound buffer, each successive loop of the programs would just add another note to the queue.)

```
 1  REM BBC
 2  REM ENVELOPE DECAY CHARACTERISTICS WILL
GIVE TREMOLO DEPTH
 3  REM PAUSE IN LINE 25 GIVES RATE
10  ENVELOPE 1,1,0,0,0,0,0,0,126,-20,0,0,12
6,106
20  SOUND 17,1,53,1
25  FOR PAUSE=1 TO 60:NEXT
30  GOTO 20
```
PROGRAM 4.9

```
 1  REM BBC
10  ENVELOPE 1,1,0,0,0,0,0,0,126,-20,0,-126
,126,106
20  ENVELOPE 2,1,0,0,0,0,0,0,126,0,0,-126,1
26,126
30  REPEAT
35  V=(1+V)MOD2 +1
40  SOUND 17,V,53,1
50  FOR PAUSE=1 TO 80:NEXT
70  UNTIL FALSE
```
PROGRAM 4.10

It is difficult to produce an effective tremolo on the BBC within an already enveloped sound, since to do this properly would mean setting all the ADSR step parameters to variables with suitably fluctuating values. The ENVELOPE command is designed for vibrato, rather than tremolo, and this design feature should probably be taken advantage of when a warbling or wavering effect is required. However, it is interesting to experiment with the sustain phase of the ADSR envelope, giving the sustain parameter an alternately positive and negative value.

```
  1 REM BBC
  2 REM S% AND DECAY CHARACTERISTICS GIVE D
EPTH: PAUSE GIVES RATE
  3 REM NOT VERY RELIABLE
 10 S%=1
 20 ENVELOPE 1,1,0,0,0,0,0,0,126,-20,S%,-12
6,126,106
 30 SOUND 17,1,53,1
 40 S%=-S%
 45 FOR PAUSE=1 TO 60:NEXT
 50 GOTO 20
```
PROGRAM 4.11

With the 64, there is little point in using the master volume register, location 54296, in a loop to create tremolo. The effect is too jerky to be useful. The SID chip contains two read-only registers (locations 54299 and 54230), which are designed for just this sort of effect.

Register 27 (54299) reads a byte which follows the amplitude of the waveform produced by oscillator 3 (location 54290). The values vary between 0 and 255 in a manner determined by the waveform and at a rate determined by the frequency of oscillator 3. Oscillator 3's audio output can and should be turned off by setting bit 2 of location 54295 (register 23) to 0 and bit 7 of location 54296 (register 24) to 0. Set oscillator 3 to a suitable frequency (say, 10 Hz) and the required waveform, PEEK register 27 and divide by 17 or more (to get a value in the range 0 to 15), then POKE that value into register 24, location 54296, to produce the required tremolo.

```
10 REM TREMOLO, C-64
20 POKE 54296,15+128
30 INPUT"MODULATED NOTE, HI AND LOW BYTES";HC,LC
40 INPUT"MODULATING FREQUENCY, HI AND LOW BYTES"
;HM,LM
50 POKE 54291,0:POKE 54292,255
```

```
60 POKE 54286,LM:POKE 54287,HM
70 POKE 54290,17
80 POKE 54277,0:POKE 54278,255
90 POKE 54276,33:POKE 54273,HC:POKE 54272,LC
95 REM HAVING LOADED CHANNEL THREE OSCILLATOR WI
TH ADSR, FREQ AND TRIANGLE WAVE
96 REM WE PEEK REGISTER 27 AND POKE THE VALUE IN
TO THE MASTER VOL REG. CH.1
98 REM DEPTH OF MODULATION GOVERNED BY VALUE OF
DIVISOR IN LINE 100
100 MV=16-(PEEK(54299))/64:REM GIVES A RELATIVEL
Y SHALLOW MODULATION
110 POKE 54296,MV+128:GOTO 100
```
PROGRAM 4.12

Register 28 works in a similar way but produces an output which depends on the channel 3 envelope (locations 54291 and 54292). This program uses that output to produce a tremolo effect.

```
10 REM C-64 CHANNEL 3 ENVELOPE TREMOLO
15 REM YOU MAY GET INTERFERENCE FROM CHANNEL
THREE DESPITE TURNING IT OFF
17 REM IN LINE 40 -- THERE SEEMS TO BE NO SOLU
TION TO THIS.
20 POKE 54277,64: POKE 54278,128
22 REM THE FOLLOWING POKES ARE CRITICAL
25 POKE 54291,7:POKE54292,32
30 READ A,B
35 REM LOOP VALUES AND PEEK DIVISOR DETERMINE
 RATE AND DEPTH
40 FOR P=1 TO 10:POKE 54290,1:FOR Q=1 TO 4:PO
KE 54296,143-PEEK(54300)/64:NEXT
45 POKE54290,0:NEXT
50 IF A=0 THEN 90
60 POKE 54273,A: POKE 54272,B
70 POKE 54276,17
80 GOTO 30
90 FOR P=1 TO 800: NEXT: POKE 54276,16
100 DATA 19,63,21,154,17,37,8,147,12,216,0,0
```
PROGRAM 4.13

Enveloped notes in practice

Finally, here are some programs for the BBC and the Commodore which play tunes using enveloped notes. The BBC program 4.14 also includes variable tempo and pitch as well as incorporating a rest (indicated by the zero in the Freq%,Dur% pair 0,5 in line 40). Program 4.15, for the BBC, uses two separately enveloped sounds. Program 4.16 for the Commodore plays our old friend, the theme from *Close Encounters*, and includes filtering to smooth the FOR . . . NEXT loop generated note envelopes. Program 4.17, again for the Commodore, plays a single-channel version of 'After the Ball' using data for frequency (in a single number form) and duration. Data is assigned to variables N and D (line 150), and N is converted into high and low bytes in line 170. The envelope is set in lines 100-110. This program also allows you to adjust tempo, and uses frequency data to signal rests and the end of the piece. Down to line 4010, the program is a skeleton for any single-channel tune. All you have to do is fill in the data. The same can be said for program 4.14.

```
   1 REM BBC-GREENSLEEVES
   2 REM VARIABLE PITCH AND TEMPO
   3 REM PLUS ENVELOPE
   4 REM AND REST
  10 DATA 165,5,177,10,185,5,193,10,197,10,1
93,5
  20 DATA 185,5,173,5,157,20,165,5,173,5
  30 DATA 177,5,165,5,165,5,165,5,161,5,165,
5
  40 DATA 173,10,161,5,145,30,0,5
  50 DATA 165,5,177,10,185,5,193,10,197,10,1
93,5
  60 DATA 185,5,173,5,157,20,165,5,173,5
  70 DATA 165,2,161,3,153,3,161,3,165,60
  80 CLS:INPUT"PITCH ADJUSTMENT";P%
  90 INPUT"TEMPO";D%
  95 ENVELOPE 1,1,0,0,0,0,0,0,64,-63,0,-63,1
26,63
 100 FOR X%=1 TO 37:READ FREQ%,DUR%
 110 IF FREQ%=0 THEN V%=0 ELSE V%=1
 120 SOUND 1,V%,P%+FREQ%,D%*DUR%:NEXT
 200 END
```

PROGRAM 4.14

```
   1 REM BBC-GREENSLEEVES
   2 REM VARIABLE PITCH AND TEMPO
   3 REM PLUS ENVELOPE
   4 REM AND REST
   5 REM NOTE THE SECOND ENVELOPE
  10 DATA 165,5,177,10,185,5,193,10,197,10,1
93,5
  20 DATA 185,5,173,5,157,20,165,5,173,5
  30 DATA 177,5,165,5,165,5,165,5,161,5,165,
5
  40 DATA 173,10,161,5,145,30,0,5
  50 DATA 165,5,177,10,185,5,193,10,197,10,1
93,5
  60 DATA 185,5,173,5,157,20,165,5,173,5
  70 DATA 165,2,161,3,153,3,161,3,165,60
  80 CLS:INPUT"PITCH ADJUSTMENT";P%
  90 INPUT"TEMPO";D%
  95 ENVELOPE 1,1,0,0,0,0,0,0,64,-63,0,-63,1
26,63
  97 ENVELOPE 2,1,0,0,0,0,0,0,30,10,-40,-20,
60,126
 100 FOR X%=1 TO 37:READ FREQ%,DUR%
 110 IF FREQ%=0 THEN V%=0 ELSE V%=1
 120 SOUND 1,V%,P%+FREQ%,D%*DUR%
 130 SOUND 2,V%*2,P%+FREQ%-48,D%*DUR%
 140 NEXT
 200 END
```

PROGRAM 4.15

```
10 REM CBMTUNE3 (CLOSE ENCOUNTERS, FOR...NEXT EN
VELOPE & FILTER)
20 POKE 54277,0:POKE 54278,240
22 POKE 54293,1:POKE54294,0:POKE54295,1
25 FOR D=1 TO 10
30 READ A,B
50 IF A=0 THEN 90
55 FOR V=15 TO 0 STEP -1
56 POKE 54296,V+16
60 POKE 54273,A: POKE 54272,B
75 POKE 54276,17
76 NEXT
78 REM INSERT POKE 54276,0 TO SEE THE EFFECT OF
SETTING GATE BIT TO ZERO
```

```
80 GOTO 30
90 RESTORE  : NEXT
100 DATA 19,63,21,154,17,37,8,147,12,216,0,0
```
PROGRAM 4.16

```
1 REM *****AFTER THE BALL C-64*****
2 REM ***  USING THE SKELETUNE  ***
3 REM ***MUSIC BY CHAS.K.HARRIS ***
4 REM ***ARRANGED  BY  G.HERMAN ***
5 REM **ORIGINAL PROGRAM B.BAYLEY**
6 REM ******************************
10 PRINT CHR$(147):GOSUB 1000: REM INITIALISE
100 A(1)=40:R(1)=40
110 POKE AD(1),A(1):POKE SR(1),R(1)
120 POKE MV,15
130 INPUT "TEMPO (1 TO 100)";T
140 IF T<1 OR T>100 THEN 140
145 PRINT"AFTER THE BALL - BY CHAS. K. HARRIS"
150 READ N,D: IF N<0 THEN POKE WF(1),0
154 IF N<0 THEN END
160 D=D*T
170 HF(1)=INT(N/256):LF(1)=N-HF(1)*256
180 POKE FH(1),HF(1):POKE FL(1),LF(1)
190 POKE WF(1),17
200 FOR X=1 TO D: NEXT
210 POKE WF(1),0
220 GOTO 150
300 REM ******************************************
999 REM REGVAR
1000 S=54272
1010 FOR X=1 TO 3
1020 CH=7*(X-1)
1030 FL(X)=S+CH:FH(X)=FL(X)+1:PL(X)=FH(X)+1:PH(X
)=PL(X)+1:WF(X)=PH(X)+1
1040 AD(X)=WF(X)+1:SR(X)=AD(X)+1
1050 NEXT
1060 HC=SR(3)+1:LC=HC+1:RF=LC+1:MV=RF+1:PX=MV+1:
PY=PX+1:O3=PY+1:E3=O3+1
1070 FOR X=0 TO 24: POKE S+X,0: NEXT
1080 RETURN
2000 REM ******************************************
3000 REM THIS SPACE FOR DATA
3100 REM IN FORM: FREQUENCY DATA, DURATION DATA
```

```
3200 REM TERMINATE WITH DATA -1,-1
3300 REM TO REPEAT, ADD LINE 152:
3400 REM "152 IF N<0 THEN RESTORE: GOTO 150"
3500 REM TO REPEAT A DEFINITE NUMBER OF TIMES
4000 REM (SAY 3, GIVING FOUR PLAYS IN ALL)
4010 REM INSERT LINE "152 IF N<0 AND B<3 THEN RE
STORE: B=B+1: GOTO 150"
5000 DATA 7381,8,4378,12,7381,4,5855,16,4915,8,4
378,24
6000 DATA 7381,8,4378,12,7381,4,5855,16,4915,8,5
519,48,0,8
7000 DATA 4378,8,6576,8,7381,8,7818,8,9848,12,78
18,4
8000 DATA 7381,16,6576,8,6204,24,6576,24,6576,8,
7381,12,6576,4
8100 DATA 5519,16,4378,8,8774,8,8774,8,7818,4,87
74,4
8200 DATA 7818,4,6576,4,5519,4,4378,4
8300 DATA 7381,8,4378,12,7381,4,5855,16,4915,8,5
855,24,4378,24
8400 DATA 4915,8,6576,12,7381,4,9848,16,8774,8,8
254,24,8254,8
8500 DATA 4127,8,7818,8,8774,8,6576,8,6576,8,657
6,8,7381,8,7818,8
8600 DATA 7381,24,4378,36,4915,36,5519,24,6576,8
,5855,16,4378,8,5855,40
9000 DATA -1,-1
```
PROGRAM 4.17

5

Controlling duration

We have seen how a sequence of frequencies can be modulated to form different notes. Now we come to a consideration of that most important of musical concepts: time. At the simplest level, the effect of changing a time parameter is to shorten or extend the duration of an individual note. This is most simply achieved by altering the duration parameter in the BBC SOUND command and by altering the delay loop in the basic Commodore routine for producing a note.

```
    1 REM BBC 5.1
    2 ENVELOPE 1,10,0,0,0,0,0,0,126,-126,0,-1
26,126,0: REM NOTE T-PARAMETER, TRY THIS WITH
 IT EQUAL 1 AND 100 AS WELL
    3 REM NOTE THAT THE PROGRAM MOVES ON BEFO
RE THE NOTES HAVE ALL FINISHED
    4 REM TRY THIS WITH THE FLUSH CONTROL (SO
UND 16+...)
    5 PRINT "PART ONE"
   10 FOR DUR=1 TO 100 STEP 10
   20 SOUND 1,1,53,DUR
   30 NEXT
   40 REM COMPARE NEXT LINES
```

```
   50 PRINT "PART TWO"
  100 FOR DUR=1 TO 100 STEP 10
  110 ENVELOPE 2,DUR,0,0,0,0,0,0,126,-126,0,-
126,126,0
  120 SOUND 1,2,53,DUR
  130 NEXT
```
PROGRAM 5.1

```
 10 REM C-64 DURATION DEMO
 15 REM NOTE HOW RAPID REPETITION OF SHORT NOT
ES RESEMBLES TREMOLO
 20 POKE 54296,15
 30 POKE 54272,34:POKE 54273,17
 40 POKE 54277,0:POKE 54278,240
 50 FOR X=1 TO 100
 60 POKE 54276,33
 70 FOR P=1 TO 10*X:NEXT
 80 POKE 54276,0
 90 NEXT
```
PROGRAM 5.2

```
 10 REM BBC DURATION DEMO
 20 FOR X=1 TO 100
 30 SOUND 1,-15,53,X
 40 FOR P=1 TO 100:NEXT
 50 NEXT
```
PROGRAM 5.3

If the changes are made to apply to a sequence of notes, the effect is to speed up or slow down the piece of music. This speed is known as the *tempo* of the piece and is traditionally referred to by a number of Italian expressions – for instance, largo (slow), moderato (medium) and allegro (fast). There are a number of conventional tempo categories, but for our purposes it is sufficient to talk of slow, medium and fast alone.

The tempo is related to standard note lengths: quaver, crochet, minim and semibreve are the commonest lengths in use (there is also the breve, the semiquaver and the demi-semiquaver). These note lengths are all relative, each defined as twice the length of its predecessor. In consequence, it often makes more sense to talk of an eighth note (quaver), quarter note, half note and whole note, extending the range where necessary. We shall employ this terminology.

Since note lengths are relative to each other, they are also relative to tempo. To define a standard, let's assume that a whole note on the BBC is obtained with a duration parameter of 20 (that is, it lasts about a second). Likewise, a whole note on the 64 results from using an upper limit in the FOR . . . NEXT delay loop of, say, 1024. These values effectively define a tempo. You may find they need adapting for your particular machine, but they are useful enough to demonstrate timing.

The Commodore program below shows the effect of altering duration parameters globally. The BBC 'Greensleeves' program 4.12 can be used similarly by responding to the 'TEMPO?' prompt. At the limits, when duration is great or small, the sense of melody begins to break down. At a very fast tempo, a sequence of notes begins to sound like a warble − a single, modulated note. At the other extreme, the melody becomes so slow that it is hard to follow the changes. Therefore, there appears to be an optimum range for tempo, if not an acceptable absolute standard. In practice, moderato will be considered the tempo defined above at which a whole note lasts for approximately one second.

```
10 REM CBMTUNE2 (CLOSE ENCOUNTERS, REPEATS AND G
ETS FASTER)
20 POKE 54296,15:POKE 54277,64: POKE 54278,128
25 FOR DL=400 TO 0 STEP-40
30 READ A,B
40 FOR P=1 TO DL: NEXT
50 IF A=0 THEN 90
60 POKE 54273,A: POKE 54272,B+TR
70 POKE 54276,17
80 GOTO 30
90 FOR P=1 TO 2*DL: NEXT: POKE 54276,16
95 RESTORE:NEXT
100 DATA 19,63,21,154,17,37,8,147,12,216,0,0
```
PROGRAM 5.4

(Try this program with different values in line 25, say, FOR DL=5000 TO 0 STEP 100. Also try adding line 35 POKE 54276,0 to see the effect).

As has been done in previous programs, duration can be controlled, globally and locally, by calculating note lengths as the product of a straightforward duration and a tempo value. The first is a local variable, the second global (similarly, pitch may be considered local and key global).

There are other techniques for controlling duration. Jumping ahead of ourselves, here is a program that plays a three-part tune (using all three sound channels on the 64). This uses the computer's internal real-time clock instead of a delay loop to measure note length (see lines 130, 210, 260 and 270). At line 270, the program waits until time (in the form of the value of system variable TI) catches up with duration before moving on to the next set of notes to play. This program is followed by a revised version, reproduced in full, which goes back to a FOR ... NEXT loop for timing. The revised program also contains some other potentially useful features.

The internal clock approach can be used on the BBC (where the variable TIME does the same job as the 64's TI). Note that in program 5.6 only one channel is gated. The other channel notes are tied, apparently gliding from one to the next. This is done by not resetting waveform/control registers to zero, and it is done because the chief difficulty with this sort of program is the timings. You could synchronize the notes on all channels, but this leads to a sterile effect; far better to miss the odd beat and slip a bit. Experimentation with duration values is usually the only reliable technique, especially since putting notes in programs tends to mess up theoretical timings. Note how the phrases in the programs below are sometimes repeated: DATA items F and E trigger flags RS and RP, which then RESTORE the DATA pointer making a repetition happen. On the BBC, you can send the DATA pointer to any line by the command RESTORE (line number), which is more versatile and very useful.

```
1 REM BUTTERFIELD BOOGIE
100 PRINT CHR$(147):GOSUB 60000
105 SW=33:WN=129:TR=17
110 POKE MV,15
120 POKE A1,9:POKE R1,0:POKE A2,36:POKE R2,36:PO
KE A3,18:POKE R3,250
130 T=TI
200 POKE W1,0:POKE W2,0:POKE W3,0
210 READ DU: IF DU=0 THEN 290
215 IF DU<>15 THEN WN=TR:SW=TR
220 READ A,B,C,D,E,F
225 IF F=1 AND RP<>1 THEN RESTORE:RP=1
226 IF E=1 AND RS<>1 THEN RESTORE:RS=1
230 POKE FH,A:POKE FL,B: POKE W1,SW
240 POKE GH,C:POKE GL,D: POKE W2,WN
```

```
250 POKE HH,E:POKE HL,F: POKE W3,TR
260 T=T+DU
270 IF T>TI THEN 270
280 GOTO 200
290 GOSUB60000
295 END
1000 DATA 15,17,37,68,149,4,73
1010 DATA 15,21,154,0,0,0,0
1020 DATA 15,25,177,0,0,6,108
1030 DATA 15,28,214,0,0,0,0
1040 DATA 15,30,141,115,88,7,163
1050 DATA 15,28,214,0,0,0,0
1060 DATA 15,25,177,0,0,6,108
1070 DATA 15,21,154,0,0,0,1
1080 DATA 15,22,227,91,140,5,185
1090 DATA 15,28,214,0,0,0,0
1100 DATA 15,34,75,0,0,8,147
1110 DATA 15,38,126,0,0,0,0
1120 DATA 15,40,200,163,31,10,60
1130 DATA 15,38,126,0,0,0,0
1140 DATA 15,34,75,0,0,8,147
1150 DATA 15,28,214,0,0,1,0
1160 DATA 100,17,37,68,149,4,73
1200 DATA 1,0,0,0,0,0,0
1210 DATA 0
59999 REM "REGSET"
60000 FOR N=54272 TO 54296:POKE N,0:NEXT
60001 V1=54272:FL=V1:FH=V1+1:PL=V1+2:PH=V1+3:W1=
V1+4:A1=V1+5:R1=V1+6
60002 V2=V1+7:GL=V2:GH=V2+1:QL=V2+2:QH=V2+3:W2=V
2+4:A2=V2+5:R2=V2+6
60003 V3=V2+7:HL=V3:HH=V3+1:RL=V3+2:RH=V3+3:W3=V
3+4:A3=V3+5:R3=V3+6
60004 LF=54293:HF=54294:RF=54295:MV=54296
60005 PX=54297:PY=54298:O3=54299:E3=54230
60006 RESTORE
60007 RETURN
60008 REM ADAPTED FROM A PROGRAM BY JIM BUTTERFI
ELD
60009 REM FIRST PUBLISHED IN 'USING THE 64' BY P
ETER GERRARD
60010 REM DUCKWORTH, 1983 - THANKS
```

PROGRAM 5.5

```
1 REM BOOGIE TWO
2 REM ENTER 5 CHORUSES FOR AN INTERESTING ARRANG
EMENT
3 REM NOTE THAT THE MELODY HAS BEEN SLIGHTLY REW
RITTEN - WHICH IS WORTH TRYING
4 REM YOURSELVES.  ALSO NOTE THAT THE TEMPO CAN
NOW BE VARIED
5 REM BY REPLACING THE FORMER 'TI' DURATION BY A
  SIMPLER DELAY LOOP
6 REM IT'S ALSO WORTH LOOKING AT HOW SECTIONS OF
 THE PIECE AND THE WHOLE PIECE
7 REM ARE REPEATED.
10 PRINT CHR$(147)
20 INPUT "TEMPO (0 TO 20)";T
30 IF T<0 OR T>20 THEN 10
40 INPUT "HOW MANY CHORUSES (1 TO 5)";R
50 IF R<1 OR R>5 THEN R=1
60 PRINT "HERE WE GO-TEMPO ";T;" NO. OF CHORUSES
  ";R
100 GOSUB 60000
105 SW=33:WN=129:TR=17
110 POKE MV,15
120 POKE A1,9:POKE R1,240:POKE A2,36:POKE R2,0:P
OKE A3,18:POKE R3,250
190 FOR N=1 TO R
200 POKE W2,0:REM ONLY THE 'SNARE' SOUND IS GATE
D, THE OTHERS PLAY CONTINUOUSLY
210 READ DU: IF DU=0 THEN 285
215 IF DU<>15 THEN WN=TR:SW=TR
220 READ A,B,C,D,E,F
225 IF F=1 AND RS<>1 THEN RESTORE:RS=1
226 IF E=1 AND RP<>1 THEN RESTORE:RP=1
227 REM RS AND RP ARE FLAGS DETERMINING THE REPE
TITION OF INDIVIDUAL PHRASES
228 REM THERE VALUES ARE CHANGED BY DATA ITEMS F
  AND E
230 POKE FH,A:POKE FL,B: POKE W1,SW
240 POKE GH,C:POKE GL,D: POKE W2,WN
250 POKE HH,E:POKE HL,F: POKE W3,TR
260 FOR P=1 TO DU*T:NEXT
280 GOTO 200
285 RS=0:RP=0:IF N>1 THEN WN=129
286 IF N>2 THEN SW=33
```

```
288 IF N>3 THEN SW=0
289 RESTORE:NEXT
290 GOSUB60000
295 END
1000 DATA 15,27,63,59,231,9,16
1010 DATA 15,21,154,0,0,0,0
1020 DATA 15,25,177,0,0,6,108
1030 DATA 15,28,214,0,0,0,0
1040 DATA 15,30,141,115,88,7,163
1050 DATA 15,28,214,0,0,0,0
1060 DATA 15,25,177,0,0,6,108
1070 DATA 15,21,154,0,0,0,1
1080 DATA 15,22,227,91,140,5,185
1090 DATA 15,28,214,0,0,0,0
1100 DATA 15,34,75,0,0,8,147
1110 DATA 15,38,126,0,0,0,0
1120 DATA 15,40,200,163,31,10,60
1130 DATA 15,38,126,0,0,0,0
1140 DATA 15,34,75,0,0,8,147
1150 DATA 15,28,214,0,0,1,0
1160 DATA 100,17,37,68,149,4,73
1200 DATA 1,0,0,0,0,0,0
1210 DATA 0
59999 REM "REGSET"
60000 FOR N=54272 TO 54296:POKE N,0:NEXT
60001 V1=54272:FL=V1:FH=V1+1:PL=V1+2:PH=V1+3:W1=
V1+4:A1=V1+5:R1=V1+6
60002 V2=V1+7:GL=V2:GH=V2+1:QL=V2+2:QH=V2+3:W2=V
2+4:A2=V2+5:R2=V2+6
60003 V3=V2+7:HL=V3:HH=V3+1:RL=V3+2:RH=V3+3:W3=V
3+4:A3=V3+5:R3=V3+6
60004 LF=54293:HF=54294:RF=54295:MV=54296
60005 PX=54297:PY=54298:O3=54299:E3=54230
60006 RESTORE
60007 RETURN
```
PROGRAM 5.6

Some points to note here are these:

The BBC will produce a never-ending note if the duration parameter is set at −1 or 255, while the Commodore will do the same as long as a non-zero sustain level is set and the waveform register remains gated on (i.e. is not POKEd with an even number). In general, note length figures in programs will increase by doubling, so that 1 may be a 32nd note (a demi-semiquaver), 2 a sixteenth, 4 an eighth, 8 a quarter, 16 a half, 32 a whole and 64 a double note. There are also intermediate values, represented in a musical score by a dot next to the note. A dotted note is one and a half times as long as the undotted note; so a dotted quarter -note, for example, will be three-eighths of a whole note. Irregular or very long note lengths are represented on a score by a tie, a curved line joining two notes, which means they must be considered as a single note whose length is equal to the sum of the lengths of the two tied notes. Computers have no problems dealing with these, except that you should remember to use a convenient scale of numbers for your note lengths, especially since, in general, duration parameters will operate as integers. Remember also that errors may creep in due to the time it takes to execute certain commands. Such commands (PRINT, for instance) can often be used as delays for note timing.

When a tie is made between two notes of different pitch, the effect is rather like a glide, a smooth transition from one pitch to the next. A smooth glide (as on a trombone) is called a glissando and sounds all the intermediate pitches between the beginning and the end note. A tie between two different notes usually means only that the release phase of the first one is ignored. On the BBC, this is achieved by flushing the note queue (that is, terminating one note with the next; any other notes waiting to be played are erased). To do this, add 16 to the channel number of the note that is to do the flushing. On the 64, the tie can be effected by not setting the appropriate gate bit to zero – that is, by allowing the first note to continue at its sustain level until the frequency data for the second note is POKEd into its registers.

In pre-programmed music (using, for example, DATA statements to provide note information), there will almost invariably be periods of silence in any piece. The periods are known as 'rests' and are treated, in music, just like notes. Rests have usually to be programmed by means of the frequency data, since they can be considered as notes of zero frequency. Unfortunately a zero frequency parameter may not work (it produces a tone on the BBC, and with the 64 you need to actively switch off a channel or POKE a zero volume to create a rest). On both computers a rest is best produced by using some arbitrary number in the DATA statement where a frequency value would be expected (say, -1), combined with a conditional branch (IF . . . THEN) which recognizes the datum and 'triggers' the silence. This technique has been used in earlier programs and a similar one used to trigger repetition of a musical phrase or to signal the end of a piece.

Note length
Note length normally matters only where you are, say, transcribing a piece of music into DATA statements. With a real-time keyboard, a note should be arranged to last as long as you hold the key down. This can be difficult to do, because of things like keyboard buffers, autorepeat of keys and note queues.

Usually a degree of trial and error is necessary to make sure notes play on time (when you strike a key) and last as long as you want them to.

The trick is to detect when a key is pressed and play the note as long as it is being pressed. When the key is released, the note should be released, but if another key is pressed the associated note should start playing immediately. Autorepeat may have to be turned off, and – on the 64, at least – the keyboard buffer may have to be emptied (by a POKE 198,0 instruction) following a key press. If only some keys are associated with notes, then the others should have no effect. In some cases you will want some other keys to have a control function (to change envelope or octave, for example), in which case pressing them should branch the program to an appropriate subroutine before they have any effect on the sound being produced. An easy solution to some of these problems is to use more than one channel on the computer to produce what is still, in effect, monophonic (single-channel) music.

The programs below are simple monophonic keyboards, with no frills. Both turn the top two rows of your QWERTY keyboard into musical keys. The Commodore program is something of a departure, because it checks the keyboard buffer itself for the value of the key pressed, and each musical key has an associated pair of frequency bytes in the DATA statements.

The envelope as it stands gives a not unpleasant repeating effect if a key is constantly pressed; try changing the envelope values. You could also change the duration value in line 3025. There are many different approaches you could take to adapting this program: relocating line 3010, introducing a delay loop, changing the GOTO in 1010 to a GOSUB and the GOTO in 3050 to RETURN, introducing a POKE W1,0 somewhere. I leave it as an exercise to play around with the program.

The BBC program is more straightforward, using INSTR to check whether a music key has been pressed (the key pressed is returned in K$) and then calculating frequency by means of a BASE+4*N statement. Even this program could be speeded up and adapted. Try adding an envelope or a second sound channel for starters.

```
1 REM "MUSIC KEYBOARD"
2 REM COMMODORE 64 KEYBOARD WITH 'TREMOLO' LIKE
AUTO REPEAT
3 REM USES KEYBOARD BUFFER TO DETECT A NOTE BEIN
G PLAYED
4 REM DATA LISTS KEY CODE, NOTE FRQUENCY VALUES
AS LISTED IN USER MANUAL
5 REM NOTE THAT THE OCTAVE RUNS FROM KEY 'E' TO
'P' (C-C)
```

```
10 GOSUB 60000
20 GOSUB 50000
30 POKE MV,15
999 POKE 198,0
1000 IF PEEK(203)=64 THEN 1000
1005 NQ=PEEK(203)
1010 FOR Z=1 TO 22:IF K(Z)=NQ THEN GOTO 3000
1015 NEXT Z
1020 GOTO 999
3000 POKE W1,0:POKE FH,H(Z):POKE FL,L(Z)
3010 POKE A1,9:POKE R1,0
3020 POKE W1,17
3025 FOR P=1 TO 100:NEXT
3050 GOTO999
3900 END
50000 DATA 56,6,206,62,7,53,59,7,163,9,8,23,14,8
,147,11,9,21,17,9,159
50001 DATA 16,10,60,22,10,205,25,11,114,24,12,32
,30,12,216,27,13,156,33,14,107
50002 DATA32,15,70,38,16,47,41,17,37,40,18,42,46
,19,63,43,20,100,49,21,154
50003 DATA 54,22,227
50004 DIM K(22),H(22),L(22)
50005 FOR X=1 TO 22: READ A,B,C:K(X)=A:H(X)=B:L(
X)=C:NEXT
50006 RETURN
50009 REM ABOVE ROUTINE SETS UP KEYBOARD WITH TO
P TWO ROWS AS KEYS
60000 FOR N=54272 TO 54296:POKE N,0:NEXT
60001 V1=54272:FL=V1:FH=V1+1:PL=V1+2:PH=V1+3:W1=
V1+4:A1=V1+5:R1=V1+6
60002 V2=V1+7:GL=V2:GH=V2+1:QL=V2+2:QH=V2+3:W2=V
2+4:A2=V2+5:R2=V2+6
60003 V3=V2+7:HL=V3:HH=V3+1:RL=V3+2:RH=V3+3:W3=V
3+4:A3=V3+5:R3=V3+6
60004 LF=54293:HF=54294:RF=54295:MV=54296
60005 PX=54297:PY=54298:O3=54299:E3=54230
60006 RETURN
60008 REM ABOVE ROUTINE GIVES VARIABLES TO ALL R
EGS & CLEARS WRITE REGS
60009 REM USEFUL ROUTINE FOR OTHER PROGRAMS
```

PROGRAM 5.7

```
  10 REM BBC MONO KEYBOARD
  20 REM KEYS FROM '1' (A£) TO '_' (G)
  30 REM ALTER BASE% FOR TUNING
  40 REM DURATION (4) IN SOUND STATEMENT
  50 REM OR ADD ENVELOPE, SECOND CHANNEL.
  60 BASE%=1
  70 N$="1QW3E4RT6Y7U8IOOP-@[\_"
  80 K$=INKEY$(0)
  90 I%=INSTR(N$,K$)
 100 IF K$<>""ANDI%>0F%=BASE%+4*I%:SOUND17,-
15,F%,4
 110 GOTO 80
```
PROGRAM 5.8

Micro-composition sequencers

Real time keyboards are fun, but micros are better suited to use as composing machines or as machines for playing ready-written music, entered in data form. The simple sequencers below demonstrate all the key principles of using a micro to compose on. It is possible to enter and display music in conventional form, but it is generally easier to understand the process if some other form of notation is used. These sequencers are essentially simple composing languages written in BASIC.

The idea of creating a music-composition language for computers is by no means new. It makes good sense, since the traditional language of staves and key signatures derives from and is closely linked to the use of conventional instruments. If the computer's promise is to be realized fully, new musical conventions will be necessary. A music-composition language makes a lot more sense to musical novices than conventional notation. Here is a simple sequencer for the BBC, which demonstrates the basic techniques.

```
  10 REM STEP-TIME BBC SEQUENCER,1984,G.HERM
AN
  20 MODE7:Q%=0:BASE%=5
  30 ENVELOPE1,1,0,0,0,0,0,0,50,-5,0,-4,126,
70
  40 DIM FREQ%(26),DUR%(999),MEL%(999),S$(99
9)
  50 N$="CN1C£1DN1D£1EN1FN1F£1GN1G£1AN1A£1BN
1CN2C£2DN2D£2EN2FN2F£2GN2G£2AN2A£2BN2CN3RST"
  60 FOR N%=1TOLEN(N$)/3:FREQ%(N%)=BASE%+4*N
%:NEXT:FREQ%(26)=0
  70 PRINT:PRINT"Key-in note (CN1,C£1...CN3)
```

```
"'"and length (01 to 80)"
   80 PRINT"AN205 plays A-natural, 2nd octave
"'"for a quarter second."'"Rest is RST & leng
th."'"To play, input PLA - to tune, TUN."
   90 PRINTTAB(5,21);:FOREX%=0TO34:PRINT" ";:N
EXT:INPUTTAB(5,21);M$
  100 M$=LEFT$(M$,5)
  110 IF M$="TUN"THEN290
  120 IF M$="PLA"THEN170
  130 FORT%=1TOLEN(N$)-2STEP3
  140 IFLEFT$(M$,3)=MID$(N$,T%,3)R%=(T%+2)/3:
Q%=Q%+1:MEL%(Q%)=FREQ%(R%):DUR%(Q%)=VAL(RIGHT
$(M$,2)):S$(Q%)=M$:SOUND1,-(MEL%(Q%)<>0),MEL%
(Q%),DUR%(Q%):PRINT" NOTE:";Q%
  150 NEXT
  160 GOTO90
  170 B%=1:F%=Q%
  180 PRINT TAB(0,8);
  190 FORT%=B%TOF%
  200 IFMEL%(T%)=0THENV%=0ELSEV%=1
  210 SOUND1,V%,MEL%(T%),DUR%(T%)
  220 PRINTCHR$(130);S$(T%);" ";
  230 IFINT(T%/5)=T%/5PRINT
  240 NEXT
  250 PRINTTAB(8,22);CHR$(131);999-Q%;" notes
left"
  260 PRINTCHR$(129)"FO TO CONTINUE"
  270 IFINKEY(-33)CLS:GOTO70
  280 GOTO270
  290 PRINT"Current base pitch ";BASE%:INPUT"
New base pitch ";BASE%:CLS:GOTO60
```
PROGRAM 5.9

Sequencers allow you to enter notes as strings – note, octave and length represented by letters or numbers; the information so entered is extracted and stored in suitable arrays. It can then be manipulated and stored on cassette or disc. Although the program above is only simple, the roots of more elaborate systems are there in the setting up of the array structure. There are some examples of more complex sequencers for the BBC and the Commodore in Chapter 8.

Meanwhile, exercises you might like to try include introducing a facility for playing your sequence in reverse order, or for repeating the whole sequence, or certain sections of it. You might like to think about introducing a facility for random restructuring of the sequence. Or you could add optional envelopes. It is a relatively simple matter to write a version of program 5.9 for the Commodore – just remember the essentials: a way of analysing an input string, some means of calculating or looking up frequency and duration, and arrays to store the values in a sequence. The pitch reckoner program of Chapter 3, which does many of these things, might be a good place to start.

These things are very much the meat of computer music, and the more elaborate programs at the end of the book go some way to introducing them. Incidentally, with more complicated programs the question of program organization becomes crucial very quickly. There are two broad solutions, both of which have been illustrated in this chapter. The first is to create special function keys to perform required tasks, and the second is to create menus. The first solution works best for real-time keyboards, the second for compositional sequencers. Where you may have difficulty choosing an approach is in the area of 'tape simulation' – that is, in programming a real-time keyboard with a note memory. In general, I recommend menu-driven programs, since these are simpler to write and easier to use.

Time signatures and DATA statements

Once you start playing with a sequencer, you need to structure your music in order to achieve a good result. The most important form of structuring is probably the use of measures or bars. Almost all compositions nowadays are divided up into 'time intervals' called measures. On a score these are indicated by a vertical line drawn in the stave (the stave is the horizontal lines along which symbols are placed to represent notes). The time interval can best be understood as a pattern of beats; it is the rhythm at which the piece must be played. The whole composition will be organized into a structure of measures, in much the same way that a poem is organized as a certain number of lines of certain length and metre.

Perhaps the most familiar compositional structure is the twelve-bar blues, which typically has three lines each consisting of four measures or bars, a structure which is reflected in the lyric. This gives the overall composition a recognizable rhythm, but each measure itself has an internal rhythm, dictated by the 'time signature' of the piece. With blues, the time signature is typically 4/4, although other signatures, such as waltz-time, 3/4, are not unknown.

A time signature can be 'simple' or 'compound' and it is made up of two parts. In simple time, the lower number represents a note length (8 is an eighth-note, 4 a quarter-note, 2 a half-note), while the upper number represents the number of such notes in the bar. These are not the notes that are played, but the notes representing beats. Thus 4/4 means each bar is long enough to include four beats and each beat is one quarter note in length; the bar is one whole note in length. Similarly 3/4 means that each bar is long enough to contain three beats and each beat is one quarter-note in length; the bar is three-quarters of a whole note in length, (so 3/4 time may seem faster than 4/4).

In compound time, the beats are considered to be dotted notes. So 6/8 time means there are two beats to the bar, and each beat is a dotted quarter-note; the bar is three-quarters of a whole note in length, but it has only two beats in it (so 6/8 time may seem slower than 3/4 time).

The best way of understanding time signatures is to experiment with your sequencer. It may even be worth adding a time signature feature to check that you are producing bars of the right length and beat structure. Most of your compositions will probably be in 4/4 time, which is almost universal in popular and folk-style music. Remember that the composition should have a suitable number of bars, and each bar should be of the right length. Think of it in terms of writing a poem: the poem divides easily into verses of fixed length; each verse divides easily into lines of fixed length; and each line divides easily into phrases of fixed length. The length of the phrase is, effectively, the number of beats to the bar. Once you've experimented with composition as rigidly structured as this, you can begin to explore what happens when you start breaking the rules. But if you break the rules from the outset, the result will most likely be chaotic and unlistenable.

More important, perhaps, is the use of metre and time signature to guide you through a composition using DATA statements. Where note lengths are passed in a DATA statement, make sure that for each line of your melody they add up to the same number. When in doubt, add a rest at the beginning or the end of a line.

Using the Commodore 'skeleton' program of Chapter 4 (program 4.17 up to line 5000), it is a simple matter to add DATA statements so as to play any tune you can successfully transcribe. Reserve one DATA statement for each bar of the piece, at least while you are entering the figure, so that it is easy to follow the composition and to correct any mistakes.

The next program (for the 64 only) is a typical data program for a short three-part composition. Data is in the form 'duration, high frequency byte channel 1, low fequency byte channel 1, hfb 2, lfb 2, hfb 3, lfb 3'; having loaded your skeleton program, you can load this data from tape or disc by following the instructions written in the data program REMs. Compositions in DATA form, can thus be permanently stored and loaded into a 'playing' program.

```
6000 REM TYPICAL DATA FOR MERGEABLE SKELETON: C-
64
6010 REM CHANNEL 1 IS MELODY, 2 IS RHYTHM, 3 IS
BASS
6020 REM MERGE INSTRUCTIONS:
```

```
6030 REM LOAD MERGEABLE SKELETON
6040 REM TYPE 'POKE 43,PEEK(45)-2:POKE 44,PEEK(4
6)'
6050 REM LOAD DATA PROGRAM SUCH AS THIS
6060 REM MAKING SURE THAT LINE NUMBERS START ABO
VE 5020
6070 REM TYPE 'POKE 43,1:POKE 44,8' TO RESET COM
PUTER
6080 REM TYPE 'RUN' TO START MERGED PROGRAMS
7000 DATA 10,8,147,172,210,3,54
7010 DATA 20,8,147,0,0,4,73
7020 DATA 10,12,216,205,133,4,73
7030 DATA 20,10,205,0,0,0,1
7040 DATA 30,17,37,137,43,3,54
7050 DATA 15,16,47,0,0,3,54
7060 DATA 15,17,37,0,0,1,0
7070 DATA 100,0,0,0,0,0,0
7080 DATA 0
```
PROGRAM 5.10

Staccato

One duration effect that remains to be dealt with is staccato. Here is a program, for the BBC, which introduces staccato – an effect achieved by breaking off a note short and completing its specified duration with a period of silence. At the right tempo the effect is like a series of sharp stabs. In musical scores it is indicated by a dot over the note. Staccato can be used to great rhythmic effect (its opposite, incidentally, is legato). At a fast tempo, staccato resembles pizzicato or the sound made by plucked strings – try altering the tempo figure in the program.

```
1 REM BBC GREENSLEEVES
2 REM WITH STACCATO EFFECT
3 REM PLUS ENVELOPE
4 REM AND REST
5 REM NOTE THE SECOND ENVELOPE
10 DATA 165,5,177,10,185,5,193,10,197,10,1
93,5
20 DATA 185,5,173,5,157,20,165,5,173,5
30 DATA 177,5,165,5,165,5,165,5,161,5,165,
5
```

```
   40 DATA 173,10,161,5,145,30,0,5
   50 DATA 165,5,177,10,185,5,193,10,197,10,1
93,5
   60 DATA 185,5,173,5,157,20,165,5,173,5
   70 DATA 165,2,161,3,153,3,161,3,165,60
   80 CLS:INPUT"PITCH ADJUSTMENT";P%
   90 INPUT"TEMPO";D%
   92 STACCATO=0
   97 ENVELOPE 2,1,0,0,0,0,0,0,30,10,-40,-126
,60,126
  100 FOR X%=1 TO 37:READ FREQ%,DUR%
  110 IF FREQ%=0 THEN V%=0 ELSE V%=1
  115 ENVELOPE 1,1,0,0,0,0,0,0,64,-16,STACCAT
O,-16,126,96
  120 SOUND 1,V%,P%+FREQ%,D%*DUR%
  130 SOUND 2,V%*2,P%+FREQ%-48,D%*DUR%
  135 STACCATO=1-STACCATO
  140 NEXT
  200 END
```
PROGRAM 5.11

Using look-up tables

So far we have used frequency numbers as data; but, as the sequencer and pitch reckoner show, it should be possible to enter alphabetic note names as data. It is a relatively simple matter, requiring only a look-up table to translate the note name into the appropriate frequency. We'll move to such a program in the next chapter, after dealing with frequency modulation.

The use of look-up tables raises an important issue. With a short composition it may not take too long or be too complicated to enter data in numerical form. Once your compositions start getting lengthy, entering data as numbers becomes tedious and prone to error. In general the use of a look-up table in the program is to be recommended. The major deficiency of such an approach is that it becomes harder to make adjustments to single notes or phrases, but this is more than compensated for by the time and temper saved.

As far as playing time goes, try to avoid calculations during the course of the 'performance' as much as possible. They only slow things down. Once again look-up tables which allocate array elements to the appropriate parameters at the start of the program will save a lot of time. One or more such tables can be stored anywhere you like in a program as DATA, so they can be saved on tape or disc with suitable line numbers and used as the kernel of a program.

6

Controlling frequency

In the previous chapter we came across the idea of a glide. Like other forms of modulation, glides are transitional phenomena. Music can be understood as an arrangement of so-called 'steady states' linked by transitions. We could consider a vibration of finite duration as a transition between steady states – the steady states being states at which the vibrating system is at rest.

Just as we can describe a piece of music using an 'outline' showing the way in which amplitude changes with time, we can draw an outline showing how frequency changes with time. The first outline would be a complex amplitude envelope, which could be broken down into single envelopes associated with individual notes. What determines when one note ends and the next begins is not so much the point at which a release phase meets an attack phase, but rather the point at which one steady state frequency gives way to another steady state frequency.

This is a perceptual phenomenon, since it depends on when we recognize the changes that constitute music as being determinate ones. A series of clicks becomes a note at around 20 to 30 Hz, for example, but if a 30 Hz note lasts only for a thirtieth of a second we will hardly be able to hear it as a note.

The short programs below take a simple tone and change the frequency using a FOR . . . NEXT loop. Another loop provides a delay between frequency changes. You should experiment with the delay and with the magnitude of the frequency change. Firstly, some curious effects can be achieved. Secondly, at a certain rate of change and using a certain magnitude of change, the effect is rather like a sequence of notes being played. Speed up the change or decrease the magnitude of change and the effect of sequence is lost; it begins to sound like a glide.

```
 1 REM BBC
10 FOR FREQ=1 TO 255 STEP 4
20 SOUND 1,-15,FREQ,10
30 FOR PAUSE=1 TO 1000:NEXT
40 NEXT
```
PROGRAM 6.1

```
10 REM C-64 FREQUENCY DEMO
20 POKE 54296,15
30 POKE 54272,17:POKE 54273,34
40 POKE 54277,0:POKE 54278,240
45 REM TRY ADDING STEP VALUES BELOW, EG.4,10,
20
50 FOR F=0 TO 100
60 POKE 54276,33
70 POKE 54273,34+F
75 REM TRY SMALLER AND GREATER 'P' END VALUES
, EG. 1,10,1000
80 FOR P=1 TO 100:NEXT
90 POKE 54276,0
95 REM LINE 100 ADDS DELAY BETWEEN NOTES
100 FOR P=1 TO 100:NEXT
110 NEXT
```
PROGRAM 6.2

There are two kinds of glide and, in a sense, one kind of ordinary transition from note to note. Glissando is the effect obtained on a trombone or by a Hawaiian guitar. It is often considered gimmicky, although both the BBC and the Commodore are happy doing it (or something that sounds so close as to be imperceptibly different). Portamento is the effect obtained when you run your finger along a piano keyboard – a series of rapid but definite steps as you move from the start note to the finish note. Portamento is considered less problematic in conventional music, since it doesn't tend to sound like an effect designed to be funny or sinister. If the steps are high enough and deep enough, portamento merges into an ordinary sequence of notes, which we do not perceive as a transitional effect at all.

Now take the above programs and use them to construct a short phrase (say, two or three notes) which repeats over and over.

```
  1 REM BBC
 10 FOR FREQ=1 TO 48 STEP 2
 20 SOUND 1,-15,FREQ,1
 40 NEXT
 50 GOTO 10
```
PROGRAM 6.3

```
  1 REM BBC
 10 FOR FREQ=1 TO 48 STEP 12
 20 SOUND 1,-15,FREQ,1
 40 NEXT
 50 GOTO 10
```
PROGRAM 6.4

```
 10 REM C-64 SIMPLE RIFF
 15 FOR X=0 TO 24:POKE54272+X,0:NEXT
 20 POKE 54296,15
 40 POKE 54277,128:POKE 54278,240
 50 FOR F=1 TO 3
 60 POKE 54276,33
 70 POKE 54273,34-F*2
 75 REM REMOVE LINES 80,90 AND 100 TO OBTAIN V
IBRATO EFFECT
 80 FOR P=1 TO 100:NEXT
 90 POKE 54276,0
100 FOR P=1 TO 100:NEXT
110 NEXT
120 GOTO 50
```
PROGRAM 6.5

If you speed up the change, the effect begins to resemble tremolo – a wavering or warbling in the sound. This is vibrato. Like tremolo, vibrato is characterized by two parameters: depth and rate. It is a form of frequency modulation in which the modulated frequency is modified by a considerably lower modulating frequency. The resulting effect is complex (the more so when the modulated frequency is not an exact multiple of the modulating frequency) and can produce a wide range of effects: horn-type sounds, bell-like tones, tinkling or shattering glass and so on.

Generally speaking, vibrato effects are dependent on the frequencies of the two tones involved and their relative amplitudes (the phase differences of the two tones can also be relevant). It is worth experimenting with vibrato effects; they are among the most useful sound modification techniques around. A new development in electronic music has recently seen the introduction of

'FM synthesizers' by the Japanese Yamaha company. FM synthesizers, which create new sounds from the modulated output of several sine waves, have raised vibrato to a fine art.

Achieving vibrato effects

The BBC micro allows simple, if somewhat crude, control of frequency changes within a note by use of the pitch envelope parameters in the ENVELOPE command. These define three intervals and specify two parameters for each: the number of steps in each interval and the change of pitch (positive or negative) per step. The pitch envelope can be selected to repeat for the duration of a note or to play only once. Further details of how the parameters work are given in Appendix 2.

Let's assume we have a note of A-above-middle-C (with a theoretical frequency of 440 Hz) and we wish to modulate it with a note of 10 Hz. Firstly, remember that much of the theory goes out of the window (or, at least, becomes very complex), since none of the waveforms we deal with on the BBC will be pure sine waves. Now, with a modulating frequency of 10 Hz, the modulated tone will repeat its shape ten times every second (this is a consequence of Fourier's theorem). The pitch envelope, then, must last for one-tenth of a second and must repeat. To last for one-tenth of a second, we set the step duration parameter (the second parameter in the ENVELOPE command) to 1 (for one-hundredth of a second with repeat) and the step numbers (parameters 6-8 of the ENVELOPE command) to, say, 5, 0 and 5. There could be other arrangements, but this one is simple and gives an envelope lasting the required time. The pitch change parameters (3-5 in ENVELOPE) can then be selected to give different effects. Between them, pitch change and number of steps define the depth and rate of the modulation.

In the following program, try values of 1, 0 and −1 to start with (which give a rise of just over a semitone in the first interval, a steady state in the second and a fall of just over a semitone in the third interval). Increase these values and then take the modulated tone through the BBC's frequency range. The effects can be dramatic.

```
  1 REM BBC
  2 REM TRY 2,5;5,2;5,5;10,5;5,1 WITH 53 AS
PITCH
 10 INPUT"DEPTH, RATE"D,R
 15 INPUT "PITCH PARAMETER"FREQ
 20 ENVELOPE1,1,R,0,-R,D,0,D,126,0,0,0,126,
126
 30 SOUND 17,1,FREQ,-1
```
PROGRAM 6.6

The 64 gives you a far greater degree of control over frequency than the BBC, but the arrangement here involves using the output of oscillator 3 to vary the frequency of the tone you wish to modulate. By POKEing a low order frequency register (say, register 0, location 54272) with the PEEKed contents of register 27 (location 54299) you will get a rapidly fluctuating frequency output from your chosen channel. This is not an exact form of modulation, but it effects a usable vibrato, and the technique is used in the Commodore 'FX-GEN' program included in this book. Here is a demonstration of how it works. Remember to turn oscillator 3's audio output off; by changing the frequency and waveform of oscillator 3, you can obtain some useful effects. (You might even try modulation using a pulse wave of variable duty cycle, although the best conventional vibrato will result from using a triangle wave in oscillator 3 at the lowest available frequency.) After the Commodore program comes a BBC program to demonstrate vibrato using the conventional technique of calculation based on sine or cosine functions. It is still effective.

```
10 REM VIBRATO, C-64
20 POKE 54296,15+128
30 INPUT"MODULATED NOTE, HI AND LOW BYTES";HC,LC
40 INPUT"MODULATING FREQUENCY, HI AND LOW BYTES"
;HM,LM
50 POKE 54291,0:POKE 54292,255
60 POKE 54286,LM:POKE 54287,HM
70 POKE 54290,17
80 POKE 54277,0:POKE 54278,255
90 POKE 54276,33:POKE 54273,HC
95 REM HAVING LOADED CHANNEL THREE OSCILLATOR WI
TH ADSR, FREQ AND TRIANGLE WAVE
96 REM WE PEEK REGISTER 27 AND POKE THE VALUE IN
TO THE LOW FREQ REG. OF CH.1
100 HM=HM+PEEK(54299):IF HM>=256 THEN HM=HM-256
110 POKE 54272,HM:GOTO 100
```
PROGRAM 6.7

```
1 REM BB VIBRATO EFFECT
2 REM ANY VALUES HAVE SOME EFFECT
3 REM BUT BEST RESULTS WITH RATE AND
4 REM DEPTH OF AROUND 100
5 REM TRY 53,100,100 AS VALUES
6 REM OR 53,100,256 OR 53,10,100
7 REM FOR INTERESTING EFFECTS
```

```
   10 CLS
   20 INPUT"PITCH VALUE"'"VIBRATO  DEPTH"'"VI
BRATO RATE"';PV%,DP%,RT%
   25 FR%=PV%:REM WITHOUT THIS, PITCH SLOWLY
SWEEPS DOWN
   30 FOR Y%=1TO2 STEPO
   35 PV%=FR%
   40 FOR X%=OTO359 STEPRT%
   50 PV%=PV%*(1+COS(X%)/(DP%))
   60 SOUND 1,-15,PV%,1
   70 NEXTX%,Y%
```
PROGRAM 6.8

Other frequency effects

A number of related effects can be obtained on the BBC and Commodore micros, and here are a few demonstration programs:

Firstly, there are glides. On both machines these may be achieved by use of a simple subroutine that may be included in a larger program. We've already seen this done in standard fashion on the BBC and the 64, but you can also use the BBC's ENVELOPE command to do the job. You may like to reserve a special envelope for glides, or you may decide to trigger the pitch envelope section of an ordinary envelope by use of a variable. For example, ENVELOPE 1,1,-1*V,0,V,5,0,5,x,x,x,x,x,x will sound a vibrato whenever V is non-zero. Similarly,

ENVELOPE 1,1,0,0,GL,0,0,FR(2)-FR(1),x,x,x,x,x,x

will glide up to frequency FR(2) from FR(1) if GL is 1, or will glide down the equivalent number of steps if GL is −1, but won't have any pitch effect if GL is 0. Here is an example of a glide subroutine.

```
   1 REM BBC
   5 DIM FR%(2)
  10 INPUT "BEGINNING AND END OF PITCH GLIDE
"FR%(1),FR%(2)
  15 INPUT"SPEED(O-FAST TO 127-SLOW)"S%
  20 GL%=1*SGN(FR%(2)-FR%(1)):REM GLIDE ON A
ND IN WHAT DIRECTION
  25 FR%=ABS(FR%(2)-FR%(1)):REM KEEPS NUMBER
OF PITCH STEPS IN ENV. POSITIVE
  30 PROCGLIDE
  40 END
 100 DEFPROCGLIDE
```

```
   110 ENVELOPE1,S%+128,0,0,GL%,0,0,FR%,126,0,
0,-126,126,126
    120 SOUND 17,1,FR%(1),-1
    130 ENDPROC
```
PROGRAM 6.9

One intriguing form of frequency modulation is so-called ring, or balanced, modulation. The effect here is for two tones to modulate each other, as a result of which neither tone can be heard at the output. With ordinary frequency modulation, the modulated frequency remains a component of the final output, but with ring modulation the output is composed exclusively of the sum and difference of the two input frequencies. The effect is weird and should be used only in small doses; once again, it is available on the FX-GEN program in this book.

The 64 has a ring modulator built in. When bit 2 of any of the control registers is set while that register is outputting a triangle wave (that is, 21 is POKEd into any of registers 4, 11 and 18 at locations 54276, 54283 and 54290; 21 being 17, for triangle, plus 4 to set bit 2), the triangle wave is replaced by the ring-modulated combination of respectively, oscillators 1 and 3, 2 and 1, 3 and 2. The effect is commonly used to mimic bells, gongs and buzzers.

This program shows how it works. The frequency of the oscillators selected affects the final output. In the example, channels 1 and 3 are modualted, with channel 1 being the 'controlling' channel. Apart from frequency, no other channel specific parameter has an effect.

```
10 REM C-64 RING MODULATION DEMO
20 REM NOTE BEAT FREQUENCIES AND HARMONICS
30 POKE 54277,9
35 FOR F3=4 TO 40 STEP 6
40 POKE 54287,F3
50 POKE 54296,15
60 FOR P=1 TO 24
65 PRINT "C3 FREQ ";F3;" C1 FREQ ";P
70 POKE 54273,P:POKE 54276,17+4
80 FOR X=1 TO 1024:NEXT
90 POKE 54276,0
100 FOR X=1 TO 1280:NEXT
110 NEXT:NEXT
```
PROGRAM 6.10

On the BBC, ring modulation can only be approximately simulated, using the fact that for input frequencies F1 and F2, the output frequencies of a ring modulator will be F1+F2 and ABS(F1−F2). This program uses calculations to provide ring modulation over a small, but still usable, range of values. It is followed by a demonstration.

```
10 REM BBC RING MODULATOR
20 REM CAN BE REWRITTEN AS PROCEDURE
30 REM TO OPERATE WITH CHANGING TONES
40 REM WARNING: SOME NOTES WILL CAUSE
50 REM TONES TO GO OUT OF RANGE
60 REM OF BBC PITCH PARAMETERS
70 REM THEY WILL STILL PLAY, BUT
80 REM THE RING MODULATION EFFECT
90 REM WILL BE LOST
100 DIM P(2),FR(2),RM(2)
110 INPUT"PITCH NUMBER 1 & 2";P(1),P(2)
120 FOR X=1TO2
130 FR(X)=(124*(1.0596444^(P(X)/4)))
140 NEXT
150 RM(1)=ABS(FR(1)-FR(2))
160 RM(2)=FR(1)+FR(2)
170 FOR X=1 TO 2
180 P(X)=4*(LOG(RM(X)/124))/(LOG(1.0596444)

190 NEXT
200 REM NOTE THE DURATION VALUES MIGHT
210 REM NEED CHANGING, BUT THEY SHOULD
220 REM OBVIOUSLY BE EQUAL.
230 SOUND 1,-15,P(1),100
240 SOUND 2,-15,P(2),100
```
PROGRAM 6.11

```
10 REM BBC RING MODULATION DEMONSTRATION
20 REM EIGHT HARMONY STEPS FOLLOWED BY
30 REM EIGHT MODULATED STEPS, REPEATING
40 REM NOTE HOW CERTAIN MODULATIONS
50 REM HAVE UNEXPECTED EFFECTS
60 REM TO EXPERIMENT TRY DIFFERENT DATA
70 REM DIFFERENT DURATIONS AND
80 REM ENVELOPING THE SOUND
90 RPT=0
```

```
100 DIM P(2),FR(2),RM(2)
110 READ P(1),P(2)
120 IF P(1)=0 THEN RESTORE:RPT=1-RPT:GOTO11

130 IF RPT=0 THEN 220
140 FOR X=1TO2
150 FR(X)=(124*(1.0596444^(P(X)/4)))
160 NEXT
170 RM(1)=ABS(FR(1)-FR(2))
180 RM(2)=FR(1)+FR(2)
190 FOR X=1 TO 2
200 P(X)=4*(LOG(RM(X)/124))/(LOG(1.0596444)

210 NEXT
220 SOUND 1,-15,P(1),8
230 SOUND 2,-15,P(2),8
240 GOTO 110
250 DATA 53,81,61,89,69,97,73,103
260 DATA 81,33,89,69,97,61,103,53
270 DATA 0,0
```
PROGRAM 6.12

When F1 and F2 are in a simple ratio to each other – say 2:1, 3:4 or 7:5 – the result of ring modulation will be two harmonics of a fundamental given by the highest common factor of F1 and F2. When F1 approaches F2 a sort of throbbing will be heard. This is called a beat frequency and its value is given by F1−F2. When F1 exactly equals F2 the beat frequency will stop, and the result of ring modulation will be just a single frequency double that of the two components or, if you prefer, one octave up. Try using these values with the programs above. At the very least, they will give you an indication of how well tuned your computer is, although equal values will return an error in the BBC program – division by zero. (An interesting envelope for program 6.12 is ENVELOPE 1, 1, 0, 0, 0, 0, 0, 0, 127, −8, 0, 0, 126, 0: don't forget to alter lines 220 and 230 to call the envelope. Unequal durations, although not giving a proper demonstration of pure ring modulation, create good effects.)

Harmonics and chords
Frequency modulation is intriguing because of the way it creates new harmonics, thus expanding the whole range of timbres available to the musician.

Where tone frequencies all have a common factor which is not 1, that factor is known as a fundamental. All the other tones are then harmonics of that fundamental. The fundamental need not be present in a composite tone for the ear to hear it. Somehow (nobody knows exactly how) the ear manages to reconstruct it from the information available. Go back to the ring modulator section above to test this out.

Each waveform has a spectrum of its own. The simplest spectrum – just a single component frequency – is, naturally, produced by a pure sine wave, which is unobtainable on either of our computers. Every simple waveform has a spectrum that includes only harmonics of a fundamental frequency (usually the lowest frequency on the spectrum diagram); this fundamental frequency will always be heard. Pulse waves are particularly interesting since their harmonic content depends on the duty cycle of the wave, a phenomenon which can be exploited on the Commodore but not on the BBC. One variant of frequency modulation is called pulse width modulation and can be demonstrated on the 64.

```
10 REM C-64 PULSE WIDTH MODULATION
20 POKE 54296,15+128
30 POKE 54272,75:POKE 54273,34
40 POKE 54277,0:POKE 54278,240
50 POKE 54290,16:POKE 54287,1
60 FOR X=1 TO 100
70 POKE 54274,PEEK(54299)
80 POKE 54276,65
90 NEXT
100 FOR X=1 TO 1000:NEXT
110 POKE 54276,0
```
PROGRAM 6.13

In some cases of frequency modulation, only harmonics are produced. These examples produce clear and pleasant tones. Where frequency modulation produces frequencies not harmonically related, however, the effect can be clangorous and discordant – a very useful phenomenon if you want to produce effects.

There is normally a considerable difference in amplitudes in the spectrum of a 'single' tone. When the component frequencies are allowed to approach each other in amplitude, tonal quality begins to change markedly. The component frequencies seem to separate out, so that what we hear sounds not like a single tone but like several tones all striving to be heard.

Where the component frequencies are harmonically related, the effect begins to resemble a chord – i.e. several notes played together and apparently integrated with each other. Where the component frequencies are not harmonically related (as in certain kinds of frequency modulation), the resultant sound is discordant.

Musical instruments are characterized by a dominant waveform. They may produce tones with different waveforms, but one will predominate. For example, a piano sound is best produced by a pulse waveform (using a spiky pulse with a low duty cycle). Woodwinds are characterized by triangle waves. Brass by sawtooth or ramp waves. Percussion is associated with noise waveforms; white noise for a snare drum, periodic noise (or discordant FM sounds) for cymbals. A triangle waveform will produce a good bass sound and should be used for other stringed instruments.

The combination of tones, whether of the same waveform or not, produces further harmonic richness. The pleasant blending of tones is really the subject of the theory of harmony and chords; since chords are at the heart of most western music, they are worth some consideration. (Appendix 1 contains a guitar chord tutor program, which may be instructive.)

In discussing harmonics, we have been dealing with frequencies that are all simple multiples of some fundamental. For example, notes of 200 Hz, 300 Hz, 400 Hz and 500 Hz are all harmonics of a note of 100 Hz. But 100 Hz, 200 Hz and 400 Hz produce the same *notes* – the second exactly one octave above the first, the third exactly one octave above the second.

What of 300 Hz and 500 Hz? These odd harmonics produce different notes, albeit notes in, respectively, the octave above the octave beginning with 100 Hz and the octave above that. If we want to produce those same notes but in the same octave as the fundamental, we have to divide 300 Hz by 2 and 500 Hz by 4. The result is notes of 150 Hz and 125 Hz. For the sake of convenience, let's assume that 100 Hz, the fundamental, is a C. Then 150 Hz will be a G and 125 Hz will be an E This triad, when all the notes are played together, is known as the chord of C-major. It is the basic chord of the key of C-major. The note C is known as the tonic, G (the fifth note on the scale C, D, E, F, G, A, B) is the dominant and E (the third note in the scale, coming between C and G) is known as the mediant. A similar procedure can be applied to arrive at all the chords of any given scale or key (but only in a system of just tuning; equal temperament deviates somewhat from the perfect mathematical norm in order to allow a less narrow sort of regularity). The basic principle of harmony, then, is that notes can be combined according to relations specified by the series of harmonics of any fundamental. The fundamental provides the tonic (upon which a conventional composition will most frequently be resolved, or end); scaled down to its octave, the odd harmonics and those even ones – like the sixth – not produced by simple doubling provide notes that can be blended with it. The result is more or less harmonious depending on the distance of the original harmonic from the fundamental. Thus a chord of C, D and B will be discordant because D is the ninth harmonic of C, and B is the fifteenth.

Harmonic theory is complicated enough to fill several volumes, but the essential thing is that chords are practical examples of the important relationships between frequency and music. There are a few areas where precise knowledge will come in handy. If, for example, you are transcribing a piece written for conventional instruments on to your computer, it is useful to know that the precise octave of every note is not necessarily crucial. Especially on the BBC, you may find yourself attempting to transcribe a bass note out of the computer's range. You can generally replace it with the same note an octave or two higher or, often more satisfactory, replace it with another note that forms a suitable chord. E, E and G will often stand in for C, E and G; so, often, will A, E and G (the chord of A-minor). Similarly if you are composing, say, a bass line to accompany an already written melody, an elementary knowledge of chords and harmonic theory will help you avoid fundamental mistakes. The rule in general is play safe: stick with major chords or with common note triads and, if necessary, dyads. With any triad, there are always two possible notes that can go in the bass line (the so-called triadic inversions) – so that, say, you have a C in the melody and either an E or a G in the bass. Then there are melodic inversions that can be experimented with so that, for example, an interval of a fifth upwards is substituted for an interval of a fifth downwards. Here again, elementary harmonic theory suggests you restrict yourself to using melodic inversions with intervals of fifths and thirds, the safest ones to play around with.

To finish this section, here is a first outing into true polyphony and a final flourish on our music-playing programs. This one, for the Commodore, plays a three-part harmony and has note data entered in note-name form. It can easily be adapted for the BBC, since all information is included as data items, apart from tempo, which is input from the keyboard.

The timing is acceptable for such an arrangement and it makes the program a lot simpler than it could be. Each note is given its own duration, and line 340 allows the program to miss playing a note on any given channel by branching over the play section wherever a duration value of zero or less is found. Thus, with suitable entries in the data table, it is relatively simple to adjust timings on each channel individually; there is no need for synchronizing them or for complex counting systems to be involved.

```
1 REM HARMONY C-64
2 REM THIS PROGRAM CUTS A FEW CORNERS
3 REM IN THE MATTER OF TIMING, AND
4 REM THE RELIANCE ON A SIMPLE
5 REM DELAY LOOP CAUSES SOME QUIRKS
6 REM TRY SYNCING THE NOTES AND ALSO
7 REM SETTING THE GATE BIT LOW BETWEEN NOTES.
8 REM A TEMPO OF 15 SOUNDS GOOD, BUT YOU COULD M
AKE SEVERAL ADJUSTMENTS
```

```
9 REM - FOR EXAMPLE, BY CHANGING WAVEFORMS.
10 REM THE TUNE REPEATS OVER AND OVER
11 REM TO STOP IT PRESS RUN-STOP
12 REM AND YOU MAY HAVE TO POKE WAVEFORM REGISTE
RS WITH ZERO
13 REM TO TURN OFF THE SOUND.
14 REM NOTE HOW THE TEMPO CHANGES AFTER THE FIRS
T CHORUS.
100 PRINT CHR$(147)
105 INPUT "TEMPO (1 TO 100)";T
106 IF T<1 OR T>100 THEN T=20
108 PRINT"PLEASE WAIT WHILE I TUNE UP"
110 T=T*10
138 DIM F$(3,99),HF(3,99),LF(3,99),D(3,99)
140 DIM N(14),DU(3),WF(3),FW(3),EN(3)
141 FOR X=1 TO 14: READ N(X): NEXT
148 GOSUB 1000
150 POKE MV,15
160 FOR V=1 TO 3
170 READ AD,SR,HP,LP,FW(V)
180 POKE AD(V),AD:POKE SR(V),SR:POKE PH(V),HP:PO
KE PL(V),LP
190 NEXT V
240 :
250 I=1
255 FOR V=1 TO 3
260 READ F$,D(V,I)
265 IF F$="R" THEN F=0:GOTO310
268 IF F$="*" THEN EN(V)=I:O=O+1:GOTO315
270 D(V,I)=D(V,I)/8
280 OC=VAL(RIGHT$(F$,1))
295 F=N(2*(ASC(LEFT$(F$,1))-64)+(LEN(F$)=2))
300 F=F*2^(OC-4)
310 HF(V,I)=INT(F/256):LF(V,I)=F-HF(V,I)*256
315 NEXT V
318 I=I+1
320 IF O=3 THEN 333
330 GOTO 255
333 FOR K=1 TO I
334 PRINT CHR$(147);"OKAY"
335 FOR V=1 TO 3
338 POKE FH(V),HF(V,K):POKE FL(V),LF(V,K)
340 IF D(V,K)<=0 THEN 380
```

L. I. M. E.
THE MARKLAND LIBRARY
STAND PARK RD., LIVERPOOL, L16 8JD

```
350 D(V,K)=D(V,K)-1
360 POKE WF(V),FW(V)
370 GOTO 340
380 NEXT V
385 FOR P=1 TO T:NEXT
390 IF Z=3 THEN END
400 NEXT K
500 GOTO 333
950 END
999 REM REGVAR
1000 S=54272
1010 FOR X=1 TO 3
1020 CH=7*(X-1)
1030 FL(X)=S+CH:FH(X)=FL(X)+1:PL(X)=FH(X)+1:PH(X
)=PL(X)+1:WF(X)=PH(X)+1
1040 AD(X)=WF(X)+1:SR(X)=AD(X)+1
1050 NEXT
1060 HC=SR(3)+1:LC=HC+1:RF=LC+1:MV=RF+1:PX=MV+1:
PY=PX+1:O3=PY+1:E3=O3+1
1070 RETURN
3000 REM***FREQUENCY DATA**********************
3010 DATA 7381,7818,8271,0,4378,4647,4915
3020 DATA 5217,5519,0,5855,6207,6576,6962
3990 REM***ENVELOPE,PULSE AND WAVEFORM DATA*****
4000 DATA 40,40,7,255,17
4100 DATA 9,127,7,255,65
4200 DATA 9,255,7,255,17
5000 REM***NOTE DATA***********************
5100 DATA A4,8,A4,8,A5,8,C4,12,C4,12,C4,12
5200 DATA A4,4,A5,4,A4,4,F3,16,F4,16,F4,16
5300 DATA D4,8,D4,8,D3,8,C4,24,C3,24,C4,24
5400 DATA A4,8,D2,8,A3,8,C3,12,E3,12,C4,12
5500 DATA A4,4,D2,4,A5,4,F4,16,C2,16,F5,16
5600 DATA D4,8,D4,8,D5,8,E4,8,E4,8,E5,8
5700 DATA C4,8,C4,8,C5,8,B4,8,B3,8,B4,8
5800 DATA C4,4,C4,4,C4,4,D4,4,D3,4,D4,4
5900 DATA E4,4,G3,4,E4,4,F4,4,F3,4,F4,4
6000 DATA G4,4,G3,4,G3,4,A4,4,A3,4,A4,4
6100 DATA A£4,8,A£4,8,A£4,8,D4,12,D5,12,G4,12
6200 DATA A£5,4,A£4,4,A£3,4,A5,16,A4,16,A3,16
6300 DATA G4,8,G3,8,D4,8,F£4,24,F£4,24,D4,24,G4,
24,G3,24,D4,24
6400 DATA G4,8,G4,8,G3,8,A4,12,C4,12,E4,12,G4,4,
```

```
E4,16,C4,8
6500 DATA C5,8,C4,8,F3,8,C4,8,C4,8,C4,8,F4,4,F4,
4,F4,4,A4,4,A4,4,A4,4
6600 DATA C5,4,C5,4,C5,4,A£4,4,C5,4,A£4,4,G4,4,E
4,4,C4,4
6700 DATA A4,8,A4,8,A4,8,C5,12,C4,12,F4,12,A4,4
6800 DATA F4,16,F3,16,F4,16,D4,8,D5,8,D4,8,F4,24
,F3,24,F4,24
6900 DATA C4,24,C3,24,A3,24,D4,8,D4,8,D4,8,F£4,1
2,D3,12,F£4,12,A4,4,A3,4,A5,4
6910 DATA D5,16,D4,16,G4,16,D4,8,A4,8,C5,8
6920 DATA B4,24,B3,24,B5,24,B4,8,G4,8,D4,8,B3,4,
D4,4,G4,4,B4,4,B4,4,B4,4
6930 DATA C5,8,C5,8,C5,8,C4,8,G4,8,C4,8,G4,8,G4,
8,C4,8
6940 DATA C4,16,E4,16,G4,16,A£4,8,C4,8,E4,8
6960 DATA A£3,8,C4,8,C3,8,F4,24,F3,24,F5,24,F4,2
4,F4,24
6970 DATA C4,24,F4,24,A4,24,C4,24,R,24,C3,24,B3,
48,B2,48,D4,48
6975 DATA A£3,32,E4,32,A£4,32,C4,24,A£4,24,C4,24
6978 DATA F4,48,F4,48,A3,24,A£3,24,B3,24,F4,24
6980 DATA C4,96,F4,96,C2,96
7000 DATA *,0,*,0,*,0
```

PROGRAM 6.14

7

Noise

The musician's definition of noise is rather like the gardener's definition of a weed: noise is a sound that you don't want, it is the wrong sound in the right place or the right sound in the wrong place. The physicist's definition of noise is different. Noise, in the general science of acoustics, is unpitched or semi-pitched sound; that is, noise is a sound that does not have a definite or discernible pitch.

For the musician, such unpitched or semi-pitched sounds can be desirable – for example, as drum or cymbal beats, or if you want to produce the sounds of wind, sea, bells or tinkling glass in a composition. Such sounds all fall under the physicist's heading of noise.

Noise is generally marked by irregular frequency spectra, which means that the spectrum of a noise will show an unpredictable harmonic content. At one extreme, the harmonic content of a sound can be completely random: any frequency may appear with equal probability, and as a result there are no fundamentals and no overtones or harmonics as such. The frequency spectrum of such a sound will be changing constantly over time. If the spectrum is sampled over a long enough period, and the component frequencies marked on a graph showing amplitude against frequency, the result will be a straight line at the level of the sound's overall amplitude.

This is the transitional sound *par excellence*, since, if any grouping of frequencies repeated in the spectrum, we would be able to detect some regularity, or a degree of 'pitchedness', to the sound. Such random sounds are described as white noise, by analogy with light, since white light is a combination of all frequencies of light in equal amounts.

White noise can be generated on both the BBC and the Commodore. As we have seen, this is not strictly white, since a pseudo-random number generator is used to produce it, but as with the RND function in BASIC, to all practical purposes the difference cannot be detected. The noise has a repetitive element, but the repetition occurs at such a low frequency (much less than 1 Hz) that it can't be heard as a repetition.

To complicate matters, the white noise produced by the BBC is effectively filtered into four different types: noise in which low frequencies predominate (called pink noise), noise in which middle frequencies predominate (which we could call yellow noise), noise in which high frequencies predominate (which we could call blue noise) and noise in which the predominant frequencies are determined by the pitch being played on channel 1.

The noise is obtained by setting the channel of a SOUND statement to 0. With the pitch number at 4, 5, 6 and 7 you get blue, yellow, pink or controlled noise. This program uses the controlled noise to give a *whoosh* effect. The sound has been enveloped by a FOR . . . NEXT loop, but you could use a standard ADSR envelope to produce a similar effect.

```
10 REM BBC WHOOSH
20 FOR V=15 TO 0 STEP -1
30 SOUND 1,0,V*17,2
40 SOUND 0,-V,7,2
50 NEXT
```
PROGRAM 7.1

If white noise is filtered narrowly enough, regularity begins to emerge, the sense of a low, high or middling frequency coloration homing in on a central frequency. The spectrum of such a sound looks like a bell, the typical shape of a sound passed through a band-pass filter. Although the waveform of such a tone will not be simply repetitive, there will be large-scale repetitions at the central frequency. An audibly similar effect can be achieved by randomly shifting the phase (or starting point) of the harmonics of a given fundamental in a square wave. The fundamental is then the central apparent frequency of the sound.

On the BBC, such 'periodic' sounds are produced by setting the pitch parameter in a SOUND command to 0, 1, 2, or 3 when the command addresses channel 0, the noise channel. The results are, respectively, high, medium and low frequency buzzes and a buzz or periodic noise whose central frequency is controlled by the pitch of channel 1. In the following effects, periodic and white noise are controlled by a channel 1 frequency. Channel 1

volume is set to 0, so the controlling frequency is unheard; but try setting it to
a suitable negative value to hear the noise and tone together.

```
10 REM BBC NOISE LINKED TO CHANNEL 1
20 FOR F=127 TO 255
30 SOUND &11,0,F,4
40 SOUND &10,-15,7,4
50 NEXT
```
PROGRAM 7.2

```
10 REM BBC PERIODIC NOISE
20 X=128-X
30 SOUND 1,0,127+X,10
40 SOUND 0,-15,3,10
50 GOTO 20
```
PROGRAM 7.3

The Commodore 64 produces white noise by setting a waveform register
to 128 + 1 (for the gate bit). This noise is always controlled by the frequency
to which the noise-producing channel has been set, and can be filtered using
the programmable filter, to give a range of colorations.

```
10 REM C-64 NOISE
20 POKE 54296,15+16
30 POKE 54295,1+240
40 POKE 54277,0:POKE 54278,255
45 POKE 54276,129
50 FOR X=255 TO 0 STEP -5
60 POKE 54294,X:POKE 54273,X
70 NEXT
80 POKE 54276,0
```
PROGRAM 7.4

The Commodore has other ways of producing noise. Ring modulation is
one technique used to produce clangorous sounds (see Chapter 6). Another
is pulse width modulation.

Since the harmonic content of a pulse wave varies according to the pulse
width (a low or high duty cycle being rich in overtones compared to a
middling duty cycle), a random effect can be achieved by varying pulse width
randomly. To do this, you feed white noise into channel 3 and use channel 3
to control the pulse width of a sound being produced on another channel.
The effect can be intriguing.

```
10 REM C-64 RANDOM PWM
15 FOR X=54272 TO 54296:POKE X,0:NEXT
20 POKE 54296,15+128:POKE 54275,7
30 POKE 54287,4:POKE 54290,129
35 REM TRY DIFFERENT FREQUENCY VALUES POKED T
0 54273
40 POKE 54273,8:POKE 54277,240
50 POKE 54278,255
52 POKE 54276,65
55 FOR Z=1 TO 1000
60 POKE 54274,PEEK(54299)
80 NEXT
90 POKE 54276,64
```
PROGRAM 7.5

Another technique uses random frequency modulation, also using channel 3 to provide a random control parameter.

```
10 REM C-64 RANDOM FM
15 FOR X=54272 TO 54296:POKE X,0:NEXT
20 POKE 54296,15+128
30 POKE 54287,240:POKE 54290,129
40 POKE 54277,240
50 POKE 54278,255:POKE 54276,33
55 FOR Z=1 TO 1000
60 POKE 54273,PEEK(54299)
80 NEXT
90 POKE 54276,64
```
PROGRAM 7.6

These techniques are, essentially, ways of producing a varied harmonic content in a wave. If the modulations are rapid enough, the effect will tend towards noise.

Very high and very low frequencies can be sources of interesting noise effects since, at the limits of the frequency scale, musical quality begins to disappear. Here are two simple programs to simulate the sound of tinkling glass on the BBC and the Commodore. The high frequency sound is enveloped to give a sharp attack and an only slightly less sharp decay/release.

```
10 REM C-64 TINKLE
15 FOR X=54272 TO 54296:POKE X,0:NEXT
```

```
20 POKE 54296,15:POKE54275,15
30 POKE 54277,21:POKE 54278,16
40 POKE 54273,240
50 POKE 54276,65
60 FOR X=1TO100:NEXT
70 POKE 54276,64
80 FOR X=1 TO INT(RND(0)*200):NEXT
90 GOTO 50
```
PROGRAM 7.7


```
10 REM BBC TINKLE
20 ENVELOPE 1,1,0,1,1,-1,0,1,1,96,-48,0,-78,1
26,78
30 SOUND 1,1,240+RND(15),RND(2)
40 FOR X=1 TO RND(1000):NEXT
50 GOTO 20
```
PROGRAM 7.8

Very low frequencies are most often used as controls rather than as signals in their own right. These should be below the audible range – between, say, 0 and 3 or 4 Hz. They can best be achieved by cycling through a sound instruction at a rate determined by some delay loop. The effect is particularly useful if you want to simulate sirens, UFOs, machinery or ominous pulsing. These programs demonstrate the effect and may be experimented with to produce other interesting sounds.


```
10 REM BBC TRAIN+MUSICAL UFO
15 N=4
20 FOR X=1 TO 100
30 FOR VOL=-15 TO 0
40 SOUND 0,VOL,N,0
50 NEXT
60 N=((N+1)MOD3)+4
70 NEXT
80 NEXT
90 :
95 REM NOTE THE USE OF AN ARRAY IN THE SECTIO
N BELOW
100 DIM M(3):DUR=10
110 FOR X=1 TO 3:READ M(X):NEXT
120 FOR X=1 TO 3: SOUND 1,-10,M(X),DUR:SOUND
1,-8,M(4-X),DUR*1.5:NEXT
```

```
130 GOTO 120
140 DATA 53,69,81
```
PROGRAM 7.9

```
10 REM C-64 EFFECT
20 FOR X=0 TO 24:POKE 54272+X,0:NEXT
30 POKE 54296,15
32 REM TRY DIFFERENT ADSR VALUES IN LINE 35 F
OR DIFFERENT EFFECTS
35 POKE 54277,40:POKE54278,8
40 FOR X=1 TO 3: READ HF(X),WF(X):NEXT
50 FOR X=1 TO 3: POKE 54273,HF(X):POKE 54276,
WF(X)
60 FOR P=1TO10:NEXT:NEXT:REM ALTER DELAY LOOP
   FOR DIFFERENT EFFECTS
70 POKE 54276,0
80 RESTORE:GOTO 40
100 DATA 17,33,68,129,34,17:FREQUENCY AND WAV
EFORM
110 REM POKE 54276,0 TO TURN NOISE OFF AFTER
BREAKING
```
PROGRAM 7.10

Rhythm and percussive effects

The idea of using a low frequency to control a sound leads naturally to a discussion of rhythm and percussion. Remember that most percussion instruments have a sharply enveloped sound, and they are often characterized by white or coloured noise or high frequency pulses. Think of snare drums and cymbals, triangles, wood blocks and even pianos. These programs produce a variety of percussive sounds as demonstrations.

```
10 REM WHITE NOISE SOUND PERCUSSIVE
20 POKE 54296,15: REM SET VOLUME
30 POKE 54277,7: REM ATTACK/DECAY
40 POKE 54278,17: REM SUSTAIN/RELEASE
50 POKE 54273,4:POKE 54272,73:REM HIGH AND LOW F
REQUENCY BYTES FOR MIDDLE C
60 POKE 54276,129:REM SET WHITE NOISE
70 FOR P=1 TO 100:NEXT:REM SET NOTE LENGTH
80 POKE 54276,128: REM TURN OFF
```
PROGRAM 7.11

```
1 REM "FUNNY EXPLOSION"
100 S=54272
110 FOR X=0 TO 24
120 POKE S+X,0
130 NEXT
140 POKE 54296,15
150 POKE 54272,116: POKE 54273,7
160 POKE 54277,25: POKE 54278,136
170 POKE 54276, 129
180 FOR X=1 TO 100
190 POKE 54273,SGN(X/10-5)*(X/10-5)
195 NEXT
200 POKE 54276, 0
```
PROGRAM 7.12

```
 10 REM BBC PERCUSSIVE SOUNDS
 20 ENVELOPE 1,1,-15,0,0,2,0,0,126,-20,0,0,
126,0
 25 ENVELOPE 2,1,0,0,0,0,0,0,127,-10,0,0,12
6,0
 27 ENVELOPE 3,1,-4,0,0,50,0,0,127,-3,-2,0,
100,0
 30 SOUND 18,1,30,20
 40 SOUND 16,1,7,20
 50 FOR P=1 TO 500:NEXT
 60 SOUND 17,1,60,20
 70 SOUND 16,2,4,10
 80 FOR P=1 TO 500:NEXT
 90 SOUND 19,3,160,20
100 SOUND 16,3,3,20
110 SOUND 17,3,150,20
120 SOUND 18,3,155,20
```
PROGRAM 7.13

If a percussive effect is enclosed within a loop (REPEAT . . . UNTIL, FOR . . . NEXT or, simply, GOTO), it will repeat at a rate or frequency that can be determined by delays in the program. In this way you can produce simple rhythms.

```
10 REM CBM NOTE - PERCUSSIVE BASS
12 REM REPEATING AT RATE SET IN LINE 90
15 PRINT CHR$(147):REM CLEAR SCREEN
```

```
20 POKE 54296,15: REM SET VOLUME
30 POKE 54277,8: REM ATTACK/DECAY
40 POKE 54278,0: REM SUSTAIN/RELEASE
50 POKE 54273,4:POKE 54272,73:REM HIGH AND LOW F
REQUENCY BYTES FOR MIDDLE C
60 POKE 54276,17: REM SET TRIANGLE WAVE
70 FOR P=1 TO 200:NEXT:REM SET NOTE LENGTH
80 POKE 54276,16: REM TURN OFF
90 FOR P=1 TO 500:NEXT P: REM SETS RHYTHM
100 GOTO 60: REM PLAY AGAIN
120 END
```

PROGRAM 7.14

```
10 REM CBM NOTE - PERCUSSIVE DRUM
12 REM REPEATING AT RATE SET IN LINE 90
15 PRINT CHR$(147):REM CLEAR SCREEN
20 POKE 54296,15: REM SET VOLUME
30 POKE 54277,8: REM ATTACK/DECAY
40 POKE 54278,0: REM SUSTAIN/RELEASE
50 POKE 54273,4:POKE 54272,73:REM HIGH AND LOW F
REQUENCY BYTES FOR MIDDLE C
60 POKE 54276,129: REM SET WHITE NOISE WAVEFORM
70 FOR P=1 TO 200:NEXT:REM SET NOTE LENGTH
80 POKE 54276,16: REM TURN OFF
90 FOR P=1 TO 500:NEXT P: REM SETS RHYTHM
100 GOTO 60: REM PLAY AGAIN
120 END
```

PROGRAM 7.15

```
10 REM PERCUSSIVE RHYTHM USING ONE CHANNEL
12 REM REPEATING AT RATE SET BY DELAYS IN LINES
90 AND 100
15 PRINT CHR$(147):REM CLEAR SCREEN
20 POKE 54296,15: REM SET VOLUME
30 POKE 54277,8: REM ATTACK/DECAY
40 POKE 54278,17: REM SUSTAIN/RELEASE
50 POKE 54273,244:POKE 54272,103:REM HIGH AND LO
W FREQUENCY BYTES FOR A£-7
60 POKE 54276,129: REM SET WHITE NOISE WAVEFORM
70 FOR P=1 TO 100:NEXT:REM SET NOTE LENGTH
80 POKE 54276,16: REM TURN OFF
90 FOR P=1 TO 100:NEXT P: REM SETS RHYTHM
95 POKE 54276,33:REM TURN ON SAWTOOTH
```

```
100 FOR P=1 TO 200:NEXT P:POKE 54276,0:GOTO 60:R
EM PLAY AGAIN
```
PROGRAM 7.16

```
10 REM CBM NOTE - PERCUSSIVE DRUM
12 REM REPEATING AT RATE SET IN LINE 90
14 REM FAST RATE
15 PRINT CHR$(147):REM CLEAR SCREEN
20 POKE 54296,15: REM SET VOLUME
30 POKE 54277,8: REM ATTACK/DECAY
40 POKE 54278,17: REM SUSTAIN/RELEASE
50 POKE 54273,244:POKE 54272,103:REM HIGH AND LO
W FREQUENCY BYTES FOR A£-7
60 POKE 54276,129: REM SET WHITE NOISE WAVEFORM
70 FOR P=1 TO 100:NEXT:REM SET NOTE LENGTH
75 REM NOTE THAT NEXT POKE ADDS A SLIGHT TINKLE
TO SOUND WHICH WOULD BE
76 REM ABSENT IF POKE 54276,128 WERE USED INSTEA
D
80 POKE 54276,16: REM TURN OFF
90 FOR P=1 TO 100:NEXT P: REM SETS RHYTHM
100 GOTO 60: REM PLAY AGAIN
120 END
```
PROGRAM 7.17

```
 1 REM BBC RHYTHM EFFECT
 2 REM WITH DELAY
 5 INPUT"DELAY ";DELAY
10 FOR VOL%=-15 TO 0
20 SOUND 0,VOL%,4,0
30 NEXT
35 FOR P=1 TO DELAY:NEXT
40 GOTO 10
```
PROGRAM 7.18

The technique can be readily adapted and improved for more complex rhythms by the use of flags that will regularly vary the number of beats or the quality of the rhythmic sound, or simply by using a variety of loops.

```
1 REM BBC RHYTHM EFFECT
2 REM WITH DELAY
3 REM CYCLES THROUGH UNPITCHED TONES
```

```
 5 INPUT"DELAY ";DELAY
 8 X=4
10 FOR VOL%=-15 TO O
20 SOUND O,VOL%,X,O
30 NEXT
32 X=((X+1)MOD3)+4
35 FOR P=1 TO DELAY:NEXT
40 GOTO 10
```
PROGRAM 7.19

```
 1 REM BBC RHYTHM EFFECT
 2 REM WITH DELAY
 3 REM MUSICAL PLINKS
 5 INPUT"DELAY ";DELAY
 8 X=0
10 FOR VOL%=-15 TO O
20 SOUND 1,VOL%,X,O
25 REM CHANGE 'O' ABOVE TO 1 FOR NEAR MUSI
C
30 NEXT
32 X=((X+1)MOD3)
35 FOR P=1 TO DELAY:NEXT
40 GOTO 10
```
PROGRAM 7.20

```
10 REM PERCUSSIVE RHYTHM USING TWO CHANNELS
12 REM NOTICE HOW MESSY THIS CAN GET AND ALSO HO
W IT DRIFTS OUT OF SYNC
14 REM IT DEMONSTRATES HOW A STRUCTURED APPROACH
 WOULD IMPROVE ON MATTERS
15 PRINT CHR$(147):REM CLEAR SCREEN
20 POKE 54296,15: REM SET VOLUME
30 POKE 54277,8: REM ATTACK/DECAY
40 POKE 54278,17: REM SUSTAIN/RELEASE
44 POKE 54284,4:POKE 54285,4:REM SET ADSR CHANNE
L 2
50 POKE 54273,244:POKE 54272,103:REM HIGH AND LO
W FREQUENCY BYTES FOR A£-7
54 POKE 54280,6:POKE 54279,16:REM SET CHANNEL 2
TO F£-2
56 POKE 54282,1:POKE 54281,O:REM SET LOW DUTY CY
CLE CHANNEL 2
58 FOR RPT=1 TO 2: REM REPEAT NEXT SECTION
```

```
60 POKE 54276,129: REM SET WHITE NOISE WAVEFORM
65 FOR P=1 TO 50:NEXT P
66 POKE 54283,129: REM SET CHANNEL 2 TO NOISE
70 FOR P=1 TO 100:NEXT:REM SET NOTE LENGTH
72 POKE 54283,0: REM TURN OFF CH.2 NOISE
80 POKE 54276,16: REM TURN OFF CH.1
82 NEXT RPT
85 POKE 54283,65:REM SET PULSE ON CHANNEL 2
90 FOR P=1 TO 200:NEXT P: REM SETS RHYTHM
92 POKE 54283,64: REM TURN OFF PULSE
94 FOR RPT=1 TO 2
95 POKE 54276,129:REM TURN ON SAWTOOTH
100 FOR P=1 TO 100:NEXT P:POKE 54276,0
105 NEXT RPT: REM REPEAT ABOVE SECTION
110 POKE 54283,129
120 FOR P=1 TO 200:NEXT
130 GOTO 58:REM REPEAT
```
PROGRAM 7.21

```
10 REM BBC EFFECTS
20 ENVELOPE 1,1,0,0,0,0,0,0,126,-48,0,0,12
6,0
30 FOR X=1 TO 3
40 SOUND 0,1,6,4
50 SOUND 1,1,250,4
60 IF X=2 THEN 70 ELSE 80
70 FOR P=1 TO 1200:NEXT:GOTO 110
80 FOR P=1 TO 600:NEXT
90 SOUND 0,1,3,4
100 SOUND 1,1,20,4
110 NEXT
120 GOTO 30
```
PROGRAM 7.22

In general, a rhythm program can be built up by setting a tempo and a bar length and using arrays to hold percussion information. The program then cycles through the bars, filling each beat with a particular percussive effect. Here you will find some useful envelopes for the BBC and a 'skeleton' to run them. A similar program could be written for the 64.

```
  10 REM BBC RHYTHM SKELETON
  20 DIM E%(50)
  30 CLS
  40 INPUT "TEMPO (1 FAST TO 100 SLOW)"T%

  50 INPUT"NUMBER OF BEATS"B%
  60 E%(0)=-1
  70 FOR X%=1 TO B%
  80 PRINTTAB(0,0)"SELECT SILENCE(0),SNARE(1
),"'"          RIMSHOT(2) SYNTH(3)"
  90 A$=STR$(E%(X%-1))
 100 IF A$="-1"THEN A$=""
 110 PRINT TAB(X%-1,4);A$;
 120 INPUT E%(X%)
 130 NEXT
 140 PRINT TAB(B%,4);E%(B%);"   "
 150 PRINT "OKAY"
 160 ENVELOPE 0,0,0,0,0,0,0,0,0,0,0,0,0,0
 170 ENVELOPE 1,1,0,0,0,0,0,0,127,-12,0,0,12
6,0
 180 ENVELOPE 2,1,-8,0,0,2,0,0,126,-60,0,0,1
26,0
 190 ENVELOPE 3,1,-4,0,0,48,0,0,127,-3,-2,0,
96,0
 200 REPEAT
 210 FOR X%=1 TO B%
 220 SOUND 17,E%(X%),160,20
 230 SOUND 16,E%(X%),4,20
 240 FOR P%=1 TO T%*100:NEXT
 250 NEXT
 260 UNTIL FALSE
```
PROGRAM 7.23

Synchronizing accents

Percussion effects are one area of music-making where the computer's ability to hard-sync sounds is invaluable. Musically speaking, a rhythm track must be synchronized with at least some of the notes in a melody.

Each bar is normally accented (or emphasized) by one beat. You can choose which beat is to be the main accenting beat, but in classical convention it is the first beat of a bar (the down beat). This marks the start of the first note of that bar. The effect of accenting the down-beat in 4/4 time is a rhythm that goes *DA-da-da-da-DA-da-da-da-DA-da-da-da*. It is also common to accent the up-beat, the one before the start of each bar, thus:

da-da-da-DA-da-da-da-DA-da-da-da-DA. Try saying these to yourself and you will see that they give quite different effects.

Even in 4/4 time, the range of possible rhythms is enormous. For example, accenting an off-beat: *da-da-DA-da* or *da-DA-da-da*; missing a beat: *DA-()-da-da*; doubling a beat: *Da-da-dada-da*; accenting more than one beat: *da-DA-DA-da*. Try saying these to yourself again (making *DA* louder and more vigorous than *da*) and you will see that the effect changes with each variation.

In a composed piece try to sync your melody to the accented beat. This gives a much crisper effect, but may require considerable working out of timings. On the BBC, sync is done by setting SOUND statements:

SOUND &nOc, x, x, x

where c is a channel number and n indicates how many channels are to be in sync (the '&' indicates HEX). The relevant commands on these other channels should take the same form.

On the 64, sync is a rather different operation. BBC sync is a gating operation; under its control, the 76489 chip is enabled only when *all* sync channels are turned on (a logical AND). The Commodore has no such procedure; gating is controlled solely by POKEing waveform registers (locations 54276, 54283 and 54290) with an odd number (usually waveform parameter plus one) writing a binary 1 to bit 0 of the register. This operation turns on the relevant oscillator's envelope. The sync bit on the registers (bit 1) synchronizes waveforms when set to 1; that is, the logical AND is performed on the oscillator output rather than on the gate input. The result is a combination of the outputs from one channel with the output of another oscillator (1 with 3, 2 with 1 or 3 with 2), giving complex harmonic structures (see the program below). The simplest way to make sure that two or more channels start playing together (the function of the BBC sync feature) is just to put the POKEs to waveform registers together in the program. Since there are no sound buffers on the Commodore, as there are on the BBC, sounds do not have to queue up and wait their turn to play (which may lead to lags and leads between channels) – gate instructions are carried out immediately. (The test bit on the waveform registers, bit 3, locks its associated oscillator at zero level until it is reset to 0. It can thus be used to ensure an oscillator starts at the same time as its envelope is switched on. First, set the test bit to 1, for channel 1, POKE 54276,8. Next set overall volume, set up frequency, ADSR and pulse width – if required – and then, simultaneously, clear the test bit, set waveform and gate envelope on: POKE 54276,0+16+1. The oscillator should start at the same moment as the envelope. This should give a sharper attack, which may be useful for percussion. In general, the test bit can be turned on without affecting other bits by POKE 54276, PEEK (54276) OR 8 and off by POKE 54276, PEEK (54276) AND 247.)

```
10 REM C-64 SYNC AND TEST BIT
15 FOR F=1 TO 3
20 FOR X=0 TO 24:POKE 54272+X,0   :NEXT
30 POKE 54296,15+128: REM VOLUME AND CHANNEL
3 OFF
40 POKE 54273,100: REM CHANNEL 1 FREQUENCY
60 POKE 54277,219:POKE 54278,255:REM CHANNEL
1 ENVELOPE
65 POKE 54287,F*30: REM OBSERVE DIFFERENT EFF
ECTS OF CHANNEL 3 FREQUENCY
70 POKE 54276,19:REM SET TRIANGLE AND SYNC, C
HANNEL ONE, AND TURN ON
80 FOR P=1 TO 10000:NEXT
90 POKE 54276,8:REM TURN CHANNEL ONE OUTPUT O
FF USING TEST BIT
100 REM TEST BIT CAN BE USED FOR STACCATO EFF
ECT
130 NEXT
```
PROGRAM 7.24

Accenting is a matter of emphasis. This can be achieved by use of greater volume, or simply by the use of a dominant sound – for example, a snare coming in on the first beat of every bar, while the other beats are marked by a cymbal sound. The bar breaks represent 'natural' accents in music, so to accent other beats is somehow going against the grain. If done carefully this can result in an interesting tension. If done sloppily the result will be a mess.

Complex rhythms can be built up from a number of simpler rhythms. A rhythm in 4/4 time may be achieved by having a snare sound repeating every fourth beat, a cymbal every second beat, a bass drum starting on the third beat and repeating every fourth beat, wood block every beat, even a tympani starting on the fourth beat and repeating every other bar on the fourth beat.

With only one noise channel, there are difficulties in building up complex rhythms. The easiest technique is to work out the rhythm pattern beforehand and fill as many bars as it takes for that pattern to complete. If you want complex rhythms, advantage can be gained from using just one other sound channel to play suitable percussive sounds like triangle, bass or blocks. In this case, two dependent rhythm patterns can be programmed; but they should be synchronized – remember that it may be important to tune the sound from the non-noise channel so that it doesn't sound discordant when played with other notes or instruments. This is not necessarily a contradiction, since many acoustic instruments used for percussive accompaniment are tunable; among them, according to the conventional definition of a percussive or rhythm instrument, are the piano, the tympani, the bass and the bass drum.

8

Real music

Part 1: Dynamic effects

We have seen how certain real instrumental sounds can be synthesized using a microcomputer. More importantly, we've seen how very complex are the sounds produced by real instruments, especially when they are playing music.

In a sense, synthesis remains a magic art. Even once you've understood waveforms, envelopes, modulation and timbre, there are certain apparently indefinable qualities of a musical sound that may stay beyond your grasp: how, for example, the timbre of a piano changes with the pitch of the note it is playing, or how an individual's playing style can extract the most startlingly unexpected effects from an apparently simple instrument like a guitar.

Most of these things can be gathered together under the general heading of 'dynamic effects'. The best-known dynamic effect – the one that features on all the synthesizer ads – is concerned with the speed or energy with which the keys on a keyboard are attacked. This is called *key velocity* and has the effect of altering the attack characteristics of a note or its peak amplitude. There is no simple way this effect can be produced just using the standard typewriter keyboard of a micro. However, other dynamic effects are available to us.

Don't forget that the synthesizer – or the computer, for that matter – is an instrument in its own right and therefore displays some dynamic effects of its own. Some of these, inevitably, are undesirable, like the dead points on some acoustic instruments when notes sound dull and lifeless. As with any instrument, playing a computer will demand a degree of practice, if only to enable you to become familiar with its quirks.

One of the major sticking points of using a computer as an instrument is the question of polyphonic sound. Many acoustic instruments, certainly the keyboard and stringed instruments, are polyphonic; i.e. you can play more than one note at a time, each note being independent of the other. The Commodore and the BBC micros both have this facility to some extent. We have so far mainly considered the computers as monophonic instruments, playing one note at a time; but with three music channels it is possible to play up to three notes simultaneously. There is another option, and this is to use the three channels under the control of a single key or data entry. In some ways this is a more satisfactory arrangement, since it lends greater body and flavour to a tone, especially if you add a hint of 'detuning', so that each channel plays at a slightly different frequency, thus adding to the timbre. Or you could have the channels playing an octave or two apart, again lending richness to the timbre.

The main problems for polyphony are the delays it introduces into the program. With both computers there are a number of techniques for speeding up programs. The first and most important is good program structure, but there are others; using short variable names, concatenating lines, reducing the number of GOTOs and GOSUBs the program has to deal with and placing those that must remain as close to the beginning of a program as possible. On the BBC you can generally replace variables by integer variables (the so-called percent variables, written A%, Bee%, C3% and so on – although if you do this on the Commodore it will have the opposite effect and slow things down. On both machines, especially the Commodore, some speed can be achieved by using variables instead of numerical constants. This is useful to remember when dealing with all the locations you have to POKE on the 64. If your keyboard still displays some tardiness after all these measures have been taken, console yourself with the thought that it is a feature of many dedicated synthesizers as well. Modifications to the attack, decay and release rates are often helpful, although you may then find the sound quality you were after has disappeared.

The best way of speeding up a program is normally to write in a well-organized and carefully thought-out fashion. Always try to find the simplest solution to a given problem, asking yourself what you really want the program to do. Sometimes a slight modification of the terms of your problem will lead to a new and more efficient solution. Try to reduce the number of things a program has to do at any one time. This is especially useful with the Commodore, where several POKEs have to be executed to produce a sound, since many of these POKEs can be executed outside of a main play loop. If you want to play different pieces of music from within a program, you could set ADSR parameters, pulse widths and any filtering parameters first and, in your main loop, include only POKEs to the frequency registers and the waveform/control registers. ADSR and other settings could be changed by branching off to another part of the program only when required. These considerations should encourage you to use menus and branches to subroutines or calls to procedures (on the BBC).

As with any programs, the ones that follow could doubtless be improved. I hope you will treat this as an exercise, and that you will find a variety of ideas on how to construct musical programs in the examples.

Dynamic effects in practice
The following program for the Commodore 64 turns the computer into a real-time keyboard with the option of playing in monophonic or polyphonic mode. The polyphonic feature is something of a compromise, but it produces an additional and interesting effect. The main loop of the program is formed by lines 200-300, which wait for a key to be pressed and then check whether it is one of the 'musical' keys (defined in line 1090). If it is, a frequency is set, the note is played and the screen display is refreshed. If it isn't, the program branches to subroutine 2000 to see whether the key is associated with a parameter (octave, waveform, mono/poly setting, duration of ADSR setting). Octave and waveform are immediately changed to a prescribed value. Duration is increased by 1 until it reaches 10 when it goes back to 0. ADSR setting is changed after another branch, to subroutine 4000, stops the program and waits for values to be INPUT. Mono and poly are toggled.

The effect of toggling poly mode on is to open all three sound channels to keyboard entries. Thus a note played on channel 1 will be followed by a note played on channel 2 and then by a note on channel 3. A maximum of three notes can play simultaneously, allowing you to produce simple chords. However, there is something of a time lag between each of the notes, and the program does not scan the keyboard to find out how many keys are being pressed simultaneously before playing. The three notes will still be played in sequence but may overlap. The effect is somewhere between true polyphony and echo.

```
1 REM CBM64 SYNTH,COPYRIGHT GARY HERMAN,1983,
2 REM TOP TWO ROWS PLAY NOTES
3 REM VARIABLE ENVELOPE, OCTAVE AND WAVEFORM APP
LY TO ALL NOTES
4 REM NOTE THE DURATION (SUSTAIN PHASE) CONTROL
MAY NEED ADJUSTMENT
5 REM NOTE HOW EVEN SINGLE NOTES SOUND RICHER IN
```

```
 POLY MODE
6 REM BUT ALSO NOTE THAT KEYBOARD SCANNING AND N
OTE TRIGGERING LOSE SOME
7 REM RELIABILITY IN THIS MODE, AND OFTEN PRODUC
E UNPREDICTED HARMONIC EFFECTS
10 POKE 54296,15
20 PRINT CHR$(147);"SETTING UP PLEASE WAIT"
30 PRINT
40 PRINT"USE F1,F3,F4,F5 TO CHANGE OCTAVE"
50 PRINT "USE F2,F4,F5,F6 TO CHANGE WAVEFORM"
60 PRINT "USE BACK ARROW TO CHANGE DURATION"
70 PRINT "USE HORIZONTAL CRSR TO CHANGE ENVELOPE
"
80 PRINT "USE SPACE BAR TO TOGGLE MONO/POLYPHONI
C"
90 PRINT
100 GOSUB 1000:REM INITIALISE
190 PRINT"OKAY"
200 GETA$: IFA$=""THEN200
210 FR=FQ(KY(ASC(A$)))/M:T=7*V:SP=S+T:CR=SP+4:IF
 FR=0 THEN GOSUB 2000
220 FOR X=5 TO 6:POKE S+7+X,0: NEXT
240 POKE SP,FR-HB*INT(FR/HB):POKE SP+1,FR/HB
250 POKE SP+6,SV:POKE SP+5,AV
260 POKE CR,WV+1:FOR X=1 TO DU:NEXT: POKE CR,WV
270 IF P=1 THEN V=V+1: IF V=3 THEN V=0
275 PRINT "♣OCTAVE: ";OC;" WAVEFORM: ";WV+1;" DU
RATION: ";DU/10;" VOICE: ";V+1
280 GOTO 200
300 END
1000 S=54272:F=7040:DIM FQ(26), KY(255)
1010 FOR X=0 TO 28:POKE S,X:NEXT
1020 FOR X=26 TO 1 STEP -1:FQ(X)=F*5.8+30:F=F/2^
(1/12):NEXT
1030 KY$="Q2W3ER5T6Y7UI9OOP@-*\^"
1040 FOR X=1 TO LEN(KY$):KY(ASC(MID$(KY$,X)))=X:
NEXT
1060 SV=255:AV=9:WV=16:W=0:M=1:OC=4:HB=256:DU=50
1070 FOR X=0 TO 2:POKE S+5+7*X,AV:POKE S+6+7*X,S
V
1080 POKE S+2+7*X,255:POKE S+3+7*X,0: NEXT
1090 RETURN
1095 REM IN FOLLOWING COMMANDS ACTUAL SYMBOLS, W
```

```
HICH DON'T PRINT CORRECTLY,
1096 REM HAVE BEEN CHANGED TO KEY NAMES
1097 REM CHANGE BACK BEFORE ENTERING
2000 IF A$="F1"THEN M=1:OC=4:RETURN
2010 IF A$="F3"THEN M=2:OC=3:RETURN
2020 IF A$="F5"THEN M=4:OC=2:RETURN
2030 IF A$="F7"THEN M=8:OC=1:RETURN
2040 IF A$="F2"THEN W=0:WV=16:RETURN
2050 IF A$="F4"THEN W=1:WV=32:RETURN
2060 IF A$="F6"THEN W=2:WV=64:RETURN
2070 IF A$="F8"THEN W=3:WV=128:RETURN
2080 IF A$="SPACE"THEN P=1-P:RETURN
2090 IF A$="BACK ARROW"THEN DU=DU+10:IF DU>100 T
HEN DU=0: RETURN
3000 IF A$="HORIZONTAL CRSR" THEN GOSUB 4000:RET
URN
3010 RETURN
4000 PRINT CHR$(147)
4010 PRINT "ATTACK/DECAY: ";AV
4020 PRINT "SUSTAIN/RELEASE: ";SV
4030 INPUT "CHANGE (Y/N)";B$
4040 IF B$<>"Y" THEN RETURN
4050 INPUT "ATTACK/DECAY (0-255)";AV
4060 INPUT "SYSTAIN/RELEASE (0-255)";SV
4070 IF AV<0 OR AV>255 OR SV<0 OR SV>255 THEN 40
00
4080 GOTO 4000
4090 PRINT CHR$(147)
5000 RETURN
```

PROGRAM 8.1

A number of different effects can be obtained by simple modifications. SID chip's sync feature can be used to produce dynamic interaction between channels (see Chapter 7). The main loop (200-280) can be speeded up by removing the print statement to a subroutine only conditionally branched to, and by relocating the POKEs dealing with ADSR parameters. In line 260 the waveform/control registers could have bits 0 and 1 set to 1 as well as the waveform bit (WV+2+1), while removing all reference throughout the program to the duration parameter, and relocating POKE CR,WV to a new line, 205. Bits 0 and 1 are, respectively, the gate and synchronization bits. Leaving the sync on (by changing 205 to POKE CR,WV+2) has some interesting effects.

Synthesizing reverberation
Polyphony gives a far richer harmonic content to the music you produce. The interaction between each of the tones in a group produces this richness, and this interaction is a dynamic effect. There are a number of different ways in which tones can be played together so as to interact. One of the most useful and natural is reverberation.

The synthesis of reverberation involves the repetition of a single tone in rapid sequence. Modifications in the tone may be introduced, in particular a reduction in volume for each repetition. If the repetitions are far enough apart, you get something resembling echo (although it is usually more mechanical sounding than real echo). If the repetitions are very close together, the notes being produced almost simultaneously, the result is like the electronic musician's flanging/phasing or chorus effect.

An understanding of the principles underlying these effects is necessary to develop useful means of synthesizing them. Reverberation is a feature of all natural sounds and is produced because in any ordinary environment sound from a single source reaches the ear by a variety of routes, directly and as a reflection from walls and other surfaces. The slight time lags involved give the sense of *space* most obvious when reverberation becomes genuine echo. The longer the delays the greater the perception of the space involved. Also involved in the time delay is a diminution of volume, and often a distortion of harmonic content (in particular a loss of bass frequencies).

Some of the harmonic distortion is a product of the delays themselves, since the two tones that combine may be identical in every respect apart from a difference in phase. The phase difference will produce an amplification of some frequencies and an attenuation of others where, respectively, peaks reinforce each other or a peak and a trough coincide. If you imagine the phases differences to vary during the course of tone being produced, the result will be like using a variable filter on a single tone. Where the variations are regular this will sound like a filter sweep or even a wah-wah; but in practice the variations are more or less random, and the effect is called phasing (for obvious reasons) or flanging (because it used to be synthesized by using two tape recorders producing identical tones and putting slight pressure on the flanges of one tape in order to vary its speed marginally). The most familiar example of flanging is the sound produced by a plane flying over a smooth runway. Here, the characteristic *whoosh* is produced by the variations in delay time for the reflected sound of the plane as it moves over the reflecting surface of the runway.

In analogue synthesis a device known as a comb filter is often used to produce phasing. The microcomputer controlling a PSG can produce a similar result by sending out the same tone through each of its three sound channels and introducing a slight delay. Usually it is unnecessary to vary the delay, since the characteristics of the computer and the program will introduce small enough variations in delay. However, it is worth experimenting with variable and even random delays.

Chorus effects are similar. They are meant to synthesize the natural sound of a group of instruments playing in unison. Since there will be slight differences in the character of the tones produced by different instruments of the same sort, there will be a complex pattern of harmonic variations in any chorus. Also, the instruments in a chorus will never all play at precisely the same time, so here too delays contribute to the effect. Producing a chorus effect on a micro involves a combination of slight discrepancies in tuning and slight delays. The more 'layers' you can add to the tone, the better.

The program that follows is for the BBC micro, although the principles are easily implemented on other micros. In essence, delays are introduced in two ways: firstly, by using three channels to produce more or less the same tone and, secondly, by looping round the tone-producing commands, introducing a delay to produce a sequence of repetitions.

The main play loop is contained in lines 280-320, which call PROCPLAY, lines 340-470. There are three separate SOUND statements (which might fruitfully be replaced with a single command embedded in a loop, as long as channel, envelope, duration and delay variables are replaced by suitable arrays). The three commands, separated by delay loops, are embedded in a FOR . . NEXT loop, which determines the number of repetitions of the three sounds. The program allows control of the number of repetitions, note duration, the delay between sounds and the rate at which the sounds die away (called 'decay constant') as well as certain features of the sound envelope. These can be changed during play by pressing the relevant function keys, and the results are shown on screen. Note frequency is determined by the variable BASE% and the calculations incorporated in line 35, which checks to see whether a note key has been pressed (using the key data in line 620) and calculates the frequency of the key as BASE% plus four times the index of the array variable (A%(X%)) associated with that key. The note keys are the top two rows of the QWERTY keyboard.

With the appropriate choice of variables, the keyboard can give mandolin-type tremolo, staccato, chorus, flanging or even (with zero delay) a full-blooded poly effect. You could experiment with the timings of the delays and decays and with the envelopes. Different envelopes will doubtless give yet more interesting effects (especially if you experiment with the pitch section of the envelopes).

```
10REM***BBC ECHO***Gary Herman,1984
20REM***a refined version of previous echo
programs***
30REM***red function keys change variables
***
40REM***delay,number of cycles, note durat
ion***
50REM***decay constant (f0-f3),envelope pa
rameters***
60REM***peak vol,sustain vol, attack/decay
and sustain release (f4-f7)
70REM***f8 resets echo, f9 resets envelope
***
80REM***you can set parameters to 0 by typ
ing RETURN***
90REM***in response to initial prompts***
100 ON ERROR MODE7
110REM"ECHO"
120MODE7:DIMA%(23):BASE%=45:L%=1:M%=2:N%=3
130FORX%=1TO23:READP%:A%(X%)=P%:NEXT
140INPUT"DELAY : "DELAY%
150INPUT"NUMBER OF CYCLES: "REPT%
160INPUT"NOTE DURATION: "DUR%
170INPUT"DECAY CONSTANT : "K%
180 PRINT
190INPUT"MAXVOL: "V%
200INPUT"SUSVOL: "S%
210INPUT"AD     : "AD%
220INPUT"SR     : "SR%
230CLS
240 INPUT "SIMPLE (S) OR COMPLEX (C) ENVELO
PES: ",A$
250IFA$="S"M%=L%ANDN%=L%
260CLS:PRINT"Okay"
270 VDU 23;8202;0;0;0;
```

```
   280 PROCPrint
   290FREQ%=-1
   300 PROCPLAY
   310 PROCCHANGE
   320 GOTO 280
   330 :
   340 DEF PROCPLAY
   350FORX%=1TO23:IFINKEY(-A%(X%))FREQ%=BASE%+
4*X%:X%=23
   360NEXT
   370 IFFREQ%=-1THEN350
   380 MAXVOL%=V%:SUSVOL%=S%
   390 PROCENV(MAXVOL%,SUSVOL%)
   400 FOR CYC%=1 TO REPT%
   410 SOUND &11,L%,FREQ%,10
   420 FOR X%=1TODELAY%:NEXT
   430 SOUND &12,M%,FREQ%,10
   440 FOR X%=1TODELAY%*2:NEXT
   450 SOUND &13,N%,FREQ%,20
   460 MAXVOL%=MAXVOL%-K%:SUSVOL%=SUSVOL%-K%:N
EXT
   470 ENDPROC
   480 DEF PROCCHANGE
   490IFINKEY(-33)DELAY%=(DELAY%+100)MOD1000
   500IFINKEY(-114)REPT%=(REPT%+1)MOD20
   510IFINKEY(-115)DUR%=(DUR%+1)MOD40
   520IFINKEY(-116)K%=(K%+8)MOD128
   530IFINKEY(-21)V%=(V%+8)MOD127
   540IFINKEY(-117)S%=(S%+8)MOD128
   550IFINKEY(-118)AD%=(AD%+8)MOD128
   560IFINKEY(-23)SR%=(SR%+8)MOD128
   570IFINKEY(-119)DELAY%=0:REPT%=0:DUR%=0:K%=
0
   580IFINKEY(-120)V%=126:S%=0
   590 ENDPROC
   600PROCPrint
   610GOTO290
   620 DATA 97,17,50,34,18,35,52,20,36,53,69,3
7,54,38,39,55,40,56,72,25,57,121,41
   630 END
   640DEF PROCENV(MAXVOL%,SUSVOL%)
   650ENVELOPE1,DUR%,0,0,0,0,0,0,AD%,AD%-127,-
SR%,(SR%=0),MAXVOL%,SUSVOL%
```

```
  660ENVELOPE  2,DUR%,0,0,0,0,0,0,2*AD%,-2*AD%
,-SR%,(SR%=0),MAXVOL%-30,SUSVOL%-3
  670ENVELOPE3,DUR%,0,0,0,0,0,0,AD%-50,-AD%+5
0,-SR%,(SR%=0),MAXVOL%-60,SUSVOL%-60
  680 ENDPROC
  690DEF PROCPrint
  700PRINTTAB(0,1)"NUMBER OF CYCLES: "REPT%"
  "
  710PRINTTAB(0,3)"DECAY CONSTANT: "K%"          "

  720PRINTTAB(0,2)"NOTE DURATION: "DUR%"      "

  730PRINTTAB(0,0)"DELAY : "DELAY%"          "
  740PRINTTAB(0,8)"MAXVOL: "V%  " SUSVOL: "S%
 '"AT/DCY: "AD%  " SUS/RL: "SR%"     "
  750ENDPROC
```

PROGRAM 8.2

Synthesizing simple echo and 'detuning'
For the Commodore owner, I include a short echo program. The effect is
about as simply achieved as you can get; the sound is produced as a series of
repetitions. The program asks for a number of repetitions, a delay and a
decay constant (between 0 and 15) and then proceeds to put out a sound and
repeat it at progressively lower volume. Only one channel is used. A more
elaborate echo could be achieved by adding sound from SID's two other
channels.

```
1 REM ECHO, C-64
10 S=54272:LF=S:HF=S+1:WF=HF+3:AD=WF+1:SR=AD+1:M
V=S+24:POKE WF,0
20 V=15:REM SET INITIAL VOLUME
30 POKE HF,17:POKE LF,37:REM MIDDLE C
40 POKE AD,9:POKE SR,240:REM FAST ATTACK/RELEASE
,     SUSTAIN, MODERATE DECAY
50 INPUT"ENTER REPEATS,DELAY,DECAY FACTOR";R,DL,
DC
60 IF DC<0 OR DC>15 THEN PRINT "DECAY OUT OF RAN
GE":GOTO 50
70 DC=DC/15
```

```
80 FOR RPT=0 TO R
85 POKE WF,16:REM TRIANGLE OFF
90 POKE MV,V
100 POKE WF,17:REM TRIANGLE ON
110 FOR DELAY=0 TO DL:NEXT
130 V=V*DC
140 NEXT
```
PROGRAM 8.3

This program could be used within a real-time keyboard program as the main play loop. Different effects can be achieved by use of different ADSR parameters, but flanging and chorus effects can be obtained only with more than one channel, since they result from the interaction of more than one sound playing at the same time. The Commodore program above achieves its echo by gating a sound off before repeating it; two sounds are never heard at the same time using only one channel.

A similar effect to flanging and chorus – in that it is the result of a dynamic interaction between two or more simultaneous sounds – is called *detuning*, and is obtained by setting the frequencies of two or more oscillators, ostensibly playing the same note, at slightly different levels. The oscillators within the 76489 and SID chips may not be exactly in tune anyway. To introduce 'user detuning' it is necessary only to load each oscillator with slightly different pitch values: perhaps plus or minus 1 in the case of the BBC's pitch parameters, and plus or minus 10 or 20 in the case of the Commodore's low frequency registers. For example:

> 100 SOUND 1,−15,53,100
> 110 SOUND 2,−15,52,100

on the BBC, and

> 100 POKE 54273,34:POKE 54272,75
> 110 POKE 54280,34:POKE 54279,60

on the Commodore.

Detuning results in the generation of so-called 'beat frequencies', heard as slight throbs within the sound. The effect is caused by the way in which the two slightly different frequencies appear to drift in and out of phase, now reinforcing each other and now cancelling out. In effect, a new component frequency is added to the sound, whose value is the difference between the two fundamentals. This is yet another method for making a sound harmonically rich.

Arpeggiating

One effect generally obtainable only on the most expensive synthesizers, similar to echo, is easily achieved using a computer. This is *arpeggiating*.

An arpeggio is the result of playing the notes that comprise a chord in rapid sequence, rather than simultaneously. It is the classic type of harp sound, also familiar if you've ever slowly strummed a guitar or played a piano chord one note at a time.

Arpeggios can be attractive. Expensive synthesizers allow you to enter an arpeggiating mode in which any chord you play will be transformed into an arpeggio that may, if required, play over and over. The technique is often used on contemporary pop and rock records to provide a rhythmic backing, on top of which a melody may be played or sung. A fully fledged arpeggiator allows an arpeggio to be played across a number of octaves (the same notes will be repeated in more than one octave) and in a number of directions – up the scale (say, C, E and G), down the scale (say, G, E and C) or cycling (C, E, G, G, E, C and so on).

On a computer with a three-channel sound generator it is an easy matter to send successive notes to different oscillators, storing the note frequencies within an array and then cycling through sound commands, calling the appropriate array elements, until a new note is played. This is the technique used in the two programs below, one for the BBC and one for the Commodore.

For the BBC arpeggiator, a note is fetched from the keyboard in lines 290-325. The note frequency is determined in our familiar way by checking against data to see which key has been pressed and then calculating the relevant frequency using the index value (X%) of an array (A%(X%)). Notes are assigned channels by the variable T%, which can take values between 1 and 3, cycling round so that the next channel after 3 is 1. Lines 340-410 then cycle round the channels and through a number of octaves determined by the variable G%, repeating each of the notes played so far until a key is pressed (UNTIL INKEY (0)). If that key represents a note, this note is added to the arpeggio, so that the fourth note played becomes the new note number one. Thus the arpeggio automatically plays in the same sequence as the notes played and automatically includes as many notes (up to three) as have been played. The arpeggio can be stopped at any point by pressing function key f3, and a new arpeggio will then start with the next note. The ADSR parameters can be changed using the function buttons, and the rate and number of octaves in the arpeggio can be altered in a similar way. One simple improvement would be to add a facility for sweeping *down* octaves or *cycling through* them. As it stands, the program allows arpeggios only to ascend through a set number of octaves (see the loop formed by lines 340 and 410).

```
 10    REM***BBC ARPEGGIATOR...ARP***
 15 REM***function keys change variables***
 16 REM***f0,f1:rate/f2:cancels hold/f3:oct
aves up and down***
 17 REM***f4-f9:envelope***
 20   REM**G.Herman, 1984***********
 30   ON ERROR GOTO 2000
 40   MODE 7:BASE%=1:G%=1:RATE%=128:V%=0:T%=
3:DIM A%(23),FREQ%(3)
 50 AS%=8:DS%=-8:SS%=0:RS%=-1:AV%=120:DV%=3
2
 60 FOR X%=1 TO 23:READ P%:A%(X%)=P%:NEXT
 70 VDU 23;8202;0;0;0;
 80 PROCSCREEN
140 IF  INKEY(-33)RATE%=RATE%/2
150 IF  INKEY(-114)RATE%=RATE%*2
160 IF  INKEY(-115)V%=1-V%
170 IF  INKEY(-116)G%=(G%+1) MOD 8
180 IF  INKEY(-21)AV%=(AV%+8) MOD 128
190 IF  INKEY(-117)DV%=(DV%+8) MOD 128
200 IF  INKEY(-118)AS%=(AS%+8) MOD 128
210 IF  INKEY(-23)DS%=(DS%-8) MOD 128
220 IF  INKEY(-119)SS%=(SS%+8) MOD 128
230 IF  INKEY(-120)RS%=(RS%-1) MOD 8
260 ENVELOPE 1,1,0,0,0,0,0,0,AS%,DS%,SS%,RS
%,AV%,DV%
290 REPEAT
300 FOR X%=1 TO 23
310 IF  INKEY(-A%(X%))T%=(T% MOD 3)+1:FREQ%(
T%)=BASE%+4*X%:V%=1:X%=24
320 NEXT
325 UNTIL INKEY(0)
330 IF V%=0 THEN  290
340 FOR F%=0 TO G%
350 REPEAT
360 FOR RPT%=1 TO T%
370 SOUND 16+RPT%,V%,48*F%+FREQ%(RPT%),-1
380 FOR P%=1 TO 65536 STEP RATE%:NEXT
390 NEXT
400 UNTIL INKEY(0)
410 NEXT
420 GOTO 80
430 DEF PROCSCREEN
```

```
440 PRINT TAB(5,5)"RATE : "INT(RATE%/16)" "
450 PRINT TAB(5,6)"HOLD : "V%
460 PRINT TAB(5,7)"RANGE : "G%+1" OCTAVES"
470 PRINT TAB(5,8)"NOTES : "T%
480 PRINT TAB(5,9)"ATTACK TARGET : "AV%" "

490 PRINT TAB(5,10)"DECAY TARGET : "DV%
500 PRINT TAB(5,11)"A STEP : "AS%" "
510 PRINT TAB(5,12)"D STEP : "DS%" "
520 PRINT TAB(5,13)"S STEP : "SS%" "
530 PRINT TAB(5,14)"R STEP : "RS%" "
540 ENDPROC
570 DATA97,17,50,34,18,35,52,20,36,53,69,37
,54,38,39,55,40,56,72,25,57,121,41
2000 MODE 7
```
PROGRAM 8.4

The next program is an arpeggiator for the Commodore 64, but it is much more besides. The program is REMmed to explain the screen display and key operations, which are quite complicated. Apart from arpeggiating (use the space bar to turn on and off), the program allows you to adjust ADSR parameters, pulse width, the bottom octave on the keyboard (which plays two octaves) and the octave range of the arpeggiator. You can also change waveforms on each channel independently, and introduce ring, pulse width and frequency modulation, as well as filtering. The main play loop is contained in lines 95-145; because of all the operations involved, it operates quite slowly. Great improvements can be made, once the program has been entered and debugged, by reducing variable names to one letter and by concatenating program lines using colon separators. The back arrow key (top left of the keyboard) allows the program to jump over several POKEs during the play loop, thus speeding it up somewhat. However, with real-time control of facilities like ring mod, there is bound to be some tardiness. A better solution may have been to menu-drive the program, but you can't doubt the attractiveness of a fully real-time keyboard.

```
1 REM ARPSYNTH***C-64***GARY HERMAN 1984
2 REM ARPEGGIATOR WITH FILTERING, VARIABLE ADSR,
 PULSE WIDTH, RING MODULATION.
3 REM THE KEY FUNCTIONS CAN BE UNDERSTOOD BY AN
EXAMINATION OF THE PROGRAM
```

```
4 REM BUT USEFUL STARTER KEYS ARE '9' WHICH TOGG
LES THE STATUS DISPLAY ON AND
5 REM OFF, THE SPACE BAR WHICH TOGGLES THE ARPEG
GIATOR FUNCTION AND
6 REM THE POUND SIGN WHICH SILENCES THE OUTPUT.
9 PRINT CHR$(147)
10 PRINT "SETTING UP, PLEASE WAIT"
12 GOSUB 1000
14 GOSUB 2000
15 GOSUB 3000
16 GOSUB 5000
17 PRINT CHR$(147)
18 REM THE FOLLOWING KEYS, ARRANGED AS ON A TWO
MANUAL ORGAN, PLAY THE NOTES:
19 REM TWO FULL OCTAVES.
20 N$="Q2W3ER5T6Y7UZSXDCVGBHNJM,"
21 REM THE STATUS DISPLAY SHOWS IMPORTANT INFORM
ATION: READING ALONG
22 REM ARPEGGIATOR ON/OFF,ADSR SETTINGS,WAVEFORM
 OF LAST NOTE PLAYED, BOTTOM
23 REM OCTAVE AND RANGE,HOLD,RING MODULATION,NOT
E DURATION,PULSE DUTY CYCLE.
24 REM PULSE WIDTH MOD ON/OFF,OSC3 WAVEFORM,STAT
US OF OSC3 OUTPUT,FILTER
25 REM INFORMATION:OSCILLATORS FED TO FILTER,CUT
-OFF FREQ,RESONANCE,FILTER TYPE
26 PRINT CHR$(19):PRINT "ARP","ADY","SUR","WFM":
PRINT
27 PRINT "OCT","HLD","RGM","DUR":PRINT
28 PRINT "M/S","PWM","WF3","OS3":PRINT
29 PRINT "OSF","COF","RES","TYP":PRINT
30 PRINT "CH","BY-PASS","FM":PRINT
32 V=0
35 GET A$:IF A$="" THEN 35
50 FOR K=1 TO 25
60 IF MID$(N$,K,1)=A$ THEN T=T+1+(T=3)*3:I(T)=K:
V=1:K=25
70 NEXT K
75 PRINT CHR$(19);SPC(20);CHR$(161-V)
80 IF V=0 THEN GOSUB 200:FW(T)=FW:GOTO 32
85 POKE 198,0
90 IF GS THEN GOSUB 4000
95 F=J
```

```
100 FOR CH=1 TO T
103 POKE WF(CH),O+PT
104 POKE MV,15+VN+CF
106 IF SY=1 THEN 125
109 POKE RF,CR+CS:POKE HC,FX
115 POKE AD(CH),AD:POKE SR(CH),SR
120 POKE PH(CH),HP:POKE PL(CH),LP
125 POKE FH(CH),FR(I(CH)+12*F):POKE FL(CH),FQ(I(
CH)+12*F)
130 POKE WF(CH),FW(CH)+RM
132 FOR DEL=1 TO DUR:POKE PH(CH),HP+IP*PEEK(RG)/
16:NEXT DEL
133 IF PEEK(198)<>0 THEN CH=T:GOTO 32
135 NEXT CH
138 FOR DEL=1 TO DUR:POKE HC,FX+XS*PEEK(RG):NEXT
 DEL
139 F=F+1:IF F<=G THEN 100
140 IF ARP=1 THEN 95
145 IF ARP=0 THEN 32
190 REM THE ITEMS ENCLOSED IN SQUARE BRACKETS BE
LOW STAND IN FOR THE SYMBOLS
191 REM ASSOCIATED WITH THE RELEVANT KEYS
192 REM BECAUSE THESE SYMBOLS DO NOT PRINT OUT.
193 REM THOSE ITEMS NOT IN BRACKETS ARE THE KEYS
 THEMSELVES.
194 REM THE KEY NAMES SHOULD BE REPLACED WITH TH
E APPROPRIATE KEY SYMBOL
195 REM FOR THE PROGRAM TO WORK.
196 REM THE SYMBOLS ARE OBTAINED BY PRESSING THE
 RELEVANT KEY WITHIN QUOTES.
200 IF A$="[F1]" THEN DUR=DUR+5+(DUR=95)*100:RET
URN:REM NOTE DURATION
210 IF A$="[F3]" THEN PT=1-PT:RETURN:REM TOGGLES
 NOTE HOLD FEATURE
220 IF A$="[F5]" THEN G=G+1+(G=4)*5:RETURN:REM S
ETS OCTAVE RANGE FOR ARPEGGIOS
230 IF A$="[F7]" THEN J=G:RETURN:REM SETS BOTTOM
 OCTAVE EQUAL TO TOP OF RANGE
240 IF A$="[SPACE BAR]" THEN ARP=1-ARP:RETURN:RE
M TOGGLES ARPEGGIO FEATURE
250 IF A$="[F2]" THEN AD=AD+8+(AD>=248)*256:RETU
RN:REM A/D SETTING UP BY 8
260 IF A$="[F4]" THEN AD=AD-1-(AD<=0)*255:RETURN
```

```
:REM A/D SETTING DOWN BY ONE
280 IF A$="[F6]" THEN SR=SR+8+(SR>=248)*256:RETU
RN:REM S/R SETTING UP BY 8
290 IF A$="[F8]" THEN SR=SR-1-(SR<=0)*255:RETURN
:REM S/R SETTING DOWN BY ONE
298 IF A$="9" THEN GS=-(GS+1):REM TOGGLES STATUS
 DISPLAY WITH NEXT NOTE PLAYED
310 IF A$="." THEN FW=17:RETURN:REM SETS WAVEFOR
M TO TRIANGLE
320 IF A$="/" THEN FW=33:RETURN:REM SETS WAVEFOR
M TO SAWTOOTH
330 IF A$="[VERTICAL CRSR]" THEN FW=65:RETURN:RE
M SETS WAVEFORM TO PULSE
340 IF A$="[HORIZONTAL CRSR]" THEN FW=129:RETURN
:REM SETS WAVEFORM TO NOISE
350 IF A$="=" THEN RM=4-RM:RETURN:REM TOGGLES RI
NG MODULATION
360 IF A$="[UP ARROW]" AND RO=1 THEN RG=03:RO=1-
RO:RETURN:REM OSC3 WAVEFORM
365 IF A$="[UP ARROW]" AND RO=0 THEN RG=E3:RO=1-
RO:RETURN:REM OSC3 ENVELOPE
370 IF A$="*" THEN HP=HP+1+(HP=15)*15:RETURN:REM
 ADJUSTS PULSE DUTY CYCLE
374 IF A$=";" THEN FX=FX+16+(FX=250)*255:RETURN:
REM SETS FILTER CUT-OFF
375 IF A$=":" THEN CF=CF+16+(CF=80)*96:RETURN:RE
M SETS FILTER TYPE:LP,HP,BP
376 IF A$="L" THEN CS=CS+1+(CS=7)*8:RETURN:REM S
ETS OSCILLATOR FED TO FILTER
377 IF A$="P" THEN CR=240-CR:RETURN:REM SETS RES
ONANCE LEVEL
378 IF A$="O" THEN XS=1-XS:RETURN:REM TOGGLES FR
EQUENCY MODULATION
380 IF A$="@" THEN IP=1-IP:RETURN:REM TOGGLES PU
LSE WIDTH MODULATION
385 IF A$="[POUND SIGN]"AND PT=0 THENPOKEWF(1),0
:POKEWF(2),0:POKEWF(3),0:RETURN
386 REM SHUTS OFF ALL OUTPUT
390 IF A$="-" THEN T=T+1+(T=3)*3:RETURN:REM SETS
 NUMBER OF CHANNELS IN USE
395 IF A$="+" THEN FW(3)=FW:RETURN:REM SETS OSCI
LLATOR3 WAVEFORM TO CURRENT ONE
396 IF A$="O" THEN VN=128-VN:REM TOGGLES OSC3 OU
```

```
TPUT
397 IF A$="[BACK ARROW]" THEN SY=1-SY:REM TOGGLE
S PULSE AND ADSR ROUTINES IN/OUT
398 REM SAVING TIME WHEN VALUES DO NOT NEED TO B
E RESET
399 RETURN
999 REM REGVAR
1000 S=54272
1010 FOR X=1 TO 3
1020 CH=7*(X-1)
1030 FL(X)=S+CH:FH(X)=FL(X)+1:PL(X)=FH(X)+1:PH(X
)=PL(X)+1:WF(X)=PH(X)+1
1040 AD(X)=WF(X)+1:SR(X)=AD(X)+1
1050 NEXT
1060 LC=SR(3)+1:HC=LC+1:RF=HC+1:MV=RF+1:PX=MV+1:
PY=PX+1:O3=PY+1:E3=O3+1
1070 FOR X=0 TO 24: POKE S+X,0: NEXT
1080 RETURN
2000 REM
2010 DIM FR(999),FQ(999)
2100 RETURN
3000 FOR Z=1 TO 73: READ FR(Z),FQ(Z):NEXT Z
3010 DATA 4,73,4,139,4,208,5,25,5,103,5,185,6,16
,6,108,6,206,7,53,7,163,8,23
3020 DATA 8,147,9,21,9,159,10,60,10,205,11,114,1
2,32,12,216
3030 DATA 13,156,14,107,15,70,16,47,17,37
3040 DATA 18,42,19,63,20,100,21,154,22,227,24,63
,25,177,27,56,28,214
3050 DATA 30,141,32,94,34,75,36,85,38,126,40,200
,43,52,45,198,48,127
3060 DATA 51,97,54,111,57,172,61,126,64,188,68,1
49
3100 DATA 72,169,76,252,81,161,86,105,91,140,96,
254,102,194,108,223,115,88
3110 DATA 122,52,129,120,137,43,145,83,153,247,1
63,31,172,210,183,25,193,252
3120 DATA 205,133,217,189,230,176,244,103
3130 DATA 3,210,4,12
3999 RETURN
4000 PRINT CHR$(19):PRINT
4010 PRINT ARP,AD,SR,FW(T):PRINT
4020 PRINT J;G,PT,-(RM=4),INT(DUR/5):PRINT
```

```
4030 PRINT HP,IP,FW(3),-(VN=0):PRINT
4040 PRINT CS,FX,CR,CF:PRINT
4050 PRINT T,SY,XS
4100 RETURN
5000 T=0:J=1:G=1:DUR=0:PT=0:LP=255:HP=7:VN=0
5010 AD=40:SR=40:FW(1)=65:FW(2)=33:FW(3)=17:FW=3
3
5100 RETURN
```

PROGRAM 8.5

The program accepts keyboard input and uses a MID$ function (in line 60) to check whether the key pressed is a note key (defined by the string N$ in line 20). If another key has been pressed, the program branches to subroutine 200, which checks to see if one of the facility keys has been pressed and takes the appropriate action. Line 90 updates the screen display, if necessary, and then the program moves into the play loop.

Note frequency data in high byte/low byte form is contained in lines 3010 to 3130 and is read in into two arrays, FR(Z) and FQ(Z). Octave values are calculated in line 125, during the play loop. A further increase in speed may be achieved by calculating the relevant frequencies in advance and assigning them to array elements.

The arpeggiator feature is implemented by means of a variable T (similarly to the BBC arpeggiator), which provides the end point of the FOR . . . NEXT loop in line 100. With the arp feature on, the program loops back to line 95, otherwise it goes back to line 32 to fetch another note from the keyboard. Line 133 checks to see whether a key has been pressed while the play loop is being performed.

Improvements to the program could include graphics as well as speed. As with the BBC arpeggiator, this program only cycles up through the octaves set by variable G – see line 139. There is room for a modification here.

Sequencing

This chapter has so far dealt with playing music from the keyboard. The micro can also be used as a composing instrument or as one that performs in its own right.

The sequencer is the fundamental compositional aid that electronic music has developed. Sequencing is simply a form of recording without tape or disc. Once again, digital techniques make the task relatively simple, since it can – in essence – be reduced to the job of storing and recalling a series of numbers. The numbers relate to the frequency, duration and, sometimes, other characteristics of a note.

The simplest way of approaching the task is to enter the numbers direct on to a computer keyboard and store them in arrays. It goes without saying that this might get tedious and confusing. There are really no better techniques for data storage than the use of arrays – which, happily, are well implemented in BASIC even though at the cost of a great deal of memory. But direct keyboard entry of numbers can be improved upon. The two chief contenders for contemporary sequencers are 'step-time' entry and 'real-time' entry. Step-time entry is by far the easiest and is the technique used by the shortish BBC program in Chapter 5.

The program is monophonic: only one melody line can be stored. To write yourself a polyphonic sequencer is an easy matter in principle. You simply replace the relevant variables – MEL%(Q%),DUR%(Q%) and S$(Q%), in this case – by two-dimensional arrays (for example, MEL%(N%,Q%)), so that note data is indexed not just by step but by sound channel as well. The playback loop, lines 170 to 280, should then include three SOUND statements (one for each channel) instead of just the one in line 210. Further modifications should also be easy. For example, it would be possible to enter a string in line 90 which, rather than giving note data, a play instruction or a tuning instruction, would give a code to trigger a new envelope. The BBC sequencer could be built up into a really useful program without too much effort.

As it stands, the program is still quite versatile. Note data is input as a string which gives the note name, accidental (sharps only, in this case) or natural, the octave and the note length. The string is dissected for information, checked against the reference string in line 50, which gives all the acceptable note names and octaves, and against instructions to play (PLA) or tune (TUN); if acceptable, the note plays and is stored. A PLA instruction sends the program to line 170, from where the sequence entered so far is played and displayed on the screen. A TUN instruction sends the program to line 290, which provides a simple routine to tune the computer by changing the value of BASE%, the base pitch value from which all pitch parameters are calculated in line 140. An RST instruction ensures that the following duration is stored but treats the note as one of zero frequency. On playback, a zero frequency triggers silence (line 200) — the intended result, since RST means rest.

The long Commodore program that follows should suggest some of the extras that could be added to any sequencer. Again, the program is only monophonic, but fairly simple modification to the play subroutine (lines 3000-3040), the associated subroutines and note entry and note data storage variables could turn it into a polyphonic sequencer. The main variables are H(S), L(S) (high and low frequency), G(S) (tie to next note) and D(S). These would need to be replaced by two-dimensional arrays. The program as it stands already identifies the registers with a specific channel by means of arrays indexed by the variable V, so WF(V) represents the waveform of channel V. The main problem with two-dimensional arrays (and with arrays in general) is the amount of memory they take up — a fact which limits the number of notes it is possible to store.

```
1 REM C-64 SEQUENCER, 1984
2 REM "_" MEANS LEFT ARROW, TOP LEFT OF KEYBOARD
3 REM £ IS HASH SIGN (SHIFTED 3)
4 REM THE PROGRAM IS DESIGNED TO BE EXPANDED INT
O A 3-CHANNEL SEQUENCER
10 GOSUB 1000
20 PRINT CHR$(147)
50 GOSUB 5000
100 Q=0:V=1:DIM N(16),Z$(999),F(999),H(999),L(99
9),D(999),G(999)
105 GOSUB 800
120 FW(V)=17:A(V)=36:S(V)=36:TEM=10
130 N$="CDEFGABR"
150 GOSUB 210
200 GOTO 150
210 PRINT CHR$(147):GR=0:DOT=1:GLS=0
211 IF Q>=999 THEN PRINT"TOO MANY NOTES":Q=999
212 POKE MV,15:POKE AD(V),A(V):POKE SR(V),S(V):P
OKE PL(V),LP(V):POKEPH(V),HP(V)
214 POKE WF(V),0
215 GOSUB 8000
220 A$=CHR$(13)+"ENTER NOTE,[£],[OCT],[DUR],[.],
[T]": GOSUB 2000
225 A$="":GOSUB 2000
230 GET A$: IF A$="" THEN 230
240 IF A$="X" THEN GOSUB 4000:GOTO 210
245 IF A$="R" THEN C$="  ":GOTO 310
```

```
250 IF A$="P" THEN GOSUB 2500:GOTO 210
252 IF A$=" " THEN GOSUB 6000:GOTO 210
254 IF A$="*" THEN GOSUB 7000:GOTO 210
255 IF A$="@" THEN GOSUB 9000:GOTO 210
258 IF ASC(A$)<65 OR ASC(A$)>71 THEN 230
260 GOSUB 2000
270 GET B$: IF B$="" THEN 270
275 IF B$="_" THEN 210
280 IF B$<>"£" THEN B$="."
290 A$=A$+B$:GOSUB 2000
300 GET C$: IF C$="" THEN 300
302 IF C$="_" THEN 210
305 IF VAL(C$)=0 OR VAL(C$)>7 THEN C$="4"
310 A$=A$+C$:GOSUB 2000
315 IF MID$(A$,1,1)+MID$(A$,3,1)="B7" THEN 210
320 GET D$: IF D$="" THEN 320
325 IF D$="_" THEN 210
330 IF VAL(D$)=0 THEN D$="4"
340 A$=A$+D$:GOSUB 2000
350 GET E$: IF E$="" THEN 350
355 IF E$="_" THEN 210
360 IF E$="." THEN DOT=1.5
362 IF E$<>"." THEN E$=" ":DOT=1
365 A$=A$+E$: GOSUB 2000
370 GET F$: IF F$="" THEN 370
375 IF F$="_" THEN 210
380 IF F$<>"T" THEN GLS=1:F$=""
382 A$=A$+F$: GOSUB 2000
384 PRINT
395 PRINT "--------ENTERING NOTE---------------"
;Q+1
400 O=0
405 FOR X=1 TO 8
410 IF LEFT$(A$,1)=MID$(N$,X,1) THEN Q=Q+1:Y=X:Z
$(Q)=A$:O=1
415 NEXT
418 IF O=0 THEN RETURN
420 IF MID$(A$,2,1)="£" THEN Y=Y+8
430 F(Q)=N(Y)
440 OC=VAL(MID$(A$,3,1))
450 F(Q)=F(Q)*2^(OC-4)
460 H(Q)=INT(F(Q)/256):L(Q)=F(Q)-H(Q)*256
470 D(Q)=(VAL(MID$(A$,4,1)))*DOT
```

```
475 G(Q)=GLS
490 S=Q:GOSUB 3000
500 RETURN
799 REM FREQUENCY DATA
800 FOR X=1 TO 15: READ N(X): NEXT
810 DATA4378,4915,5519,5855,6576,7381,8271,0,464
7,5217,5855,6207,6962,7818,8756
820 RETURN
998 END
999 REM REGVAR
1000 S=54272
1010 FOR X=1 TO 3
1020 CH=7*(X-1)
1030 FL(X)=S+CH:FH(X)=FL(X)+1:PL(X)=FH(X)+1:PH(X
)=PL(X)+1:WF(X)=PH(X)+1
1040 AD(X)=WF(X)+1:SR(X)=AD(X)+1
1050 NEXT
1060 HC=SR(3)+1:LC=HC+1:RF=LC+1:MV=RF+1:PX=MV+1:
PY=PX+1:O3=PY+1:E3=O3+1
1070 RETURN
1999 REM SCREEN DISPLAY
2000 PRINT "| ": REM HOME
2010 FOR X=0 TO 20: PRINT: NEXT
2020 PRINT TAB(10);A$;"-"
2025 POKE 198,0
2030 RETURN
2500 REM SEQUENCE
2510 PRINT CHR$(147);999-Q;" NOTES LEFT:";Q;"IS
LAST NOTE"
2520 PRINT:PRINT"TYPE 'P' TO PLAY,ANY OTHER KEY
FOR PART":PRINT
2530 GET P$:IF P$=""THEN 2530
2540 IF P$="P" THEN A=1:B=Q:C=1:RPT=1:GOTO 2600
2550 INPUT "START NOTE      ";A
2560 INPUT "FINISH NOTE     ";B
2570 C=1*SGN(B-A)
2580 INPUT "REVERSE (Y/N) ";AN$
2590 IF AN$="Y" THEN I=A:J=B:A=J:B=I:C=-C
2595 INPUT "NUMBER OF PLAYS   ";RPT
2600 PRINT CHR$(147)
2610 FOR R=1 TO RPT
2620 FOR S=A TO B STEP C
2625 PRINT CHR$(19);"       ]";CHR$(19);"[";S;
```

```
2630 GOSUB 3000
2640 NEXT S,R
2645 PRINT CHR$(147)
2650 RETURN
2999 REM PLAY ROUTINE
3000 POKE FH(V),H(S):POKE FL(V),L(S):POKE WF(V),
FW(V)
3020 FOR P=1 TO 2^D(S)*TEM: NEXT
3030 POKE WF(V),FW(V)-G(S)
3040 RETURN
3999 REM EXIT TO SYSTEM
4000 PRINT CHR$(147)
4005 FOR X=1 TO 200:NEXT
4010 INPUT "ARE YOU SURE (Y/N)";AN$
4020 IF AN$<>"Y" THEN RETURN
4030 FOR X=1 TO 3:POKE WF(X),0:NEXT
4040 END
4999 REM INSTRUCTIONS
5000 PRINT"COMMODORE 64 SEQUENCER"
5030 PRINT"ENTER NOTES IN THIS FORM:"
5040 PRINT"NOTE[£][OCTAVE][DURATION][DOT][TIE]"
5050 PRINT"SO THAT 'C£45.T' WILL PLAY "
5060 PRINT"C-SHARP ABOVE MIDDLE-C FOR "
5070 PRINT"A DOTTED SEMITONE, TIED TO "
5080 PRINT"THE NEXT NOTE."
5090 PRINT: PRINT"PRESSING THE SPACE BAR AFTER E
NTERING"
5100 PRINT"A NOTE NAME (EG. C) WILL GIVE DEFAULT
S"
5110 PRINT"[NATURAL][OCTAVE4][QUARTER NOTE]"
5120 PRINT"   [NO DOT][NO TIE]"
5130 PRINT: PRINT"TEMPO, AND SOUND SETTINGS CAN
BE "
5140 PRINT"CHANGED BEFORE EVERY NOTE"
5150 PRINT"DURATION IS DETERMINED BY A NUMBER"
5160 PRINT"BETWEEN 1 AND 9-AN INCREASE OR DECREA
SE"
5170 PRINT"OF 1 DOUBLES OR HALVES NOTE DURATION"
5180 PRINT"OCTAVES CAN BE 1 (LOW) TO 7 (HIGH)"
5190 PRINT"HIGHEST NOTE IS A£7"
5200 PRINT:PRINT"PRESS SPACE BAR"
5210 GET A$: IF A$="" THEN 5210
5220 IF A$=" " THEN RETURN
```

```
5999 REM CHANGE SETTINGS
6000 PRINT CHR$(147);"VOICE              ";V
6010 PRINT"TEMPO              ";TEM
6020 PRINT"ATTACK/DECAY       ";A(V)
6030 PRINT"SUSTAIN/RELEASE ";S(V)
6040 PRINT"WAVEFORM           ";FW(V)
6050 PRINT"HIGH PULSE         ";HP(V)
6060 PRINT"LOW PULSE          ";LP(V)
6070 INPUT"CHANGE ANY (Y/N)";AN$
6080 IF AN$<>"Y" THEN PRINT CHR$(147):RETURN
6090 PRINT CHR$(19);
6100 INPUT"VOICE              ";V
6110 INPUT"TEMPO              ";TEM
6120 INPUT"ATTACK/DECAY     ";A(V)
6130 INPUT"SUSTAIN/RELEASE";S(V)
6140 INPUT"WAVEFORM           ";FW(V)
6150 INPUT"HIGH PULSE         ";HP(V)
6160 INPUT"LOW PULSE          ";LP(V)
6170 GOTO 6070
6180 IF AN$<>"Y" THEN PRINT CHR$(147):RETURN
6999 REM EDIT
7000 PRINT CHR$(147)
7002 A$=STR$(Q)+")"+Z$(Q)+"LAST NOTE":GOSUB2000
7010 PRINT"PRINT(P),INSERT(I),DELETE(D),RETURN(R
)":PRINT:INPUT AN$
7015 IF AN$="R" THEN RETURN
7020 IF AN$="I" THEN 7200
7030 IF AN$="D" THEN 7100
7040 PRINT CHR$(147)
7045 PRINT"PRESS SPACE BAR TO PLAY NOTE SEQUENCE
"
7050 INPUT"ENTER FIRST AND LAST NOTES,OR RETURN"
;FF,LL
7052 POKE 198,0
7055 IF FF<=0 OR FF>Q THEN FF=1
7056 IF LL<=0 OR LL>Q THEN LL=Q
7057 PRINT CHR$(147);"FIRST:";FF;"LAST";LL;" PRE
SS SPACE BAR"
7058 POKE 198,0
7060 FOR S=FF TO LL
7065 GET S$:IF S$<>" " THEN 7065
7070 PRINT"[";S;Z$(S);"]";
7072 IF S/3=INT(S/3) THEN PRINT
```

```
7075 GOSUB 3000
7080 NEXT
7082 PRINT:PRINT:PRINT"PRESS ANY KEY TO CONTINUE
"
7083 FOR P=1 TO 2000:NEXT
7084 POKE 198,0
7085 GET X$:IF X$="" THEN 7085
7090 GOTO 7000
7100 INPUT "FIRST NOTE TO DELETE ";F
7110 INPUT "NUMBER OF NOTES       ";N
7115 IF N<1 OR N>Q OR F>Q OR F<1 THEN 7000
7120 FOR S=F TO Q:Z$(S)=Z$(S+N):H(S)=H(S+N):L(S)
=L(S+N)
7125 D(S)=D(S+N):G(S)=G(S+N):NEXT
7128 FOR S=Q-N+1 TO Q:Z$(S)="":H(S)=0:L(S)=0:D(S
)=0:G(S)=0:NEXT
7130 Q=Q-N
7140 FF=1:LL=Q
7150 GOTO 7057
7200 INPUT "INSERT NOTE AFTER ";F
7205 Q=Q+1
7210 FOR S=Q TO F+1 STEP-1:Z$(S)=Z$(S-1):H(S)=H(
S-1):L(S)=L(S-1)
7215 D(S)=D(S-1):G(S)=G(S-1):NEXT
7220 QQ=Q:Q=F:GOSUB210:Q=QQ
7230 POKE WF(V),0
7240 FF=1:LL=Q
7300 GOTO 7057
7999 REM MENU
8000 PRINT"SPACE BAR TO CHECK SETTINGS"
8010 PRINT"* TO PRINT AND EDIT SEQUENCE"
8020 PRINT"P TO PLAY SEQUENCE OR PART"
8030 PRINT"R FOR REST,C,D,E,F,G,A,B FOR NOTES"
8040 PRINT"_ WILL DELETE ANY NOTE BEFORE ENTERIN
G"
8045 PRINT"@ PUTS YOU IN DISC/TAPE MODE"
8050 PRINT"X EXITS TO SYSTEM":PRINT
8060 PRINT "CURRENT NOTE: ";Q+1
8100 RETURN
8999 REM LOAD/SAVE
9000 PRINT CHR$(147)
9010 CR$=CHR$(13)
9020 PRINT"FILE NAME 'END' RETURNS TO PROGRAM":P
```

```
RINT
9050 INPUT"TAPE (T) OR DISC (D)";AN$
9100 INPUT"READ (R) OR WRITE(W)";BN$
9101 IF BN$="W" THEN 9110
9102 IF BN$<>"R" THEN 9100
9105 INPUT"MERGE WITH EXISTING SEQUENCE (Y/N)";C
N$
9106 PRINT"CURRENT END OF SEQUENCE";Q:EQ=Q
9107 INPUT"READ NEW SEQUENCE TO START AT NOTE";F
S
9108 IF CN$="Y" THEN 9110
9109 FOR S=1 TO FS-1:Z$(S)="":H(S)=0:L(S)=0:D(S)
=0:G(S)=0:NEXT
9110 INPUT"FILE NAME...........";DT$
9120 IF DT$="END" THEN RETURN
9150 IF AN$="T" THEN FILE=1:DEVICE=1:CHANNEL=1:G
OTO9200
9160 FILE=15:DEVICE=8:CHANNEL=15
9170 OPEN FILE,DEVICE,CHANNEL:PRINT£FILE,"IO"
9180 GOSUB 9600
9184 DT$="0:"+DT$+",S,"+BN$
9186 FILE=2:CHANNEL=2
9200 IF BN$="W" THEN 9500
9400 OPEN FILE,DEVICE,CHANNEL+(AN$="T"),DT$
9405 G=FS
9410 IF AN$="D" THEN GOSUB 9600
9420 INPUT£FILE,Z$(G),H(G),L(G),D(G),G(G)
9430 G=G+1
9435 IF G>=999  THEN G=999
9440 IF ST=0 THEN 9410
9450 CLOSE FILE:CLOSE 15
9455 G=G-1
9460 IF G<EQ AND CN$="Y" THEN Q=EQ:RETURN
9470 Q=G
9480 IF Q>=999 THEN PRINT"TOO MANY NOTES":Q=999
9490 RETURN
9500 OPEN FILE, DEVICE,CHANNEL,DT$
9510 FOR I=1 TO Q
9520 PRINT£FILE,Z$(I);CR$;H(I);CR$;L(I);CR$,D(I)
;CR$;G(I);CR$;
9525 IF AN$="D" THEN GOSUB 9600
9530 NEXT
9540 CLOSE FILE:CLOSE 15
```

```
9590 RETURN
9600 INPUT£15,W$,X$,Y$,Z$
9610 IF W$="00" THEN RETURN
9620 PRINT "DISC ERROR ";X$:CLOSE15:CLOSE2:RETUR
N
```
PROGRAM 8.6

Although REMmed and reasonably well documented, the program has several features which may repay attention. Notes are entered in lines 210-500, a subroutine called in line 150. They are entered as a series of single-character strings eventually forming the value of the string variable A\$, which also serves to hold a variety of messages from time to time. The note is checked against string N\$ (line 130), which is formed by all the acceptable note names (C, D, E and so on) plus R for rest. Other characters are checked for in individual lines, including the full-stop, which indicates a dotted note, and the character T which indicates a note tied (or gliding) to another note.

Note data is provided in line 810; the frequency of notes belonging to each octave is calculated in lines 440-460. Subroutine 2000 is the screen display, 2500 the routine called when the sequence is to be played (any part of the sequence can be played, repeated and reversed), and 3000 actually plays each note. Subroutine 4000 is the 'exit to system' routine, 5000 the instructions screen. Subroutine 6000 allows you to change tempo, ADSR, pulse and waveform parameters (which are then set for the sequence and for all future notes); 7000 allows you to edit out any number of notes or to insert any single note, renumbering the sequence as appropriate. Pressing the space bar during the edit routine allows you to hear the sequence, as it were, one note at a time. Subroutine 8000 prints the main menu during the note-entering phase, and 9000 allows you to save or load the sequence to or from tape or disc. On loading, the saved sequence may be located anywhere in the current sequence, thus allowing you to repeat or re-arrange subsequences. This routine is a fairly standard Commodore filing routine, and something similar could easily be added to the BBC sequencer above. Something of the sort is useful for serious composition, although for many purposes a tape recorder and/or a notebook may be quicker, easier and — although I hate to admit it — more reliable.

Part 2: Putting It All Together

The next two programs are real-time sequencers. The first program is just a new top half for the Commodore step-time sequencer above. Everything from line 999 in the program above should be tacked on to the program below, with these exceptions: line 1045 POKE WF(X),0 should be added; the instructions (subroutine 5000) should be revised, and the menu (subroutine 8000) has been omitted. Some changes have been made to the play subroutine at line 3000, and I include the revised lines below. For the rest, the lines should be entered unchanged.

Real-time note entry is effected using the top two rows of the keyboard (see line 810). Frequencies are calculated in subroutine 800 (you may wish to adjust the values in line 800). The stored frequency can be adjusted by changing the octave (variable MM, which is altered by keys f1, f3, f5 and f7). As played, the note can be adjusted by altering the value of the variable TU (keys M and N, which appear in lines 680 and 690), though this is a crude form of tuning and is not stored: it is more like the pitch bend facility on a conventional synthesizer. The action of most of the keys is indicated in the menu (lines 710 to 760), although non-storable filtering is obtainable by use of the even (shifted) function keys (see line 220). (This feature could be expanded and improved.)

The thinking behind the program is illuminating, since the program illustrates that the important thing with sequencing is arriving at the note data and storing it in appropriate variables. Any method you use for doing this is acceptable, as long as it works. There is no reason, in principle, why your sequence should not contain control information that is not directly played, but which alters the stored parameters that follow it. For example, octave information is treated this way; so too could be waveform, tempo or tuning information. The chief problem here, as always, is getting the timing right. The hoped-for standard for interfacing micros with synthesizers and other digital instruments, known as MIDI (musical or microprocessor interface for digital instruments), is simply a protocol for serial data transfer, which treats note and control information in the same way. Unlike other microcomputer serial interfaces (RS232, cassette interfaces and so on), MIDI operates very fast (at around 31 Kbauds or thousand bits per second). Even then, MIDI is often too slow to be effective.

I leave it to you to devise methods of storing note and control information quickly enough to make a real-time polyphonic sequencer with all the features available on the Commodore workable. Meanwhile, here are the listings to alter the step-time program above into an imperfect but useful real-time program.

```
1 REM REAL-TIME SEQUENCER-C-64
2 REM GARY HERMAN, 1984
3 REM ON-SCREEN INSTRUCTIONS SHOULD BE ADEQUATE
4 REM THE SEQUENCER IS LIKE A DIGITAL TAPE-RECOR
DER
5 REM MEMORISING WHAT YOU HAVE PLAYED SO THAT IT
```

```
   CAN BE PLAYED BACK TO YOU
6 REM TEMPO, ADSR AND SO ON CAN BE CHANGED
7 REM AND THE SEQUENCE CAN BE EDITED AND STORED
ON TAPE OR DISC.
8 REM YOU CAN EVEN PLAY IT BACKWARDS.
10 GOSUB 1000
20 PRINT CHR$(147)
30 PRINT "HANG ON A MO'"
100 Q=0:V=1:MM=1:DIM N(16),Z$(999),F(999),H(999)
,L(999),D(999),G(999)
104 F=7040:TU=0:DIM FQ(26),KY(255)
105 GOSUB 800
120 FW(V)=17:A(V)=9:S(V)=69:TEM=20:VM=15:GLS=0
130 PRINT"PRESS ANY KEY TO START"
140 GET A$: IFA$="" THEN 140
150 WA=0
210 GOSUB 700
220 POKE MV,VM+COF*16+RIN*32:POKE RF,COF+RES*240
:POKE HC,RND(O)*MOD*15
225 POKE AD(V),A(V):POKE SR(V),S(V):POKE PL(V),L
P(V):POKEPH(V),HP(V)
230 IF Q>=999 THEN PRINT"TOO MANY NOTES":Q=999
250 GET A$:WA=WA+1
260 IF A$="" THEN 250
400 FR=FQ(KY(ASC(A$)))/MM
405 IF FR=0 THEN GOSUB 600:GOTO 150
410 Q=Q+1
420 D(Q)=WA
430 H(Q)=INT(FR/256):L(Q)=FR-H(Q)*256
440 G(Q)=GLS
450 S=Q:GOSUB 3000
460 GOTO 150
600 IF A$="[F1]" THEN MM=1:RETURN
601 IF A$="[F3]" THEN MM=2:RETURN
602 IF A$="[F5]" THEN MM=3:RETURN
603 IF A$="[F7]"]THEN MM=4:RETURN
604 IF A$=":" THEN GOSUB 2500:RETURN
605 IF A$="[BACK ARROW]" THEN FOR P=1 TO 3000:NE
XT:RETURN
606 IF A$="[F2]" THEN MOD=1-MOD:RETURN
607 IF A$="[F4]" THEN COF=1-COF:RETURN
608 IF A$="[F6]" THEN RES=1-RES:RETURN
609 IF A$="[F8]" THEN RIN=1-RIN:RETURN
```

L.I.M.E.
THE MARKLAND LIBRARY
STAND PARK RD., LIVERPOOL, L16 9JD

```
610 IF A$="Z" THEN Q=O:RETURN
620 IF A$=";" THEN GLS=1-GLS:RETURN
625 IF A$="," THEN POKE WF(V),O:RETURN
630 IF A$="X" THEN GOSUB 4000:RETURN
640 IF A$="/" THEN GOSUB 6000:RETURN
650 IF A$="." THEN GOSUB 7000:RETURN
660 IF A$="," THEN GOSUB 8000:RETURN
670 IF A$="=" THEN GOSUB 9000:RETURN
680 IF A$="M" THEN TU=1+TU:RETURN
690 IF A$="N" THEN TU=TU-1:RETURN
699 RETURN
700 PRINT CHR$(19)
710 PRINT"Q2W3ER5T6Y7UI9OOP@-*\^...RECORD NOTES"
720 PRINT"[:] PLAYBACK, [X] EXIT, [Z] RESET"
730 PRINT"[?] CHANGE SETTINGS, [.] EDIT,[=] R-W"
740 PRINT"[;] TOGGLE HOLD, [M/N] TUNE,[,] DAMP"
750 PRINT"[F1/3/5/7] CHANGE OCTAVE"
760 PRINT"[_] PAUSES"
770 PRINT:PRINT"NOTE:";Q;"   "
780 RETURN
799 REM FREQUENCY DATA
800 FOR X=26 TO 1 STEP -1:FQ(X)=F*5.8+30:F=F/2^(
1/12):NEXT
810 KY$="Q2W3ER5T6Y7UI9OOP@-*\^"
820 FOR X=1 TO LEN(KY$):KY(ASC(MID$(KY$,X,1)))=X
:NEXT
830 RETURN
998 END
```
PROGRAM 8.7

```
2999 REM PLAY ROUTINE
3000 POKE WF(V),FW(V)-G(S-1)
3010 POKE FH(V),H(S)+TU:POKE FL(V),L(S):POKE WF(
V),FW(V)
3020 FOR P=1 TO D(S):NEXT
3030 POKE WF(V),FW(V)-G(S)
3040 RETURN
```
PROGRAM 8.8

The BBC is altogether a faster machine than the Commodore 64. A preliminary polyphonic real-time sequencer is relatively easy to write. This program was the result of totally revising my approach after having worked fruitlessly on a similar sequencer that was just increasing hourly in length and getting more bogged down with bugs at each stage.

The problem here was how to get three channels to play, so that (i) you could 'record' while one or two other channels were playing and (ii) playback proceeded at the same speed as 'recording'. Without going into detail, earlier attempts at doing this had become entangled by the complexity of keeping track of all the steps needed to be dealt with simultaneously – and especially with the problem of avoiding the need to start notes and rests on two or three channels at the same time. The answer was to build a program from the core outwards and, in the process, to revise my self-imposed specifications so that the eventual program looks less sophisticated than its predecessors but does all the really important things it should.

The core of the program is the play procedure, PROCPLAY (defined in lines 640-880 and called in line 440). The central loop is contained in lines 730-810, which run through all three channels every time the procedure is called, checking to see if there is a frequency to play or if the channel is waiting to receive input from the keyboard (dealt with by PROCKEY, lines 890-960). Most of the detailed workings of the program, with respect to how key presses are interpreted and stored, should by now be familiar. The music sounds best with no envelope, but this may simply be my choice of envelopes. It would be a simple matter to allow envelope parameters to be set from the keyboard.

Perhaps the most interesting feature of the program is its treatment of frequency. During play or record, it is possible to bend frequencies by pressing function keys f1 and f2 (f3 resets frequency 'offset' to zero). During record, these bends are stored as part of the note data. Also the keyboard can be tuned before recording by inputting a base 'offset' (lines 250-280) which holds for all future recording.

After inputting the offset (or just pressing RETURN) the program puts up a display, which allows you to set the start and finish of your record or playback sequence, to adjust the tempo, to select an envelope and to choose which channels to play back and which to record on. In this last respect, the program is like a tape recorder. When the main menu comes up each time, all channels are off. Function keys f1, f2 and f3 select their respective channels, and function key f9 is like pressing a record button for the channel you have just selected (f7 resets the channels in case of mistakes). Key f0 will start the whole thing playing and it carries on until it runs out of steps or until key 9 is pressed. Steps are recorded in line 830 (variable S%), and PROCPLAY loads a SOUND command with the data indexed by each step and channel, or calls PROCKEY to fetch such data from the keyboard. Since each step is once round the play loop, enveloped sounds (which are gated off by the '16' in the SOUND command in line 800) seem jerky. Non-enveloped sounds are smooth, but you might try to slow the loop down or, better, to slow the step counter down. Getting rid of the '16' (the flush parameter) has the effect of hanging the note sequence up.

```
  10 REM BBC SEQUENCER,1984,G.HERMAN
  20 REM REAL-TIME SEQUENCER ALLOWING THREE
  30 REM CHANNELS TO BE MIXED.
  40 REM THERE ARE 4 PRESET ENVELOPES PLUS A
NO-ENVELOPE OPTION AS DEFAULT
  50 REM YOU MIGHT ELABORATE ON THE ENVELOPE
ROUTINE
  60 REM TUNING CAN BE EFFECTED BEFORE PLAYI
NG, DURING RECORDING OR PLAYBACK
  70 REM THUS ALLOWING GLIDES ON ANY TRACK.
  80 REM ALSO A RECORDED TRACK CAN BE MIXED
ONTO OR WIPED BEFORE RE-RECORDING
  90 REM SUGGESTED IMPROVEMENT WOULD BE TO A
DD DISC FILING OF COMPOSITONS.
 100 REM 600 AVAILABLE STEPS.
 110 ON ERROR GOTO 1080
 120 MODE 7
 130 VDU12,23;8202;0;0;0;
 140 PROCINIT
 150 PROCMENU
 160 DEF PROCINIT
 170 BASE%=1:FR%=0:I%=0:T%=64:L%=0:S%=0
 180 DIM CH%(3),R%(3),CH$(3),R$(3),F%(3,600)
,FR%(3,600),A%(23),E%(3)
 190 FOR X%=1TO3:E%(X%)=-15:NEXT
 200 FORK%=1TO23:READA%(K%):NEXT
 210 DATA 97,17,50,34,18,35,52,20,36,53,69,3
7,54,38,39,55,40,56,72,25,57,121,41
 220 ENDPROC
 230 DEF PROCMENU
 240 CLS
 250 PRINT"current tuning base: "BASE%
 260 INPUT"enter required offset (or RTN):
"OF%
 270 BASE%=(BASE%+OF%)MOD256
 280 PRINT"new base: "BASE%:PRINT
 290 PRINT"f0 to play"
 300 PRINT"f1 to select channel 1"
```

```
310 PRINT"f2 ................. 2"
320 PRINT"f3 ................. 3"
330 PRINT"f4 to select start interval"
340 PRINT"f5 ......... finish ......."
350 PRINT"f6 to adjust speed"
360 PRINT"f7 to reset"
370 PRINT"f8 to select envelope"
380 PRINT"f9 to record"
390 PRINT:PRINT"To record, select channel t
hen press f9"
400 PRINT"To playback, select channel"
410 PRINT:PRINT"f0 starts sequencing -press
 firmly"
420 IFS%>I%THENI%=S%
430 CH%(1)=0:CH%(2)=0:CH%(3)=0:CH%=0:F%=0:L
%=I%:R%(1)=0:R%(2)=0:R%(3)=0:R%=0
440 IFINKEY(-33)PROCPLAY:R%=0:PROCMENU
450 IFINKEY(-114)CH%(1)=1:CH%=1
460 IFINKEY(-115)CH%(2)=1:CH%=2
470 IFINKEY(-116)CH%(3)=1:CH%=3
480 IFINKEY(-21)F%=(F%+1)MOD1000
490 IFINKEY(-117)L%=(L%-1)MOD1000
500 IFINKEY(-118)T%=((T%+8)MOD256)
510 IFINKEY(-23)THEN430
520 IFINKEY(-119)PROCENV:PROCMENU
530 IFINKEY(-120)R%(CH%)=1
540 PRINT TAB(0,19)"speed:";T%"   start:";F%
"  finish:";L%;"   "
550 IFL%>=1200PRINT"OUT OF MEMORY"
560 FOR X%=1TO3
570 IFCH%(X%)=1THENCH$(X%)=" ON"ELSECH$(X%)
="OFF"
580 IFR%(X%)=1R$(X%)="RECORD   "ELSER$(X%)="
PLAYBACK"
590 IFR%(X%)=1R%=X%
600 PRINTTAB(0,20+X%)"channel:"X%;" ";R$(X%
);" ";CH$(X%)
610 NEXT
620 GOTO 440
630 ENDPROC
640 DEF PROCPLAY
650 FORP%=1TO200:NEXT
660 FR%=0
```

```
  670 CLS:PRINTTAB(O,5);"fO to wipe erase dur
ing record"
  680 PRINT"f1 to tune up, f2 to tune down"
  690 PRINT"f3 to reset tuning"
  700 PRINT"f9 to return to main menu"
  710 S%=F%
  720 REPEAT
  730 FOR CH%=1TO3
  740 IFINKEY(-114)FR%=(FR%+1)MOD256
  750 IFINKEY(-115)FR%=(FR%-1)MOD256
  760 IFINKEY(-116)FR%=0
  770 FR%(CH%,S%)=FR%:Q%=1
  780 IFR%(CH%)=1PROCKEY:Q%=0
  790 IFF%(CH%,S%)=OV%=OELSEV%=E%(CH%)
  800 SOUND16+CH%,V%*CH%(CH%),F%(CH%,S%)-FR%*
(R%=0),T%
  810 NEXT
  820 FORP%=OTO-4*T%*(R%=0):NEXT
  830 S%=S%+1:L%=L%+R%
  840 PRINTTAB(O,18);"interval: ";S%
  850 PRINT"tuning offset: ";FR%;"    "
  860 IFINKEY(-120)THENENDPROC
  870 UNTIL S%>=L%+1
  880 ENDPROC
  890 DEF PROCKEY
  900 REPEAT
  910 FORK%=1TO23
  920 IFINKEY(-A%(K%)):F%(CH%,S%)=BASE%+4*K%+
FR%(CH%,S%):K%=23
  930 IFINKEY(-33)THENF%(CH%,S%)=0
  940 NEXTK%
  950 UNTIL INKEY(O)
  960 ENDPROC
  970 DEF PROCENV
  980 CLS:INPUT"which channel";N%
  990 IFN%<1ORN%>3THEN980
 1000 PRINT:INPUT"enter envelope number (1-4)
or zero";E%(N%)
 1010 IF E%(N%)<O OR E%(N%)>4 THEN980
 1020 IF E%(N%)=0 THEN E%(N%)=-15
 1030 ENVELOPE1,1,0,0,0,0,0,0,127,-20,0,-112,
126,40
 1040 ENVELOPE2,1,-1,2,-1,1,1,1,30,0,0,-20,12
```

```
6,126
 1050 ENVELOPE3,1,0,0,0,0,0,0,40,-8,0,-112,12
6,112
 1060 ENVELOPE4,1,1,-1,1,2,4,2,63,24,0,-1,63,
126
 1070 ENDPROC
 1080 MODE7
 1090 PRINT "ERROR- TRY AGAIN (Y/N)";
 1100 INPUT AN$
 1110 AN$=LEFT$(AN$,1)
 1120 IF AN$="Y"CLEAR:RUN
 1130 END
```
PROGRAM 8.9

An interesting and unforeseen effect results from the fact that a note stays on its channel until it is positively wiped (by pressing f0 during record). Thus you can set a channel to record and you will hear the sounds already on it but also be able to add infills or play over any note. This can be used to create rapid runs, triplets and 'warbling' effects. Another interesting effect is achieved by setting all channels to record. In this case the program plays and stores chorus-like or flanged sounds as the same note plays on each channel. By use of the tuning feature, you can detune two channels for even more acoustic interest.

Random composition, mode and scale
So far, the computer has remained a dumb receptacle for, or instrument of, your musical desires. Perhaps it has its own ambitions. The term 'computer music' often brings to mind nothing more musical than the sound of random and discordant blurps and gurgles. However, musical composition tends to follow certain well-defined rules; if the computer can be instructed to operate within these rules, it can produce something at least resembling music apparently with an intelligence of its own.

Random, or aleatoric, music has a long and respectable pedigree. The very name *aleatoric* suggests some smart soul has been at it for some time. The Aeolian harp, whose music was created by the wind blowing across its strings, was an influential aspect of life in ancient Greece before the birth of Christ. Yet there is random and random; or rather, there is first- and higher-order randomness.

First-order randomness is what everybody understands by the term 'random'. A series of events occurs in such a way that the probability of any one event occurring is the same as that of any other event occurring. In musical terms, any note can be played and probably will – the result being a discordant shambles. Even here, the idea of a note introduces an element of order into potential chaos; we could, after all, have suggested a random distribution of frequencies (i.e. white noise) rather than notes. So the simplest programmed random music would take the notes of an octave, say, and select one according to the result of calling an RND function. Try it: the result will be all but unlistenable.

There are ways of introducing more regularity into such randomness, some of which result in acceptable musical effects. You could take a subset of the notes of an octave (say, C, E, G and A) knowing them to be found commonly in each other's company. This assigns a probability of zero to the occurrence of other notes. You could go one step further and assign a greater probability to C and G occurring than to E and A, knowing that C and G are found more often in music written in the key of C. In programming terms, you might say that if RND returned a value less than 0.5, play a C; if it returned a value between 0.5 and 0.8, play a G; if it returned a value between 0.8 and 0.9 play an E and, if it returned a value between 0.9 and 1, play an A. Systems like this result in something very acceptable, especially if the probability distribution is worked out on chords (C-major, F, G7 and A-minor, say) and not just on individual notes. The more restrictions you place on the choice of events, the less random you are getting. At some point the music so created begins to sound repetitive and predictable instead of just regular.

What you would be doing in such a project was working on higher-order randomness, but in a slapdash way. A true second-order probability distribution works like this: instead of just deciding the probability of the occurrence of a particular note, you decide the probability of the occurrence of a pair of notes. Instead of saying C will occur perhaps four times out of every ten notes, you say that C will occur perhaps five times following a G out of every ten times a G occurs. Third-order randomness will then look at groups of three notes, fourth-order at groups of four notes and so on.

We are driving into the territory of style. By the time you get randomness order nine or ten, the piece of music you produce will begin to resemble closely the piece or pieces you may have examined in order to work out your probability tables. The higher the order of randomness, the more predictable the piece, just as though you had reduced the number of possible events in a first-order random probability distribution to one or two — the occurrence of the note C or the notes C and G, perhaps.

The subject will repay investigation. Music, like any other form of expression, walks a narrow line between the predictable or familiar and the novel or challenging, and random music can be constructed to represent this conflict taking place. The place to start an investigation is a program; here is one, in a version for the BBC and the Commodore, which might set you on the road.

The idea is simple, although it offers scope for experimentation. The programs take a short cut to second-order randomness by establishing patterns of *note intervals* from which to select random events. Using W to stand for a whole tone and S to stand for a semitone, we can say that the pattern of intervals in a common major scale is:

W...W...S...W...W...W...S

There is a whole tone between C and D, another between D and E, a semitone between E and F and so on.

Such patterns of intervals characterize a *mode* in music. A particular series of ascending notes separated according to the intervals of a mode is called a *scale*. Thus the major mode (the most common in western music) is associated with twelve scales, each starting from one of the twelve notes that comprise the mode. The terms 'scale' and 'mode' are often used interchangeably; remember that scales and modes alike are associated with fixed intervals between notes, and these intervals provide the characteristic flavour of the mode or scale. In terms of randomness, they represent a probability distribution on the set of possible musical tones and frequencies, and this distribution bears some of the marks of second-order randomness.

For the modes used below I am indebted to Jim McGregor and Alan Watt, whose book, *The BBC Micro Book* (Addison Wesley, 1983), is well worth a look. There are plenty of other modes; for example, there is the melodic scale of the minor mode as well as the harmonic scale. This is particularly interesting, since ascending and descending forms differ: W, S, W, W, W, W, S going up and W, W, S, W, W, S, W going down. You can construct your own intervals (this is considerably easier to do on the BBC) and, indeed, your own pattern of probabilistic distribution within the intervals.

I have included two versions for the BBC: the first, a basic monophonic version, and the second a composer that produces 'chords' and rhythm, includes a procedure for stopping the 'performance' and offers a variety of envelopes. Although ostensibly similar, the output of each program is startlingly different. There is only one program for the Commodore, based on the second BBC program.

```
1 REM RANDOM COMPOSITION 1
2 REM BASIC VERSION FOR BBC B
3 REM IMPROVEMENTS COULD INCLUDE
4 REM OCCASIONAL RESTS, MORE
5 REM STRUCTURE IN THE NEXT NOTE
6 REM PROCEDURE (EG. ASCENDING
7 REM SEQUENCES FOLLOWED BY
8 REM DESCENDING SEQUENCES),
9 REM USE OF ENVELOPE, POLYPHONY,
10 REM SELECTION OF START NOTE...
```

```
 20 CLS
 30 DIM NTE%(25):BASE%=45
 40 V%=-10
 50 PRINT "SELECT MODALITY/SCALE"
 60 PRINT "MAJOR - M"
 70 PRINT "DIMINISHED MINOR - D"
 80 PRINT "WHOLE NOTE - E"
 90 PRINT "BLUE - B"
100 PRINT "RAGA - R"
110 PRINT "DORIAN - O"
120 PRINT "AEOLIAN - A"
130 PRINT "HARMONIC MINOR - H"
140 PRINT "PENTATONIC - P"
150 PRINT "CHROMATIC - C"
160 INPUT M$
170 INPUT"TEMPO, BAR"TEMPO%,BAR%
180 PROCMODALITY
190 PROCSCALE
200 PROCSTART
210 PROCNXT
220 PROCPHRASE
230 PROCPLAY
240 GOTO 210
250 DEF PROCMODALITY
260 REPEAT
270 READ MDE$
280 UNTIL MDE$=M$
290 ENDPROC
300 DATA M,14,8,8,4,8,8,8,4
310 DATA 8,8,4,8,8,8,4
320 DATA D,16,4,8,4,8,4,8,4,8
330 DATA 4,8,4,8,4,8,4,8
340 DATA E,12,8,8,8,8,8,8
350 DATA 8,8,8,8,8,8
360 DATA B,12,12,8,4,4,12,8
370 DATA 12,8,4,4,12,8
380 DATA R,14,8,8,4,8,4,8,8
390 DATA 8,8,4,8,4,8,8
400 DATA O,14,8,4,8,8,8,4,8
410 DATA 8,4,8,8,8,4,8
420 DATA A,14,8,4,8,8,4,8,8
430 DATA 8,4,8,8,4,8,8
440 DATA H,14,8,4,8,8,4,12,4
```

```
450 DATA 8,4,8,8,4,12,4
460 DATA P,10,8,8,12,8,12
470 DATA 8,8,12,8,12
480 DATA C,24,4,4,4,4,4,4,4,4
490 DATA 4,4,4,4,4,4,4,4
500 DATA 4,4,4,4,4,4,4,4
510 DEF PROCSCALE
520 NTE%(0)=BASE%
530 READ SL%
540 FOR N%=1 TO SL%
550 READ I%
560 NTE%(N%)=NTE%(N%-1)+I%
570 NEXT
580 ENDPROC
590 DEF PROCSTART
600 START%=RND(SL%)
610 ENDPROC
620 DEF PROCNXT
630 X%=RND(2)*(1+RND(2)*(RND(2)=2))
640 ENDPROC
650 DEF PROCPHRASE
660 PH%=RND(BAR%)
670 DUR%=BAR%/PH%
680 ENDPROC
690 DEF PROCPLAY
700 S%=START%
710 FOR I%=1 TO PH%
720 SOUND 1,V%,NTE%(S%),DUR%*TEMPO%
730 S%=S%+X%
740 PRINT TAB(0,20)S%
750 IF S%>SL% OR S%<1 THEN S%=INT(SL%/2)
760 NEXT I%
770 ENDPROC
```

PROGRAM 8.10

```
 1REM CF WITH PROG ABOVE
 2:
 3:
10 REM RANDOM COMPOSITION 5
20 REM BBC MODEL B
30 REM BY G. HERMAN, 1984
40 REM ALTHOUGH APPARENTLY
50 REM MORE COMPLEX, THIS
```

```
  60 REM PROGRAM PRODUCES A MORE
  70 REM REGULAR RESULT, WITH
  80 REM PROCPHRASE RELOCATED TO
  90 REM GIVE A MORE FIXED RHYTHM.
 100 REM ENVELOPE SELECTION ALLOWS
 110 REM NO ENVELOPE OR ONE OF
 120 REM 4 PRESETS WHICH CAN
 130 REM BE CHANGED OR ADDED TO.
 140 REM ALSO NOTE THE INTRODUCTION
 150 REM OF 'BASS' AND 'TREBLE'
 160 REM LINES IN THE 'MELODY'.
 170 CLS
 180 DIM NTE%(25):BASE%=93
 190 PROCENV: Q%=0
 200 PRINT "SELECT MODALITY"
 210 PRINT "MAJOR - M"
 220 PRINT "DIMINISHED - D"
 230 PRINT "EQUAL INTERVAL - E"
 240 PRINT "BLUE - B"
 250 PRINT "RAGA - R"
 260 PRINT "DORIAN - O"
 270 PRINT "AEOLIAN - A"
 280 PRINT "HARMONIC - H"
 290 PRINT "PENTATONIC - P"
 300 PRINT "CHROMATIC - C"
 310 INPUT M$
 320 INPUT"TEMPO, BAR, LENGTH "TEMPO%,BAR%,F
%
 330 INPUT "ENVELOPE NUMBER (0-4) "V%
 340 IF V%=0 THEN V%=-10
 350 PROCMODALITY
 360 PROCSCALE
 370 PROCSTART
 380 PROCPHRASE
 390 C%=1
 400 REPEAT
 410 FOR CH%=1 TO 3
 420 PROCNXT
 430 PROCPLAY(CH%)
 440  SOUND 0,1,-4,TEMPO%*DUR%
 450 NEXT CH%
 460 C%=C%+1
 470 UNTIL C%>=PH%
```

```
  480 ENVELOPE 1,4,0,0,0,0,0,0,127,-40,0,-1,1
26,0
  490   SOUND 0,1,-4,TEMPO%*DUR%
  500 IF S%=START% AND DUR%=BAR% PROCEND
  510 GOTO 380
  520 DEF PROCMODALITY
  530 REPEAT
  540 READ MDE$
  550 UNTIL MDE$=M$
  560 ENDPROC
  570 DATA M,14,8,8,4,8,8,8,4
  580 DATA 8,8,4,8,8,8,4
  590 DATA D,16,4,8,4,8,4,8,4,8
  600 DATA 4,8,4,8,4,8,4,8
  610 DATA E,12,8,8,8,8,8,8
  620 DATA 8,8,8,8,8,8
  630 DATA B,12,12,8,4,4,12,8
  640 DATA 12,8,4,4,12,8
  650 DATA R,14,8,8,4,8,4,8,8
  660 DATA 8,8,4,8,4,8,8
  670 DATA O,14,8,4,8,8,8,4,8
  680 DATA 8,4,8,8,8,4,8
  690 DATA A,14,8,4,8,8,4,8,8
  700 DATA 8,4,8,8,4,8,8
  710 DATA H,14,8,4,8,8,4,12,4
  720 DATA 8,4,8,8,4,12,4
  730 DATA P,10,8,8,12,8,12
  740 DATA 8,8,12,8,12
  750 DATA C,24,4,4,4,4,4,4,4,4
  760 DATA 4,4,4,4,4,4,4,4
  770 DATA 4,4,4,4,4,4,4,4
  780 DEF PROCSCALE
  790 NTE%(0)=BASE%
  800 READ SL%
  810 FOR N%=1 TO SL%
  820 READ I%
  830 NTE%(N%)=NTE%(N%-1)+I%
  840 NEXT
  850 ENDPROC
  860 DEF PROCSTART
  870 START%=RND(SL%)
  880 ENDPROC
  890 DEF PROCNXT
```

```
 900 Z%=RND(4)
 910 X%=RND(Z%)*(1+RND(2)*(RND(2)=2))
 920 ENDPROC
 930 DEF PROCPHRASE
 940 PH%=RND(BAR%)+1
 950 DUR%=BAR%/PH%
 960 ENDPROC
 970 DEF PROCPLAY(CH%)
 980 S%=START%
 990 FOR I%=1 TO PH%
1000 SOUND CH%,V%,NTE%(S%)+48*(CH%=1),DUR%*T
EMPO%
1010 S%=S%+X%
1020 IF S%>SL% THEN S%=S%-Z%
1030 IF S%<1 THEN S%=S%+Z%
1040 NEXT I%
1050 ENDPROC
1060 DEF PROCEND
1070 Q%=Q%+1
1080 IF Q%<F%*10/BAR% THEN ENDPROC
1090 SOUND 1,0,0,0
1100 SOUND 2,0,0,0
1110 SOUND 3,V%,NTE%(S%),DUR%*TEMPO%
1120 PRINT "THAT'S ALL FOLKS"
1130 END
1140 DEF PROCENV
1150 ENVELOPE 1,4,0,0,0,0,0,0,127,-40,0,-1,1
26,0
1160 ENVELOPE 2,4,0,0,0,0,0,0,40,-16,0,-1,12
6,32
1170 ENVELOPE 3,4,0,0,0,0,0,0,127,-16,-8,-2,
126,80
1180 ENVELOPE 4,4,1,-2,1,1,1,1,60,-80,0,-8,1
26,40
1190 ENDPROC
```

PROGRAM 8.11

```
1 REM RANDOM COMPOSITION C-64
2 REM BASED ON BBC RND 5
3 REM TRY SYNCING BY ADDING 2 TO WAVEFORM/COMTRO
L REGISTER OF ONE CHANNEL
4 REM COULD ALSO INCORPORATE A LOWER OCTAVE ON O
NE CHANNEL FOR BASS
```

```
5 REM NOTE THE WAY IN WHICH NOTE DATA IS ENTERED
10 PRINT CHR$(147)
15 POKE 54296,15
20 DIM NT(25),HF(25),LF(25)
25 DIM H(25),L(25)
30 GOSUB 2000: Q=0: REM ENVELOPES
40 PRINT "SELECT MODALITY"
50 PRINT "MAJOR - M"
70 PRINT "WHOLE TONE-W"
120 PRINT "HARMONIC - H"
130 PRINT "PENTATONIC -P"
140 PRINT "CHROMATIC -C"
150 INPUT M$
160 INPUT "TEMPO, BAR, LENGTH";TE,BA,F
170 FOR X=1 TO 22: READ H(X),L(X):NEXT
200 GOSUB 535: REM MODALITY
210 GOSUB 600: REM SCALE
220 GOSUB 700: REM START NOTE
230 GOSUB 800: REM SELECT PHRASE
255 FOR I=1 TO PH
270 GOSUB 900: REM NEXT NOTE
280 GOSUB 1000: REM PLAY CHANNELS
345 NEXT I
360 POKE 54290,33
390 IF S=BG AND DU=BA THEN GOSUB 3000:REM END
400 GOTO 230
530 DATA 17,37,18,42,19,63,20,100,21,154,22,227,
24,63
531 DATA 25,177,27,56,28,214,30,141,32,94,34,75,
36,85,38,126
532 DATA 40,200,43,52,45,198,51,97,57,172,64,188
533 DATA 68,149
534 END
535 READ Y$
536 IF Y$=M$ THEN RETURN
537 GOTO 535
550 DATAP,10,2,4,7,9,11,14,16,19,21,23
560 DATAW,13,1,3,5,7,9,11,13,15,17,19,21,23,25
570 DATAC,25,1,2,3,4,5,6,7,8,9,10,11,12,13,14,15
,16,17,18,19,20,21,22,23,24,25
580 DATAH,15,1,3,4,6,8,9,12,13,15,16,18,20,21,24
,25
590 DATAM,15,1,3,5,6,8,10,12,13
```

```
595 DATA15,17,18,20,22,24,25
600 READ SL
610 FOR N=1 TO SL
620 READ I
630 HF(N)=H(I):LF(N)=L(I)
640 NEXT N
650 RETURN
700 XX=RND(-TI)
710 BG=INT((SL-1)*RND(1))+1
715 S=BG
720 RETURN
800 PH=INT((BA-1)*RND(1))+2
810 DU=10*INT(BA/PH)
820 RETURN
900 Z=INT(3*RND(1))
910 X=INT(Z*RND(1)+1)*(1+INT(4*RND(1))*(RND(1)<=
0.5))
920 RETURN
1000 FOR CH=0 TO2
1020 POKE 54272+7*CH,LF(S):POKE 54273+7*CH,HF(S)
1030 POKE 54276,17:POKE 54283,33
1035 REM  FOR P=1 TO DU*TE:NEXT
1040 S=S+X
1045 IF S>SL THEN S=S-Z
1050 IF S<0 THEN S=S+Z
1052 IF Z=0 THEN Z=BG
1055 IF S>SL OR S<0 THEN 1045
1060 NEXT CH
1070 RETURN
2000 POKE 54277,9:POKE 54278,143
2010 POKE 54284,40:POKE 54285,143
2020 POKE 54291,136:POKE 54292,255
2100 RETURN
3000 Q=Q+1
3010 IF Q<F*10/BA THEN RETURN
3020 FOR ZZ=0 TO 2: POKE 54276+7*ZZ,0:NEXT
3030 PRINT "THAT'S ALL FOLKS"
3040 END
```

PROGRAM 8.12

Taking the second BBC version as our model, the program works as follows. A scale or mode is selected by inputting a key letter, which is the first item on the corresponding data list. The data lists (lines 570-770) give key letter, number of following items and values for intervals. You are also asked to input tempo, bar length and the length of the composition. (Some of the details differ significantly on the Commodore program since note intervals are nowhere near as easy to handle.)

PROCMODALITY and PROCSCALE calculate note values, given a base pitch value BASE% (this could also be randomly selected). PROCSTART selects a start note from among the calculated values, PROCPHRASE (defined in lines 930-960 and called in 380) selects a random number of notes in a bar and then calculates their duration. From lines 390 to 500 an interval is chosen to the next note by PROCNXT, and PROCPLAY plays each channel. This section also plays the rhythm (lines 440 and 490) and checks to see if the end of the composition might have been reached – PROCEND being called whenever the start note recurs at a duration equal to the bar length. PROCEND then counts the occurrences of this note and ends the program when a suitable number comes up (lines 1060-1130), printing out a message and playing a final note. Until this happens, the program loops around from line 510 to line 380, selecting new phrase lengths and next notes every time.

(On the BBC, RND(Y) will repeat the sequence based on X if Y is first set by Y=RND(–X), while on the Commodore – which produces random numbers only in the range $0<x<1$ – and on the BBC, RND(0) will return the same value as the last random number chosen. On the Commodore, new fractional random numbers can be produced by setting the first selection to RND(–TI).)

There are any number of approaches to the subject of random composition, and any number of refinements can be made to the above program. Often it results in sounds described by a friend as reminiscent of Albanian wine-pressing chants. Sometimes – when it feels like it? – it produces delightful pieces of melody, rhythm and harmony. They often surprise with their ingenuity, proving just how musical the micro can be.

Appendix 1

Guitar tutor program and sound effects generator program

Guitar chord tutor

This program is an example of how micros can be adapted for educational use in the musical sphere. Written by Nick Holmes, it asks for a chord, shows you the fingering on a guitar fretboard with standard tuning and plays an arpeggio of the notes in the chords, following the simulated strum of the guitar – all in glorious colour.

Much of the interest in the program is achieved by the graphics. Chord information is input in line 2610 as a string CHORD$, which is compared against the data held in lines 2700 and 2710. There is built-in room for expansion here. Using the BBC's RESTORE X command (where X is a line number), the data pointer is moved to relevant parts of the program in order to pick out the required data. Data is provided to determine frets, strings and associated frequencies (see line 2800); PROCFINGERPLOT, PROCSET and PROCPLING handle the screen and sound output. The appealingly named PROCWOBBLE makes the strings appear to vibrate.

```
1 REM*******************************************
2 REM* SILLY SOFTWARE INC. PRESENT *
3 REM*                                      *
4 REM*    A GUITAR CHORD DATABASE      *
5 REM*                                      *
```

```
   6 REM*   COPYRIGHT HOLMES & HOLMES   *
   8 REM*********************************
  10 MODE2:PROCINTRO:CLS:GOTO10000
  17 DEFPROCNECK
  20 A=816:COLOUR 128:GCOL 0,7:CLS:REPEAT:MO
VE 0,A:DRAW 1279,A:A=A-32
  80 UNTIL A<650:PROCFRETS
  90 ENDPROC
 100 DEFPROCFRETS
 110Y=128:GCOL 0,4:FOR Z=0TO10:IF Z=10 THEN
GCOL 0,5
 140 MOVE Y*Z-2,816:DRAW Y*Z-2,656:NEXTZ:MOV
E 1279,816:DRAW 1279,656:DRAW Y*Z-2,656:GCOL
0,2:RESTORE 200
 180 FOR P=1TO5:READ X,Y:FOR N=-3TO3:FOR M=-
3TO3:PLOT 69,X+N,Y+M:NEXT M:NEXTN:NEXTP
 200 DATA 447,800,447,672,703,736,959,736,19
1,736
 210ENDPROC
 500 DEFPROCWOBBLE
 508 *FX9,3
 509 *FX10,2
 510GCOL 0,10:COLOUR 0:MOVE 0,848-(STRING*32
):LETF%=848-STRING*32
 520 IF S%=0 AND T%=0 THEN DRAW 1279,F%
 530 IF S%=1 THEN DRAW 1279-(FIF1F-100)*128,
F%
 540 IF NOT(T%=1)THEN ENDPROC
 550 IF FIF1S=STRING THEN DRAW 1279-FIF1F*12
8,F%
 560 IF FIF2S=STRING THEN DRAW 1279-FIF2F*12
8,F%
 570 IF FIF3S=STRING THEN DRAW 1279-FIF3F*12
8,F%
 580 IF FIF4S=STRING THEN DRAW 1279-FIF4F*12
8,F%
 590 ENDPROC
 999DEFPROCINTRO
1000 COLOUR 131:COLOUR 5:CLS:FOR N=1TO8:PRIN
T:NEXTN:PRINT;"    GOOD   MORNING":FOR N=1TO200
0:NEXTN:PRINT''''
1022 COLOUR 13:PRINT;"        ARE YOU":PRINT:P
RINT;"        SITTING":PRINT:PRINT;"    COMFORT
```

ABLY?"
```
 1050 PROCSCAN:PRINT':IF A$="Y" THEN 1200
 1065IF A$="N" THEN1080
 1070 GOTO 1050
 1080 COLOUR 4:PRINT " WELL, WHAT DO YOU":PRI
NT:PRINT "  EXPECT ME TO DO":PRINT:PRINT "
   ABOUT IT?":FORN=1TO1000:NEXTN
 1200 ENDPROC
 1500 DEFPROCSCAN
 1510 A$=INKEY$(500)
 1520 ENDPROC
 2300DEFPROCINSTRUCT
 2320 CLS:VDU 146,141:PRINT "           INSTRU
CTIONS"
 2321 VDU 146,141:PRINT"           INSTRUCTION
S":PRINT''
 2330 VDU 145:PRINT"THIS PROGRAM WILL SHOW TH
E FINGERINGS"
 2340 VDU 145:PRINT"AND PLAY THE NOTES FOR A
SELECTION OF"
 2350 VDU 145:PRINT"        SIMPLE GUITAR CHOR
DS"
 2370 PRINT'':VDU 134:PRINT" MAJOR AND MINOR
CHORDS ARE KNOWN BY":VDU 134:PRINT" THEIR INI
TIAL LETTERS: FOR EXAMPLE:":VDU134:PRINT" A M
AJOR IS";:VDU 131:PRINT"A";:VDU134:PRINT"& C
SHARP MINOR IS";:VDU131:PRINT"C£M"
 2380 PRINT':VDU 132:PRINT"NOTE THAT FLATS CA
NNOT BE TYPED IN ON"
 2390 VDU 132:PRINT "THE KEYBOARD, SO FLAT NO
TES ARE KNOWN"
 2400 VDU 132:PRINT "BY THEIR RELATIVE SHARPS
: FOR EXAMPLE,"
 2410 VDU 132:PRINT" D FLAT MAJOR IS 'C£', G
FLAT MINOR ":VDU 132:PRINT"         IS 'F£M' ET
C."
 2450 PRINT: VDU 133:PRINT"     <SPACE BAR>";:
VDU 130:PRINT"TO CONTINUE"
 2460 IF GET$=" " THEN ENDPROC ELSE 2460
 2500 ENDPROC
 2600 DEFPROCASK
 2610 COLOUR2:PRINT TAB(1,15);"WHICH CHORD WO
ULD"TAB(2,17);"YOU LIKE ME TO"TAB(6,19);"PLAY
```

```
?":INPUT TAB(7,21),CHORD$:A%=1:RESTORE 2700:F
OR C=0TO95:READ A$:IF CHORD$=A$ THEN 2800
 2665 NEXT C
 2670 COLOUR 1:PRINT TAB(1,23);"I'M SORRY, I
DON'T":PRINT TAB(3,25);"KNOW THAT ONE"
 2675 FOR N=0TO2000:NEXTN:PRINT TAB(0,23);"
               ":PRINT TAB(0,25);"
                         ":PRINT TAB(7,21);"
        ":GOTO2610
 2700 DATA "A","AM","A£","A£M","B","BM","C","
CM","C£","C£M","D","DM","D£","D£M","E","EM","
F","FM","F£","F£M","G","GM","G£","G£M","A7","
AM7","A£7","A£M7","B7","BM7","C7","CM7","C£7"
,"C£M7","D7","DM7","D£7","D£M7","E7","EM7","F
7","FM7","F£7"
 2710DATA "F£M7","G7","GM7","G£7","G£M7","A",
"A","A","A","A","A","A","A","A","A","A","A","
A","A","A","A","A","A","A","A","A","A","A","A
","A","A","A","A","A","A","A","A","A","A","A
,"A","A","A","A","A","A","A","A","A","A","A",
"A","A","A"
 2800 R=4000+C:RESTORE R:READ FIF1F,FIF1S,FIF
2F,FIF2S,FIF3F,FIF3S,FIF4F,FIF4S
 3510 ENDPROC
 4000 DATA 2,3,2,4,2,5,0,0
 4001 DATA 1,5,2,3,2,4,0,0
 4002 DATA 101,6,3,3,3,4,3,5
 4003 DATA 101,6,2,5,3,3,3,4
 4004 DATA 102,6,4,3,4,4,4,5
 4005 DATA 102,6,3,5,4,3,4,4
 4006 DATA 1,5,2,3,3,1,3,2
 4007 DATA 103,6,4,5,5,3,5,4
 4008 DATA 104,6,6,3,6,4,6,5
 4009 DATA 104,6,5,5,6,3,6,4
 4010 DATA 2,4,2,6,3,5,0,0
 4011 DATA 1,6,2,4,3,5,0,0
 4012 DATA 106,6,8,3,8,4,8,5
 4013 DATA 106,6,7,5,8,3,8,4
 4014 DATA 1,4,2,2,2,3,0,0
 4015 DATA 0,0,2,2,2,3,0,0
 4016 DATA 101,6,2,4,3,2,3,3
 4017 DATA 101,6,0,0,3,2,3,3
 4018 DATA 102,6,3,4,4,2,4,3
```

```
4019 DATA 102,6,0,0,4,2,4,3
4020 DATA 2,2,3,1,3,5,3,6
4021 DATA 103,6,0,0,5,2,5,3
4022 DATA 104,6,5,4,6,2,6,3
4023 DATA 104,6,0,0,6,2,6,3
4024 DATA 0,0,2,3,2,5,0,0
4025 DATA 1,5,2,3,0,0,0,0
4026 DATA 106,6,7,4,8,2,0,0
4027 DATA 106,6,0,0,8,2,0,0
4028 DATA 1,3,2,2,2,4,2,6
4029 DATA 102,6,3,5,4,3,0,0
4030 DATA 1,5,2,3,3,2,3,4
4031 DATA 103,6,4,5,5,3,0,0
4032 DATA 104,6,0,0,6,3,6,5
4033 DATA 104,6,5,5,6,3,0,0
4034 DATA 1,5,2,4,2,6,0,0
4035 DATA 1,6,1,5,2,4,0,0
4036 DATA 106,6,0,0,8,3,8,5
4037 DATA 106,6,7,5,8,3,0,0
4038 DATA 1,4,2,2,0,0,0,0
4039 DATA 0,0,2,2,0,0,0,0
4040 DATA 101,6,2,4,3,2,0,0
4041 DATA 101,6,0,0,3,2,0,0
4042 DATA 102,6,3,4,4,2,0,0
4043 DATA 102,6,0,0,4,2,0,0
4044 DATA 1,6,2,2,3,1,0,0
4045 DATA 103,6,0,0,5,2,0,0
4046 DATA 104,6,5,4,6,2,0,0
4047 DATA 104,6,0,0,6,2,0,0
4200 DEFPROCFINGERPLOT
4202 COLOUR 0:COLOUR 129:FOR F=1TO4:PROCSET:
IF B%=1 THEN 4225
4210 IF FINGERF>100 THEN FOR X=1TU6:PRINT TA
B(20-2*(FINGERF-100),5+X);CHR$(48+F):NEXT X:G
OTO 4225
4220 PRINT TAB(20-2*FINGERF,5+FINGERS);CHR$(
48+F)
4225 NEXT F:ENDPROC
4300 DEFPROCSET
4320 B%=0
4330 IF F=1 THEN 4340 ELSE 4350
4340 FINGERS=FIF1S:FINGERF=FIF1F
4350 IF F=2 THEN 4360   ELSE 4370
```

```
 4360 FINGERS=FIF2S:FINGERF=FIF2F
 4370 IF F=3 THEN 4380 ELSE 4390
 4380 FINGERS=FIF3S:FINGERF=FIF3F
 4390 IF F=4 THEN 4400 ELSE 4420
 4400 FINGERS=FIF4S:FINGERF=FIF4F
 4420 IF FINGERS=0 THEN B%=1
 4430 ENDPROC
 5000 DEFPROCPLING
 5015 FOR E=0TO3:ENVELOPE E,2,0,0,0,0,0,0,80,
-8,-1,-1,120,100:NEXTE
 5040 FOR STRING=1TO6
 5045 LET T%=0:RESTORE (6000+STRING):READ PIT
CHO:LET PITCH=PITCHO
 5060 IF FIF1S=STRING THEN PITCH=PITCH+4*FIF1
F:LET T%=1
 5070 IF FIF2S=STRING THEN PITCH=PITCH+4*FIF2
F:LET T%=1
 5080 IF FIF3S=STRING THEN PITCH=PITCH+4*FIF3
F:LET T%=1
 5090 IF FIF4S=STRING THEN PITCH=PITCH+4*FIF4
F:LET T%=1
 5093 LETS%=0
 5095 LETS%=0:IF FIF1F>100 AND (NOT (FIF2S=ST
RING)) AND (NOT (FIF3S=STRING)) AND (NOT (FIF
4S=STRING)) THEN PITCH=PITCHO+4*(FIF1F-100):L
ETS%=1
 5100 IF STRING<4THEN SOUND STRING,STRING,PIT
CH,25
 5110 IF STRING>3THEN SOUND STRING-3,STRING-3
,PITCH,25
 5120 PROCWOBBLE:FORW=1TO550:NEXTW:NEXT STRIN
G:ENDPROC
 6001 DATA 21
 6002 DATA 41
 6003 DATA 61
 6004 DATA 81
 6005 DATA 97
 6006 DATA 117
10000 MODE7
10010 PRINT TAB(3,12);"DO YOU WANT INSTRUCTIO
NS?";:PROCSCAN
10015 IF A$="Y" THEN PROCINSTRUCT
10025 MODE2:PROCNECK:PROCASK:PROCFINGERPLOT:P
```

```
ROCPLING
10030 COLOUR128:COLOUR5:PRINT TAB(0,23);"
   <SPACE>":COLOUR4:PRINT"  GIVES NEW CHORD":C
OLOUR5:PRINT:PRINT"       <RETURN>":COLOUR4:PR
INT"GIVES THIS ONE AGAIN":IF GET$=" "THEN 100
25 ELSE PROCPLING:GOTO10030
```

Effects unit

The next program allows you to explore most of the features of the
Commodore 64's sound generator to produce many intriguing effects. The
program sets up the top two rows of the 64 keyboard as a musical keyboard
(see line 510). As with previous programs, it checks a key press (returned by
GET A$ in line 110) to see if the key is associated with a note. Base
frequencies are listed in DATA in lines 610-630, and calculations (using the
octave setting held in variables M and N, which specify the full range of
Commodore octaves as, respectively, a base octave and an upward range)
are performed in line 150. Perhaps the most interesting feature of this
program is the tuning facility (lines 800-995), which allows you to reset the
tuning of the keyboard by calculating a set of new values for the frequency
variables.

Other features include three-channel sound, ring modulation, pulse-width
modulation and frequency modulation. The full range of filter commands is
accessible, and the filter cut-off frequency can be controlled from channel 3.
Waveforms can be changed in real-time, by pressing the shifted function keys
(f2, f4, f6 and f8). The first three keys cycle through waveform values for each
channel, and the current logged channel waveform is shown on the screen
(the logged channel can be changed by pressing the comma key). Function
key f8 sets all the channel waveforms equal to the current waveform on
channel 3.

The best effects are obtained by use of the various modulation controls (all
of which toggle on and off with their status shown on screen). Ring
modulation and frequency modulation can be particularly effective. The
keyboard can be played as an instrument, but it is a little slow because of all
the possible variables that must be taken into acount. The central play loop is
contained in lines 100-190; here all the relevant checks for key presses are
done, and all the necessary POKEs to and PEEKs from sound registers are
made. Line 180, IF PEEK(198)=0, checks to see whether the keyboard
buffer is empty. If it is (and is equal to zero), the program loops back to line
155 and continues playing the note it was playing. If the PEEK returns a
non-zero value, then a key must have been pressed since the keyboard buffer
was effectively wiped in line 118. The new key must then be handled, so the
program loops back to line 100.

This loop could be speeded up with a little rewriting and reorganizing of the lines. Inevitably there will be less superficial structural changes that could be made. As it stands the program produces some weird and wonderful effects with a little imagination. I've called it FX-GEN, although more musical applications are also available.

```
1 REM FXGEN-C64. GARY HERMAN, 1984
2 REM A KEYBOARD WITH NUMEROUS EFFECTS INCLUDING
 FILTERING,MODULATION
3 REM FULL OCTAVE SPAN, VARIABLE TUNING AND ATNS
TR$READDIM
4 REM THE PLAYING KEYS ARE LAID OUT ACROSS THE T
OP TWO ROWS
5 REM AND THE PROGRAM FEATURES REASONABLY COMPLE
TE INSTRUCTIONS
6 REM THE STATUS DISPLAY INDICATES WHICH KEY HAS
 WHICH EFFECT
7 REM BUT, IF IT'S NOT CLEAR, TRY EXPERIMENTING
8 REM THIS PROGRAM GENERATES SOME VERY UNUSUAL E
FFECTS AND IT'S WORTH
9 REM EXPERIMENTING WITH.
10 REM IN THE LISTING, SOME KEY SYMBOLS HAVE BEE
N CHANGED FOR THE NAME OF THE
11 REM KEY.  WHERE THIS HAS BEEN DONE, THE NAME
IS IN SQUARE BRACKETS.
12 REM IT SHOULD BE REPLACED WITH THE ACTUAL SYM
BOL WHEN KEYING IN.
20 PRINT CHR$(14);CHR$(147)
30 GOSUB 500
40 GOSUB 600
50 GOSUB 1000
60 GOSUB 700
70 GOSUB 300
90 FOR X=1 TO 3:POKE WF(X),0: NEXT
99 REM PLAY LOOP
100 P=0:IF Y<>0 THEN J=2:GOTO 110
105 J=3
110 GET A$:IF A$="" THEN 110
115 IF A$="_" THEN GOSUB 300:GOSUB700:GOTO 100
118 POKE 198,0
120 FOR X=1 TO 17
130 IF MID$(N$,X,1)=A$ THEN I=X:V=V+1+(V>=J)*J:P
```

```
=1:X=17:GOTO 150
135 NEXT
140 IF P=0 THEN GOSUB 200:GOSUB 700:GOTO 100
150 N(I)=FR(I)*2^(N-M):H(I)=INT(N(I)/256):L(I)=N
(I)-H(I)*256
155 POKE MV,RM+F+Y+U:POKE RF,O+R
160 POKE HC,K*PEEK(O3+L)+Z*(1-K):POKE LC,O
165 POKE PH(V),PP*PEEK(O3+L)/16+HP*(1-PP)
170 POKE FH(V),H(I):POKE FL(V),(1-H)*L(I)+H*PEEK
(O3+L)
175 POKE WF(V),FW(V)+1
180 IF PEEK(198)=0 THEN 155
185 POKE WF(V),FW(V)+G
190 GOTO 100
199 REM SWITCH BANK
200 IF A$="[F1]" THEN M=0:RETURN
210 IF A$="[F3]" THEN M=1:RETURN
220 IF A$="[F5]" THEN M=2:RETURN
230 IF A$="[F7]" THEN M=3:RETURN
240 IF A$="[F2]" THEN FW(1)=FW(1)+16+(FW(1)=128)
*144:RETURN
241 IF A$="[F4]" THEN FW(2)=FW(2)+16+(FW(2)=128)
*144:RETURN
242 IF A$="[F6]" THEN FW(3)=FW(3)+16+(FW(3)=128)
*144:RETURN
243 IF A$="[F8]" THEN FW(1)=FW(3):FW(2)=FW(3):RE
TURN
245 IF A$="[POUND SIGN]" THEN F=F+16+(F=64)*80:R
ETURN
250 IF A$="-" THEN O=O+1+(O=15)*16:RETURN
255 IF A$="," THEN V=V+1+(V=3)*3:RETURN
260 IF A$="+" THEN R=R+16+(R=240)*256:RETURN
265 IF A$="/" THEN L=1-L:RETURN
270 IF A$="[UP ARROW]" THEN K=1-K:RETURN
275 IF A$="*" THEN Y=128-Y:RETURN
280 IF A$="@" THEN Z=Z+16+(Z=240)*256:RETURN
285 IF A$="=" THEN G=1-G:RETURN
290 IF A$=";" THEN U=4-U:RETURN
292 IF A$=":" THEN PP=1-PP:RETURN
293 IF A$="M" THEN GOSUB 800:RETURN
294 IF A$="." THEN H=1-H:RETURN
295 IF A$="N" THEN N=N+1+(N=2)*3:RETURN
296 RETURN
```

```
299 REM ENV/PULSE/FILTER SETTINGS
300 PRINT CHR$(147)
305 POKE PH(V),7:POKE PL(V),255
308 POKE AD(V),AD:POKE SR(V),SR
310 PRINT "ATTACK/DECAY";AD
320 PRINT "SUSTAIN/RELEASE";SR
325 PRINT "FILTER CUT-OFF";Z
326 DC=INT((HP*256+LP)*100/4095)
327 PRINT "PULSE DUTY CYCLE";DC"%"
330 INPUT "CHANGE ANY(AD/SR/FC/DC)-OR NO";AN$
340 FOR X=1 TO 3:POKE AD(X),AD:POKE SR(X),SR:POK
E HC,FC:POKE PH(X),HP:NEXT
360 IFAN$<>"AD"ANDAN$<>"SR"ANDAN$<>"FC"ANDAN$<>"
DC" THEN PRINT CHR$(147):RETURN
370 PRINT:PRINT "PRESS THE SPACE BAR TO ROLL VAL
UES"
375 PRINT "RELEASE AT NEW VALUE AND HIT RETURN"
380 FOR X=0 TO 255
390 AD=AD+(AN$="AD")*(1+(AD=0)*256)
400 SR=SR+(AN$="SR")*(1+(SR=0)*256)
404 Z=Z+(AN$="FC")*(1+(Z=0)*256)
406 DC=DC+(AN$="DC")*(1+(DC=0)*100)
407 HP=INT(DC/256):LP=DC-256*HP
410 PRINT CHR$(19):PRINT TAB(12);"    ---";AD
420 PRINT TAB(15);"    ---";SR
424 PRINT TAB(14);"    ---";Z
426 PRINT TAB(16);"    ---";DC"%"
430 GET A$:IF A$="" THEN 430
435 FOR WT=1 TO 100:NEXT
440 IF A$=" " THEN NEXT
450 X=255
455 PV=DC*40.95:HP=INT(PV/256):LP=PV-HP*256
460 GOTO 300
499 REM VARIABLE INIT
500 AD=9:SR=255:HP=7:LP=255:V=0:Z=128:Y=0:FW(1)=
32:FW(2)=32:FW(3)=32:RM=15:N=1
510 N$="Q2W3ER5T6Y7UI9OOP"
520 DIM FR(17),N(17),H(17),L(17)
580 RETURN
599 REM FREQUENCY TABLE
600 FOR Q=1 TO 17: READ FR(Q): NEXT
610 DATA 4291,4547,4817,5103,5407,5728
620 DATA 6069,6430,6812,7217,7647,8101
```

```
630 DATA 8583,9094,9634,10207,10814
690 RETURN
699 REM PRINT OUT
700 PRINTCHR$(19):PRINT:PRINT:PRINT:PRINT
740 PRINT "VOICE>"V"OCT<F1-7>"N-M"WVFM<F2-8>   -
  --"FW(V)+1" -"
750 PRINT "HOLD<=>"G,"FILTER TYPE<\>"F/16,"OSC<-
>"O
760 PRINT "RS<+>"R/16,"FILTER MOD<^>"K,"O3/E3</>
"L+1
770 PRINT "FIXED CUT-OFF<@>   ---"Z,"RING<;>"U/4
,"PWM<:>"PP
780 PRINT"OSCILLATOR 3<*>"1-Y/128,"CHANGE VOICE<
,>"
790 PRINT"FM(VIB)<.>"H,"RANGE<N>"N,"TUNE<M>"INT(
FR(10)*0.0595)"A"
795 RETURN
799 REM TUNING FACILITY
800 PRINT CHR$(147)
810 RESTORE
820 INPUT"'-' OR '+' TO TUNE DOWN OR UP";AN$
830 IF AN$="-" THEN TN=-1:GOTO 860
840 IF AN$="+" THEN TN=+1:GOTO 860
850 GOTO 800
860 MC=FR(1):SU=0
865 PRINT:PRINT"PRESS SPACE BAR TO TUNE...":PRIN
T"?/ TO REVERSE DIRECTION"
868 PRINT"RELEASE AND RETURN TO SET VALUE"
870 FOR X=1 TO 3:POKE WF(X),0:NEXT
872 XX=MC+SU*TN
875 HF=INT(XX/256):LF=XX-HF*256
880 POKE FH(1),HF:POKE FL(1),LF
890 POKE WF(1),17
900 PRINT CHR$(19)"MIDDLE-C",XX,FR(1);
920 GET A$:IF A$="" THEN GOTO 920
930 IFA$=" "THENSU=SU+1+(SU=255)*256:PRINTCHR$(1
9)"MIDDLE-C",XX,FR(1);:GOTO872
931 IF A$="/" THEN TN=-TN:MC=XX:SU=0:PRINTTAB(32
)TN:GOTO 872
932 PRINT"DONE":FR(1)=XX
935 FOR X=1 TO 300:NEXT:PRINTCHR$(147)
938 PRINT"NEW VALUE",,"OLD VALUE":PRINT
939 REM CHANGE 1.0595 IF NOT APPROPRIATE
```

```
940 FORQ=2TO17:READ AA:FR(Q)=INT(FR(Q-1)*1.05953
5):PRINTQ-1">"FR(Q-1),AA:NEXT
945 READ AA:PRINT 17">"FR(17),AA
950 POKE WF(1),0
960 FOR Q=1 TO 13:IF (Q=2)+(Q=4)+(Q=7)+(Q=9)+(Q=
11) THEN NEXT Q
970 HF=INT(FR(Q)/256):LF=FR(Q)-HF*256
980 POKE FH(1),HF:POKE FL(1),LF
990 POKE WF(1),17:FORX=1TO300:NEXTX,Q
992 PRINT:PRINT "HIT ANY KEY TO RETURN"
993 GET A$:IF A$="" THEN 993
994 POKE WF(1),0:PRINT CHR$(147)
995 RETURN
999 REM REGVAR
1000 S=54272
1010 FOR X=1 TO 3
1020 CH=7*(X-1)
1030 FL(X)=S+CH:FH(X)=FL(X)+1:PL(X)=FH(X)+1:PH(X
)=PL(X)+1:WF(X)=PH(X)+1
1040 AD(X)=WF(X)+1:SR(X)=AD(X)+1
1050 NEXT
1060 LC=SR(3)+1:HC=LC+1:RF=HC+1:MV=RF+1:PX=MV+1:
PY=PX+1:O3=PY+1:E3=O3+1
1070 RETURN
```

Appendix 2

BASIC sound commands

BBC microcomputer
The two BASIC commands are SOUND and ENVELOPE. The former is followed by four parameters: channel information/cueing, volume, frequency and duration. It takes the form:

SOUND channel, amplitude, pitch, duration

SOUND can be used independently of ENVELOPE and, when it is, the last two parameters present no problems. Frequency can take an integer value between 0 and 255. As with all parameters, positive or negative values outside the acceptable range are all corrected by means of repeated addition or subtraction until a value within the range is reached.

The frequency range is exponential and is meant to be thought of as pitch. One unit is roughly equivalent to one-quarter of one semitone, so that adding 48 to any pitch value should give you a pitch exactly one octave above the original – i.e. adding 48 to a value specifying a particular note gives a note of twice the original frequency. Because this is meant to be an equal temperament tuning, the results are not exact. Errors can creep in, particularly at the low and high ends of the scale. It is wise to keep well within the range. There is a nominal spread of a little over five octaves. The notes and associated values are listed in a subsequent appendix. Middle-C (which should have a frequency of 261.624 Hz) is associated with a value of 53 in the BBC user guide. Independent measurements suggest that 51 or 52 is closer to real middle-C, and an equivalent correction might have to be made on all values if you want your computer to be in tune with other instruments.

Duration also takes integer values between 0 and 255. A unit represents a duration of one-twentieth of a second, with 255 (or −1) being an indefinite duration. The longest note of definite length is, therefore, 254 * 1/20, or 12.7, seconds. Independent timings show that this is reasonably accurate.

Volume, or amplitude, is only marginally more complicted. Zero is off and −15 is the loudest, the level increasing by 2 dB steps. A 6 dB increase (a doubling in amplitude) is therefore realized as an increase of −3 units. A 3 dB increase (a doubling in power or sound intensity, which is roughly what we mean by loudness) cannot be directly obtained.

Using positive values for volume parameters causes an ENVELOPE command to be called. In a program where data is not being stored, these values can be between 1 and 16 and each will be associated with the ENVELOPE command with the same number as its first parameter. Where data is being stored to tape or disc, only 1, 2, 3 and 4 are acceptable envelope numbers.

In use, SOUND information is loaded into a buffer, directly accessible by an OSWORD call. ADVAL(n) – where n is −5, −6, −7 or −8 – may be used to check whether the buffer for a given sound channel is empty or not. ADVAL(n) returns a value equal to the number of spaces in the channel n buffer. There are four channels, channel 0 being used for noise, while 1, 2 and 3 are musical channels. A 2 byte number as the first parameter of the SOUND command specifies channel and also the order in which notes will be played. Acceptable values for this number (in hex) are given by '&abcd', where 'a' can be 0 or 1, 'b' can be 0 to 3, 'c' can be 0 or 1 and 'd' can be 0 to 3. The 2 byte number therefore has sixty-four possible values. It can be expressed in decimal by adding any four values, one each from the following groups: 0,4096; 0,256,512,768; 0,16; 0,1,2,3.

The first hex digit, 'a', determines whether the specified note is a dummy (1) or not (0). If it is a dummy then the preceding note continues playing until its end; this is relevant only when considering the release phase under an ENVELOPE command. The second digit determines the number of notes to be played in unison with the specified one. For example, if this number is 2, then the note will not sound until two other notes on two other channels have been specified using the same format. This so-called 'hard sync' feature allows you to play chords without staggering the notes. However, in most cases the difference between three notes specified in one line or in three consecutive lines of a BASIC program not using hard sync and three notes using hard sync is all but impossible to detect.

```
10 REM BBC NO-SYNC
20 SOUND 1,-15,53,100
30 SOUND 2,-15,69,100
40 SOUND 3,-15,85,100


10 REM BBC SYNC
20 SOUND &201,-15,53,100
30 SOUND &202,-15,69,100
40 SOUND &203,-15,85,100
```

Hard sync is most useful when you want the computer to do something while it is accepting SOUND commands, because it enables you to specify a note without playing it immediately. In these examples, the trigger command plays a silence.

```
10 REM BBC SYNC-DELAY
20 SOUND &101,-15,53,40
30 PRINT"WAITING":FOR X=1 TO 5000:NEXT
40 SOUND &102,0,0,0:REM TRIGGER
```

The third hex digit in the first SOUND parameter, 'c', determines whether the buffer queue for a given channel is to be flushed (1) or not (0). If it is flushed then the note preceding the specified note is terminated, and all other notes already entered into the relevant channel buffer are erased and will not play. This is useful, for example, in real-time keyboards when you may want to terminate one note immediately a new one starts.

The final digit, 'd', determines which channel the specified note will be played on. If this number is 0, then the result will be noise – white noise if the pitch parameter is 0 to 3, semi-pitched periodic noise if it is 4 to 7. On channel 0, frequency numbers 3 and 7 will give noise that is modulated by the tone playing on channel 1. If the channel 1 tone is given a zero volume, the effect will be of hearing noise with an apparent pitch.

```
10 REM BBC NOISE LINKED TO CHANNEL 1
20 FOR F=0 TO 255
30 SOUND &111,0,F,-1
40 SOUND &110,-15,7,-1
50 NEXT
```

In most cases, the channel number is the only value used in the SOUND command's first parameter. In all cases, the parameter may be entered as a decimal number or as a hex number, and any out-of-range numbers will be converted into a number within the range. This short program gives some indication of how sound cueing operates in conjunction with pauses and a variety of durations. It is worth playing around with.

```
10 REM BBC SOUND DEMO
20 FOR N=0 TO 3
30 SOUND 1,-15,20,100
40 FOR PAUSE=1 TO 1000:NEXT
50 SOUND &11,-10,150,100
60 SOUND &101,-15,60,100
70 SOUND N,-10,5,100
80 SOUND &102,-15,100,200
90 FOR WAIT=1 TO 30000:NEXT:NEXT
```

The SOUND command is, at heart, pretty simple, not to say conventional. Most micros have some similar means of specifying channel, volume, frequency and duration. The ENVELOPE command, on the other hand, is both unique and complicated, but it is the most interesting feature of the BBC's sound facilities.

ENVELOPE affects the music or noise generated by the SOUND command. It has no independent life and must be interpreted by a program before any associated SOUND command. It is worth placing ENVELOPEs at the beginning of a program or in a procedure called at the beginning of a program, or you may find your computer becomes suddenly dumb for no apparent reason.

There are fourteen ENVELOPE parameters. The first is the envelope number, which must be the same as the 'volume' number in the associated SOUND command. The rest of the parameters fall into two categories: seven relate to the so-called 'pitch' envelope, and six relate to the amplitude or ADSR envelope. The form of the command is:

ENVELOPE N,T,S1,S2,S3,P1,P2,P3,AS,DS,SS,RS,AV,DV

Where N is envelope number, T is the step duration for the pitch and ADSR envelopes, the next three parameters are step values for the pitch envelope, P1, P2 and P3 are the numbers of steps in each of the three sections of the pitch envelope and the final parameters are step values for each of the phases of an ADSR envelope, an attack phase target level and a decay phase target level. Confusing, isn't it?

L. I. M. E.
THE MARKLAND LIBRARY
STAND PARK RD., LIVERPOOL, L16 9J

The first parameter, N, specifies which SOUND command will call that particular ENVELOPE command. Setting the SOUND command to, say, SOUND 1,3,101,10 will call envelope 3. So 3 has to be the first parameter following the ENVELOPE command relating to this SOUND command.

The second parameter, T, determines the length of each step in the pitch envelope (in units of one-hundredth of a second) and turns on or off autorepeat for the pitch envelope. Firstly, any integer value between 0 and 127 means that the pitch envelope will repeat, if necessary, for the total duration of a note (as given in the SOUND command). A value between 128 and 255 means that the pitch envelope will not repeat. Thus a T value of 2, say, gives a repeating pitch envelope while a value of 130 (128+2) gives a non-repeating envelope of the same duration.

SOUND 1,1,53,40 specifies a sound of two seconds' duration (40 * 1/20th). ENVELOPE 1,10, . . . specifies that each step in the associated pitch envelope will be ten-hundredths of a second long, or one-tenth of a second. So there can be at most twenty steps in the two-second sound. Now we come to the hard bit.

The ENVELOPE command breaks the sound up into three parts. Parameters S1, S2 and S3 specify the pitch change for each step in each of the three parts, while parameters P1, P2 and P3 specify how many steps there will be in each part. The units of the S parameters are quarter-semitones (as with the SOUND command's pitch parameter) and they can be positive or negative – giving a rise or fall in pitch, respectively. For example:

```
5 REM BBC ENVELOPE ARPEGGIO
10 ENVELOPE 2,25,0,16,12,1,1,1,127,0,0,-126,1
26,126
20 SOUND 1,2,53,120
```

gives a most interesting effect – three distinct notes repeating for a period of six seconds. The six-second duration is given by the figure '120' in line 20 (interpreted as 120 * 1/20th seconds). Line 20 also specifies an initial pitch value of 53, middle-C, opens channel 1 and calls envelope 2. Envelope 2 is defined in line 10. Each step lasts 25 * 1/100th seconds (a quarter of a second), and there is one step only in each of the three sections of the envelope (the '. . . 1,1,1 . . .' in the command).

The first section shows no change in the specified pitch (indicated by the first zero in the envelope command). Therefore middle-C is played for a quarter of a second. After that, the pitch rises by 16 units for the second section of the envelope: E-above-middle-C plays for a quarter-second. Finally the pitch rises by a further 12 units: G-above-middle-C plays for a quarter-second. This C-E-G arpeggio lasts for a total of 0.75 seconds; since the step duration parameter, 25, is less than 128, it will repeat until six seconds are up (which is eight times in all). Replacing 25 by 152 (25 + 128) plays C for a quarter-second, E for a quarter-second and G for the rest of the time, 5.5 seconds – the pitch envelope does not repeat. Replace the 25 by, say, 1 and you get a rapid arpeggio rather like an exaggerated vibrato. Replace it by, say, 100 and you will hear C, E, and G lasting for one second each and the seqeunce repeating once.

So much for the pitch envelope. The next six parameters in the ENVELOPE command deal with the amplitude envelope, which is a more familiar thing. This assumes the usual ADSR form in which a sound is divided into four phases: attack, decay, sustain and release.

Parameter 13 (AV) gives the target level for the attack phase. Assuming you are following a conventional ADSR envelope, this figure will be the peak volume of the sound. Its maximum value is 126. Parameter 14 (DV) gives the target level for the decay phase. There is no technical reason why this can't be greater than AV, in which case the note would just rise through its attack and decay phases, but conventionally it is equal to or lower than the attack target level. A tone is assumed to fall from a peak volume to a plateau volume, or even all the way to zero. Maximum value for DV is also 126.

Parameters AS, DS, SS and RS set the change of amplitude per step in each of the ADSR phases. Unlike the pitch envelope section, the amplitude envelope parameters give no explicit indication of the number of steps in each phase. It is, however, divided into discrete steps, and it works as follows.

The attack target level, AV, divided by the attack step parameter, AS, gives the number of steps in the attack phase, always remembering that these values are already divided into bands for the convenience of the hardware. The main result of this is that transitions are not always as smooth as they should be. Make all parameters as high as they can be within their bands: using 7 for all amplitude levels or parameters between 0 and 7, 15 for all between 8 and 15 and so on. This will avoid most problems.

The attack phase will last for (AV/AS)*T–hundredths of a second (if T is greater than 127, subtract 128 from it to find the value). Similarly the decay time is the number of steps in the decay phase multiplied by step length, which can be calculated by subtracting the plateau level from the attack target level, dividing by the decay step parameter and multiplying the result by T: (AV-DV)*T/DS. Since the total duration of the note is given by the SOUND command's fourth parameter, the length of the sustain phase is given by subtracting the lengths of the attack and decay phases combined from this total duration.

A sound is released only if there is no other sound waiting to be played on the same channel. The release phase extends the sound beyond the time given by the SOUND command, and its length can be calculated by dividing the plateau level by the release step parameter and multiplying the result by the step length: (DV/RS)*T. If the SOUND command specifies a note of shorter duration than the result of adding attack, decay and sustain phase lengths together, then the note will be cut short before the phases are completed. Thus:

```
10 REM BBC ENVELOPE DEMO
100 ENVELOPE 1,100,0,0,0,0,0,0,1,-1,0,-127,12
6,0
200 SOUND 1,1,53,-1
```

gives an attack time of 126 seconds and an equal decay time. The sustain level is zero, and since duration in line 200 is −1, the note continues indefinitely, at a zero volume after some 4'2". Press ESCAPE to stop it. Change the 100 in line 100 to 20 and you get a note 49 seconds long. With this parameter, T, set to 1, the audible part of the note lasts 2.5 seconds. Such indefinitely long notes may be terminated by flushing the sound buffer by adding 16 to the channel parameter of the next SOUND command to come along.

```
10 REM BBC ENVELOPE DEMO
100 ENVELOPE 1,20,0,0,0,0,0,0,12,-12,0,-127,1
08,0
200 SOUND 1,1,53,100
```

gives a total duration of five seconds (from line 200) and attack and decay times of 1.8 seconds each. So the sustain time at zero volume is now 1.4 seconds.

Change the sound duration parameter in line 200 to 50, and the note is cut short during the decay phase about 1.1 seconds before its amplitude reaches zero. To hear the note release from this level, change the release step parameter from −127 to −1. The note now dies away gradually.

Now make the attack sharper by changing the attack step parameter in line 100 from 12 to 36. This gives an attack duration of (108/36)*(20/100), or 0.6 seconds. Decay stays at 1.8 seconds. The note then continues for 2.5 − (0.6+1.8) or 0.1 seconds, but it has already reached zero amplitude so there is no release. Change the duration parameter in line 200 from 50 to 40 (2 seconds) and the note will be cut off before the decay phase ends − but you will then be able to hear it die away.

If the step length parameter, T, in line 100 is changed from 20 to 5, attack time will be 0.15 seconds and decay time 0.45 seconds; there will be no audible sustain or release. But if the last parameter in line 100 (decay target level) is given a positive value, say 48, you will be able to hear sustain and release. The decay phase is shorter, lasting only 0.25 seconds. Since the attack phase still lasts 0.15 seconds, the note sustains for 1.6 seconds. The release takes about 2 more seconds.

Now make T equal to 1 and the decay step equal to −1. Attack time is 0.03 seconds and decay time 1.08 seconds. There will be a 0.89 second sustain and a quick release (0.48 seconds).

So far we have not mixed pitch and amplitude envelopes, but let's try it.

```
10 REM BBC PITCH AND AMPLITUDE ENVELOPES
100 ENVELOPE 1,1,-1,36,0,108,3,0,36,-1,0,-1,1
26,48
200 SOUND 1,1,53,40
```

imposes a pitch envelope on the last produced sound. The pitch envelope lasts for (108+3)*1/100, or 1.11, seconds − equal to the combined length of the attack and decay phases of the ADSR envelope. Pitch falls by 108 quarter-semitones in the first section, rises by 36*3, or 108, quarter-semitones in the second section and stays where it is in the third section. After that, the pitch variations repeat until the note is over. Change the step parameter in line 100 from 1 to 128 and the pitch envelope does not repeat. Now swap pitch parameters around:

ENVELOPE 1,128,36,−1,0,3,108,0,36,−1,0,−1,126,48 or
ENVELOPE 1,128,−1,0,36,108,0,3,36,−1,0,−1,126,48

and you should hear how the pitch changes occur differently at different points in the note. More musical effects can be achieved by levelling out the pitch changes:

ENVELOPE 1,128,−1,1,−1,28,56,28,36,−1,0,−1,126,48

gives a pitch envelope that lasts 1.12 seconds with an attack-decay lasting 1.11 seconds. Change the . . . 28,56,28 . . . to 10,20,10 or 1,2,1 and you will get some pleasant effects, substantially altered if the step length parameter is changed to 1 and the pitch envelope repeats. Finally, it is possible to place pitch changes in different places in the note, as in:

ENVELOPE 1,128,0,1,−1,80,20,20,36,−1,0,−1,108,48

which gives a bend to the note after 0.8 seconds lasting for 0.4 seconds. This bend straddles the decay and sustain phases of the note and therefore produces an effect rather like using the tremolo arm on an electric guitar.

Commodore 64

Commodore BASIC is the worst thing about the Commodore 64. From the musical point of view, all the instructions are realized as POKEs (or PEEKs in some instances) to memory locations corresponding to particular registers on the machine's 6581 programmable sound generator.

Details of what each POKE or PEEK will give you can be found in the fuller discussion of the 6581 in the next appendix. For BASIC use, all you really need to know is that locations 54272 on the 64 corresponds to register zero on the 6581 chip, and the locations like the registers are numbered in steps of one from there upwards. There are a number of points to bear in mind, however, which make for easier use of the 64's facilities.

In general, POKEing a memory location can best be understood as setting certain data lines high and others low. There are three independent sound channels on the Commodore, each requiring at least five and at most seven different locations to be POKEd. Then there are seven locations that relate to all three channels: three write-only locations and four read-only locations.

The procedure is to POKE location 54296 with a volume setting, which, as it were, sets up all the channels. This setting is a value between 0 (off) and 15 (maximum). Thus 54296 can be divided into two nybbles (4 bit numbers), the least significant or right-hand nybble comprising bits number 3, 2, 1 and 0 of the byte addressed at location 54296. Thus POKEing 54296 with, say, 9 sets bit 3 high (1), bit 2 low (0), bit 1 low (0) and bit 0 high (1). This gives 1001 as our nybble, in binary code, and 1001 binary is equivalent to 9 decimal. The other, high-order nybble at location 54296 is made up of the four most significant bits of the byte: numbers 7, 6, 5 and 4. Setting 6, 5 and 4 high or low has the effect of switching on or off one of the 6581 chip's filter modes. Setting bit 7 high or low has the effect of turning off or on the audio output of channel 3.

Having set a volume, you then select the desired channel for output, and POKE the two associated locations with bytes which set attack, decay, sustain and release characteristics. The ADSR values must be entered before the note is turned on.

ADSR values are represented by nybbles; attack is the high-order nybble of one byte, and decay the low-order nybble of the same byte, while sustain and release are the high- and low-order nybbles, respectively, of the byte entered into the next location in memory. Thus there are sixteen possible values for each of the ADSR parameters, corresponding to the sixteen possible values of one nybble. Decay values, for example, are – in decimal – any number between 0 and 15, while attack values (as the high-order nybble) are any multiple of 16 between 0*16 and 15*16. They can be added together to give a combined setting for attack and decay, since we can visualize this process simply as one in which bits are set low or high in both nybbles by determining a value for a single byte.

The table below gives the real values corresponding to ADSR parameter settings. A, D and R are given as rates (the lower their value, the faster that phase of the envelope is over), while S is a proportion of peak volume. During the attack phase, the sound rises to the level set by POKEing 54296 (the peak level). During the decay phase, the sound diminishes to a level set by the sustain value (the plateau level). This can be any of sixteen values from the peak value itself (if sustain is set at 15) to zero. Setting sustain to 8, for example, would give a plateau level of roughly half the peak value; that is, for all practical purposes plateau level = peak value * (sustain value/16). All amplitude values on the 64 increase linearly, i.e. amplitude increases by a fixed absolute amount with each unit step. To get a relative doubling of amplitude (which the ear hears as a linear increase) you need to double the setting: thus an amplitude of 8 is twice an amplitude of 4 (which is not the case on the BBC).

Value		Attack	Decay/release	Sustain
0	(&0)	2 mS	6 mS	0
1	(&1)	8 mS	24 mS	0.07
2	(&2)	16 mS	48 mS	0.14
3	(&3)	24 mS	72 mS	0.20
4	(&4)	38 mS	114 mS	0.27
5	(&5)	56 mS	168 mS	0.34
6	(&6)	68 mS	204 mS	0.41
7	(&7)	80 mS	240 mS	0.48
8	(&8)	100 mS	300 mS	0.54
9	(&9)	250 mS	750 mS	0.60
10	(&A)	500 mS	1.5 S	0.68
11	(&B)	800 mS	2.4 S	0.74
12	(&C)	1 S	3 S	0.80
13	(&D)	3 S	9 S	0.87
14	(&E)	5 S	15 S	0.94
15	(&F)	8 S	24 S	1.00

(The sustain figures are only approximate. Also the timings are based on a 1 MHz clock. The attack figures give the amount of time taken for the note to rise from zero to whatever the peak amplitude is. Therefore, with a low peak amplitude, the attack will appear gentler than with a high peak amplitude. Similarly decay and release rates give the amount of time taken for the note to decay or release to zero amplitude. If a non-zero sustain value is set, the decay will be interrupted before the specified time is up. If a note decays from a low peak value, or is released from a low plateau value, then the time taken is as specified, so that the decay or release will be gentler than if the peak or plateau values were higher.)

Having set overall amplitude and envelope parameters, the next step is to set frequency. The Commodore has a range of almost eight octaves. The nominal frequencies can be calculated using the formula in the next appendix. Data are entered as a 2 byte number (that is, as 2 bytes in consecutive locations) and is, unlike the BBC, linearly related to frequency rather than pitch. This means that errors may creep in at the bottom end of the scale, where small numerical differences can have a large effect on frequency. Since the resolution is so good – 65535 values covering a range of ninety-plus notes – accurate tuning is easy, if tedious. The most accurate, if least efficient, method for entering frequencies is to specify the frequency data for each note to be used in a program as one or two items in a DATA statement. (The relationship between the 2 byte representation of frequency and a single number value is given by $FN=256*HB+LB$, where FN is a frequency number and HB and LB are the equivalent high and low bytes in decimal.) This method makes overall tuning difficult; it is often the best compromise to calculate values from a core of one octave's worth of data in your program, including a tuning variable in the calculation.

Frequency data are entered as a low byte and a high byte in consecutive locations – the low byte allowing fine tuning, the high byte allowing coarse sweeping through octaves. The range of values is 0 to 255 for each byte and, unlike the BBC, out-of-range values will – in this and all other cases – either return an error and stop the program or interfere with other parameters (for example, when you POKE the volume register with a value greater than 15 you will interfere with the filtering parameters).

After frequency comes waveform. There are four 'pure' waveforms: triangle, sawtooth, pulse and white noise. They can be 'mixed' but the effects are unpredictable. If pulse is chosen, it is necessary to set a pulse width or duty cycle. There are 4096 possible values set by POKEing a byte and a nybble into consecutive locations. The byte has a range of 0 to 255, and the nybble a range of 0 to 15. The reason for setting different pulse widths is that pulse width does affect timbre, because the harmonic content of a pulse wave at a given frequency depends on duty cycle. A value of 0 POKEd into both registers or a value of 4095 (that is, 15 in the high nybble and 255 in the low byte) will give a constant DC output. A value of 2048 (8 in the high nybble and 0 in the low byte) will give a square wave.

Setting the waveform should be the last POKE in any series of commands, because the waveform registers are also the control registers for any channel. The values for waveforms are 16 (triangle), 32 (sawtooth), 64 (pulse) and 128 (noise), but the sound will be heard only if bit 0 of the control register is set to 1. This is known as the gate bit, and it triggers the start of the attack phase of any sound. If it is set to 0, the sustain phase of the note terminates and it enters its release phase. Thus to start a note playing, say, a sawtooth wave, the location corresponding to the relevant waveform/control register must be POKEd with 33. To turn the note off, POKE the same location with 0 or any even number. Thus a note duration is governed by the attack time (given in the table above), *plus* the proportion of the decay time it takes to reach the sustain level (given by decay time *) (1 − sustain level), where decay time and sustain level are the figures given in the table above for the relevant values POKEd into their associated locations), *plus* the duration of the sustain phase, *plus* the release time (given above). Sustain duration is set by means of a delay in the program. This can be almost any command, but typically a FOR . . . NEXT loop is used. Other common delay techniques use the 64's internal clock to measure a fixed amount of time (the variable TI holds clock data), a WAIT command to detect a particular event or a GET command to detect the pressing of a key. Problems sometimes occur with the 64's keyboard buffer, which should be cleared by a POKE 198,0 instruction if a key is pressed to initiate a note.

The other sound locations are more fully dealt with in Appendix 3, but here is a simple program to test the above basic commands. All locations and data used have been ascribed to variables to simplify the POKEs. This not only makes the program easier to understand, but it also saves time, since the 64 deals with variables more quickly than it does with numeric constants.

```
1 REM C-64 SOUND DEMO
10 S=54272:LF=S:HF=S+1:W=S+4:AD=S+5:SR=S+6:V=
S+24
20 L=75:H=50:DUR=100:A=13:S=128:DEL=10:WF=33
30 POKE AD,A:POKE SR,S:POKE W,WF
40 FOR VOL=150 TO 0 STEP -DEL
60 POKE V,VOL/10
70 H=ABS(H-VOL)
80 POKE HF,H:POKE LF,L
90 FOR D=1 TO DEL:NEXT
100 NEXT
110 FOR D=1 TO DUR*DEL:NEXT
120 GOTO 30
130 REM TYPE 'POKE W,0' TO STOP NOTE
```

Changing any of the values in line 20 will create interesting effects. Replacing VOL in line 70 by 2*VOL will give a marked alternation between high and low frequencies. The changes all occur during the note's sustain phase, so it is not gated off at any point. Try gating it off by inserting a line 95 POKE W,0.

Appendix 3

Inside the 76489 and 6581 chips

Texas Instruments SN76489

The 76489 is a digital, programmable sound generator designed to be controlled by a microprocessor via an 8 bit parallel interface. The chip contains three tone generators, one noise generator, a mixer and a buffer amplifier. The tone and noise generators can be individually attenuated for control of amplitude.

The chip runs at a clock frequency of up to 4 MHz applied to pin 7 (3.579 MHz is typical). The clock pulse like all other inputs is at TTL levels – 5 volts high, 0 volts low.

Unlike many chips designed for microprocessor control, the 76489 is not accessed through the address bus. Instead there are two enable inputs and a status output, and the data itself selects the requisite register. There are eight registers selected by the second, third and fourth bits (D1, D2 and D3) of the data byte.

To control the chip's noise channel and the attenuation of all four channels requires only one byte to select the appropriate register and load the data. However, setting the frequency of the tone generators requires two bytes. A second byte in any sequence is indicated by a 0 in bit 1 (D0). In all other cases, D0 is set to 1.

If D0 is 1, then the 76489 interprets the next three bits of the data byte as the address of a register:

D0	D1	D2	D3	D4	D5	D6	D7	register
1	0	0	0	x	x	x	x	frequency 1
1	0	0	1	x	x	x	x	attenuation 1
1	0	1	0	x	x	x	x	frequency 2
1	0	1	1	x	x	x	x	attenuation 2
1	1	0	0	x	x	x	x	frequency 3
1	1	0	1	x	x	x	x	attenuation 3
1	1	1	0	x	x	x	x	noise
1	1	1	1	x	x	x	x	attenuation of noise

A frequency byte must be followed by a second byte with a zero value on D0. The frequency is determined by the last four bits of the first byte (D4, D5, D6 and D7) and the last six bits of the second byte (D2 to D7). Since this is a 10 bit number, there are 1024 possible frequencies.

The tones are produced as pulses from a count-down register, which means that the higher the 10 bit number, the lower the frequency. Nominal frequency is given by the formula $f = N/(32*n)$, where N is the clock frequency, n is the decimal equivalent of the 10 bit number and f is the resultant frequency in Hertz. With a 3.579 MHz clock, this gives a theoretical range from 109.33 Hz to about 112 KHz (far beyond the top limit of human hearing). A 2 MHz clock gives a nominal range from about 61 Hz to around 62.5 KHz. (Crafty BBC programmers might like to try to get at that 61 Hz.)

Frequency data is input in the following form:

	D0	D1	D2	D3	D4	D5	D6	D7
byte 1:	1	R1	R2	R3	F6	F7	F8	F9
byte 2:	0	x	F0	F1	F2	F3	F4	F5

where R1, R2 and R3 give the address of the relevant frequency register, and F0 to F9 give the 10 bit frequency number with F0 as the most significant bit. The 'x' means that the bit is not used.

Noise is generated by addressing the noise register − a high-speed shift register configured as a pseudo-random number generator, producing semi-pitched and apparently unpitched tones. If the sixth bit of the noise byte is 0, the noise is periodic (buzzes and suchlike); if the sixth bit is 1, the pulses are randomized, and the noise resembles white noise. Bits 7 and 8 determine the rate of the shift register and thus the apparent pitch of the noise. The available noise bytes are:

D0	D1	D2	D3	D4	D5	D6	D7	'pitch'
1	1	1	0	x	t	0	0	high
1	1	1	0	x	t	0	1	medium
1	1	1	0	x	t	1	0	low
1	1	1	0	x	t	1	1	follows tone generator 3

where t is 0 for periodic noise, and 1 for white noise. The shift register rate for the first three of these bytes is given by r=N/(512*n), where N is the clock frequency and n is 1, 2 or 4 for high, medium and low apparent pitches respectively.

Attenuation is controlled by the last four bits (a nybble) of any byte addressed to an attenuation register. There are sixteen possible values ranging from 0 dB attenuation (maximum amplitude) to 28 dB attenuation (minimum amplitude) and sound off. Attenuation values are simply 2 dB multiplied by the decimal value of the attenuation nybble: 0000 is zero, 0001 is 2 dB, 0010 is 4 dB, 0011 is 6 dB and so on.

Data is loaded into the 76489 by the following procedure: chip enable is taken low (0 volts applied to pin 6); the data byte is set up on the data bus; write enable is taken low (0 volts applied to pin 5); the ready signal goes low and is read by the microprocessor (0 volts output on pin 4); the microprocessor waits until the ready signal goes high (5 volts ouput on pin 4); write enable is taken high (5 volts applied to pin 5). This cycle of operations is now repeated for the same or any new data bytes. Each byte takes thirty-two clock cycles to load in this way; at 3.579 MHz this is about 9 microseconds, about 16 at 2 MHz.

Typically, two frequency bytes will be loaded first. If subsequent bytes have bit 1 (D0) set to zero, then they are used to update the last register addressed. This facility enables the six most significant bits of the frequency data to be quickly changed, thus allowing fast frequency sweeps, a feature used in the BBC's pitch envelope.

The output of the tone and noise generators is fed through their respective attenuators and mixed together. The final output is available as an audio signal on pin 7. This pin must be taken to ground (pin 8) through a 10 Kohm, 0.4 watt resistor in series with a 100 nF polyester capacitor; the signal can then be fed through an appropriate decoupling capacitor to an audio amplifier (the TBS820M or LM380N ICs are recommended).

On the BBC, audio output is obtainable from pin PL 16 on the computer's circuit board. This could be fed to a suitable amplifier or even to analogue or digital treatment devices. Pin 16 should be connected to ground through a 10 Kohm resistor, and the signal may need to be DC decoupled using a 10-100 microfarad capacitor and filtered with a low value capacitor taken to ground.

The 76489 requires a single 5 volt, 30 mA supply (on pin 16). The audio output level is not high enough to drive a loudspeaker without amplification. The chip may be turned off by taking write enable and chip enable simultaneously high (5 volts applied to pins 5 and 6).

Mostek 6581 Sound Interface Device
SID, as this chip is affectionately known, comes in a 28 pin DIL package and is considerably larger than the 16 pin 76489. This is not surprising, since SID

has twenty-nine separate registers, as against the 76489's eight. While the 76489 requires a fair amount of software to make it work, SID can be much more directly accessed by hardware. This difference is reflected in the sound features of the BBC (76489) and Commodore 64 (SID) computers.

The SID requires a clock pulse on pin 6, 1 MHz being the preferred value, and two supply voltages: 5 volts on pin 25 and 12 volts on pin 28. These DC voltages should be AC-decoupled near the chip. Pin 27 is audio output, a maximum of 2 volts peak-to peak at a DC level of 6 volts, which should be taken to ground (pin 14) through a 1 Kohm resistor and to an external amplifier through a 1 microfarad capacitor. The 6581 ground should be kept separate from system ground to minimize digital noise, as should be the two supply rails. Pin 26 is audio input (a facility that allows a number of SIDs to be chained together in a dedicated musical application), and the signal should be DC-decoupled through a 1 microfarad capacitor. The input impedance is about 100 Kohm, and the input should not exceed 3 volts peak-to-peak from a 6 volt DC level. Through this pin an audio signal can be routed via SID's unity gain amplifier or via the filter first (see register HEX 17 for details). Attenuation levels (as set by the volume register, HEX 18) affect this input.

Pins 24 and 23 are analogue inputs for the chip's two built-in A-to-D converters, requiring 5 volts input through a 470 Kohm variable resistor and a 1000 pF capacitor tied to ground for each input. The A-to-D converters then read the AC voltage appearing at the junction of the variable resistor and capacitor. Pins 1 and 2 and 3 and 4 require to be linked as two pairs by appropriate capacitors to enable the chip's filter. Preferred values for these capacitors are 2200 pF each. At this value (both capacitors should be as closely matched as possible) the filter has a workable range of cut-off frequencies from around 30 Hz to about 12 KHz. The maximum cut-off frequency is given by the formula $F=2.6/(C*10^5)$, where C is the capacitor value in farads). As this is not clock dependent, the filter − although programmable − works on an analogue process. All the other pins on SID are TTL compatible and relate to the chip's digital inputs and outputs.

The 6581 is designed to be interfaced with the 6502 family of microprocessors (the Commodore uses a 6510). The chip is accessed by setting chip select (pin 8) low. Assuming the clock signal on pin 6 is high, SID is ready to read or write data. In the Commodore system, chip select is connected to the eleven most significant bits of the microprocessor's address bus (lines A5 to A15) and is accessed by setting the address bus to HEX D400 (54272 decimal). Pin 7, connected to the microprocessor's read/write line, selects a read operation if high and a write operation if low.

Individual SID registers are addressed through address lines A0 to A4 on the system bus. They are active high − that is, they access registers when the relevant bits are set to 1 − and connected to the SID on pins 9 to 13.

With five available address lines, the SID could handle thirty-two registers. In fact, there are only twenty-nine, numbered 0 (HEX 0) to 28 (HEX 1C) and located at addresses 54272 (HEX D400) to 54300 (HEX D41C) on the Commodore. The remaining three locations are not used and will return garbage if PEEKed. Data is transferred between the registers and the system on the data bus (D0 to D7 on pins 15 to 22). These pins are connected to data buffers, which are held in a high impedance, off state for a write operation. When SID outputs data, the buffers turn on, and the microprocessor can read the data on the lines. The chip may be reset by taking pin 5 low for at least ten clock cycles. This turns off sound output and clears the registers to zero. Pin 5 is connected to the system reset line emanating from the microprocessor.

Of the twenty-nine registers, the last four – 25, 26, 27 and 28 – are read-only. The remaining registers are write-only. The write-only registers are loaded with data bytes from the data bus when addressed by lines A0 to A4. The read-only registers load data on to the bus when addressed by lines A0 to A4. In each case, chip select must be on and read/write set to the appropriate level.

The table below identifies the function of each bit making up the data bytes held in SID's registers:

register	D0	D1	D2	D3	D4	D5	D6	D7
0 – H00	f0	f1	f2	f3	f4	f5	f6	f7
1 – H01	f8	f9	fA	fB	fC	fD	fE	fF
2 – H02	p0	p1	p2	p3	p4	p5	p6	p7
3 – H03	p8	p9	pA	pB	x	x	x	x
4 – H04	0	s	rm	ts	tr	rp	pu	wn
5 – H05	d0	d1	d2	d3	a0	a1	a2	a3
6 – H06	r0	r1	r2	r3	s0	s1	s2	s3

(The next two groups of seven registers repeat these functions for channels 2 and 3.)

	D0	D1	D2	D3	D4	D5	D6	D7
21 – H15	c0	c1	c2	x	x	x	x	x
22 – H16	c3	c4	c5	c6	c7	c8	c9	cA
23 – H17	o1	o2	o3	oe	q0	q1	q2	q3
24 – H18	v0	v1	v2	v3	1	b	h	vo
25 – H19	x0	x1	x2	x3	x4	x5	x6	x7
26 – H1A	y0	y1	y2	y3	y4	y5	y6	y7
27 – H1B	w0	w1	w2	w3	w4	w5	w6	w7
28 – H1C	e0	e1	e2	e3	e4	e5	e6	e7

The symbols are interpreted as follows:

f0-f7: low byte setting frequency.

f8-fE: high byte setting frequency.
p0-p7: low byte setting pulse width.
p8-pB: high nybble setting pulse width.
x: not used.
g: gates oscillator on if high (set to 1).
s: syncs relevant oscillator with one behind it
    (1-3, 2-1, 3-2) if high.
rm: ring modulates output of triangle wave on relevant oscillator with
    frequency of oscillator 3.
ts: resets and locks relevant oscillator off when high; unlocks when low.
tr: sets triangle waveform in relevant oscillator when high.
rp: sets ramp or sawtooth waveform in relevant oscillator when high.
pu: sets pulse waveform in relevant oscillator when high (requires a non-zero
    pulse width).
wn: sets noise in relevant oscillator dependent on frequency setting.
d0-d3: set decay time for envelope.
a0-a3: set attack time for envelope.
r0-r3: set release time for envelope.
s0-s3: set sustain level for envelope.
c0-c2: low bits of filter cut-off frequency.
c3-cA: high byte of filter cut-off frequency.
o1-03: select oscillators (1, 2, 3 or a combination) to be fed through filter.
oe: selects external signal to be fed through filter (pin 26 input).
q0-q3: nybble setting resonance value.
v0-v3: nybble setting overall volume level.
l,b,h: set low, band or high pass filter or combination.
vo: turns oscillator 3's audio output off when set high.
x0-x7: byte representing analogue voltage level on pin 24.
y0-y7: byte representing analogue voltage level on pin 23.
w0-w7: byte representing level of signal produced by oscillator 3.
e0-e7: byte representing level of envelope 3.

(*Notes:* Noise waveform displays a pitched effect dependent on oscillator frequency. Waveforms cannot be simply combined – for example, POKEing 54276 with 48 produces a logical AND of the waveforms, which most often results in silence. Experimenting with combinations may produce interesting results, however; it is easy when doing so to set the test bit and lock the oscillator output. In general, frequency is given by the formula $F=N*C/16777216$ Hz, where N is the decimal equivalent of the 16 bit – 2 byte – frequency number, and C is the system clock frequency. At 1 MHz, this reduces to: $F=N*0.05960465$ Hz, which is a nominal value – especially since the Commodore clock actually operates at 1.02 MHz. Pulse width is given by the formula $P=N/40.95\%$, where N is the decimal equivalent of the

12 bit pulse width number. The gate bit turns on the attack cycle of a note, which is why the waveform register, which contains this bit, should be POKEd last in any program. When reset to zero, the release phase starts immediately; so to obtain an instantly ending note, set release nybble to the minimum value of 0. The sustain nybble determines a level and not a rate – that is, it sets the level at which the decay phase terminates and from which the release phase commences. In most cases, bits can be set independently and the resultant effect will be the combination of effects of setting the individual bits.)

Among the features offered by the 6581 are a high resolution for frequency, pulse width and filter cut-off controls, which enables many useful effects – frequency and pulse-width modulation, filter sweeps and the like. The A-D or POTX and POTY feature allows you to attach a potentiometer (plugging into the Commodore's game controller ports), which can be used as a 'note bender' or to produce a number of playing effects, familiar from modern synthesizers.

A low frequency wave on oscillator 3 can be used as an LFO (low frequency oscillator) to produce tremolo, vibrato or other less familiar effects. Channel 3 envelope can be used to produce filter sweeps and even, with a little ingenuity, something resembling keyboard dynamics.

The Commodore sound output (which can be found on one of the DIN sockets on the computer's back panel) is not suitable to drive a loudspeaker directly, but it can be fed into almost any general-purpose audio amplifier (such as the TBA820M or LM380N IC chips) and even treated by further analogue or digital means. A word of warning: the amplifier should be well screened and decoupled, and the signal may need to be filtered (by means of a low value capacitor taken to ground) for high frequencies generated by interference from the computer.

A number of manufacturers have begun to produce musical keyboards which utilize the 6581's A-D facilities to control the chip's output. With such an add-on (which could be designed with the aid of some experimentation by any competent amateur) and a real audio output, the Commodore with its 6581 can serve as a more than adequate synthesizer.

Appendix 4

Notes, tuning and scales

Note data as given in the BBC and Commodore 64 user guides may not be reliable. Individual machines are bound to display individual differences, however slight. Note values will also change due to temperature variations. Measurements sometimes reveal that the published note tables are not accurate; to some degree the complexity of the waveforms present at the output of the computers may explain this, since they include strong harmonics, which may affect measuring equipment. Since the user manuals already include tables, there is little point in repeating them here. Achieving an acceptable tuning is a matter of the individual ear and demands a certain amount of trial and error.

The Commodore offers the greatest degree of 'tunability', since the 16 bit frequency parameter gives a full eight-octave range with frequencies tunable to a degree below the limits of human discrimination. The lowest resolution (at the bottom octave) gives around 275 values to cover one octave, a resolution of about 0.04 of a semitone. The BBC's nominal resolution, by comparison, is 0.25 of a semitone over its five-and-a-bit-octave range. In practice, this doesn't matter too much, since the ear can stand a degree of inaccuracy, at best – but only at best – being able to discriminate a difference of 0.05 of a semitone. Slight detuning, in any case, can have an interesting effect.

The accepted standard for tuning is the note of A-above-middle-C (nominally, pitch parameters of 89 on the BBC and 28,214 on the

Commodore). This has a conventionally determined frequency of exactly 440 Hz. Middle-C is the note that comes exactly half-way between the bass and treble clefs on a piece of sheet music (also in the middle of a piano keyboard). Using this standard, the table below gives frequency values for notes spanning eight octaves using both an equally tempered scale (in which the ratio of one note to the next is 1.05946 or the 12th root of 2) and a just tuning based on A at 440 Hz (in which the notes follow Pythagorean ratios).

Note	Equally tempered		Just tuning	
	Ratio	Frequency	Ratio	Frequency
A0	0.0625	27.500	0.0625	27.500
A1	0.1250	55.000	0.1250	55.000
A2	0.2500	110.000	0.2500	110.000
A3	0.5000	220.000	0.5000	220.000
A#3	0.5297	233.068		
B3	0.5612	246.928	0.5625	247.500
C4	0.5946	261.426		
C#4	0.6300	277.200	0.6250	275.000
D4	0.6674	293.656	0.6667	293.333
D#4	0.7071	311.124		
E4	0.7942	329.648	0.7500	330.000
F4	0.7937	349.228		
F#4	0.8410	370.040	0.8333	366.667
G4	0.8910	392.040		
G#4	0.9439	415.316	0.9375	412.500
A4	1.0000	440.000	1.0000	440.000
A#4	1.0594	466.136		
B4	1.1224	493.856	1.1250	495.000
C5	1.1892	523.248		
C#5	1.2600	554.400	1.2500	550.000
D5	1.3348	587.312	1.3333	586.667
D#5	1.4142	622.248		
E5	1.4984	659.296	1.5000	660.000
F5	1.5874	698.456		
F#5	1.6820	740.080	1.6667	733.333
G5	1.7820	784.080		
G#5	1.8878	830.632	1.8750	825.000
A5	2.0000	880.000	2.0000	880.000
A6	4.0000	1760.000	4.0000	1760.000
A7	8.0000	3520.000	8.0000	3520.000

The advantage of equal temperament is that a note will have the same frequency regardless of what key it is played in. On a just scale, note frequencies are specifically related to the key, hence the gaps in the above table, since it includes only those notes in the key of A-major.

Keys and scales are important. As mentioned in Chapter 8, we can consider a mode to be a pattern of intervals and a scale a pattern of notes. Because ancient modes (Aeolian, Dorian and so on) did not use an equally tempered scale, mode and scale often meant the same thing. In other words, some modes had meaningful intervals only if they were considered to start from a particular note. Thus the Aeolian mode was and is a scale in A.

If we use mode and scale interchangeably, for convenience, we can simply describe some common examples by reference to note intervals (whole tone or semitone), allowing them to start from any given note. This oversimplifies the matter and assumes an equally tempered scale (it also ignores microtonality, in which note intervals of less than a semitone may be used; as, for example, in Indian music. The twelve-note system is often known as the diatonic scale).

The commonest mode is then the major with a pattern of intervals: W, W, S, W, W, W, S. This is typified by the notes allowed in the key of C-major: C, D, E, F, G, A and B. (These notes are all the *naturals* that exist. Sharps and flats are described as *accidentals* in musical terminology, and a key is identified by the number of accidentals it contains.)

There are two minor modes: the harmonic minor (W, S, W, W, S, W+S, S) and the melodic minor, which differs between ascending and descending notes (W, S, W, W, W, W, S-W, W, S, W, W, S, W). Thus C, D, D#, F, G, G#, B is the key of C-minor in harmonic mode, and C, D, D#, F, G, A, B, C, D, E, F, G, A, A# is C-minor in melodic mode.

Pentatonic scales include only five notes, typified by the five black notes, or accidentals, on a keyboard. The interval pattern is W, W+S, W, W, W. A final interval could be included in all these patterns, which would take us back to the start note an octave or two up.

Chromatic scales include all twelve notes of any octave. The interval pattern is then S, S, S, S, S, S, S, S, S, S, S, S. The whole tone scale allows only whole tone intervals: W, W, W, W, W (from C it goes C, D, E, F#, G#, A#, a scale particularly associated with the music of Debussy). The medieval hexachord scale consisted of the intervals W, W, S, W, W, in notes from C: C, D, E, F, G, A, thus missing out B and requiring a tone and a semitone interval to get back to C.

Any number of similar scales may be devised, the random composer in Chapter 8 borrowing a number employed by Jim McGregor and Alan Watt and using self-devised names, or names borrowed from modal music of the medieval period (which is more complicated than just setting out intervals). You might try using just tunings and a limited number of notes to construct composing programs with a degree of originality.

Bear in mind that the starting and finishing notes of a piece of music are important in determining its character and may dictate whether the piece is in, say, D-minor or some curious mode. For example, the interval sequence W+S, W, W, W+S may be written W+S, W, W, W+S, W if we include the whole tone to take us back to the beginning. Another sequence, W, W, W+S, W, W+S (including the last interval to get back to the beginning), could include the same notes, since it is the first sequence shifted left by one interval. The first might be realized by the notes F, G#, A#, C#, D#, while the second could be C#, D#, F, G#, A#. The first note in the sequence (as with the C in the C-major scale) or some other simply related note (such as the dominant in a major scale), which starts a piece off, then determines much of the character of the piece that follows, as it were, on its way back to the 'key note'. This sense of character is at the heart of the whole topic of modes and scales. A case in point is the Dorian mode, which, from the sixteenth century on, was defined as the note sequence D, E, F, G, A, B, C, (D) – with D as the tonic or final note and A as the dominant note. This is just a C-major scale shifted one place to the left, with exactly the same intervals but with a different character altogether. Likewise the Aeolian mode is just a C-major scale but starting from A (the tonic), with E as the dominant note. The Ionian mode is identical to a modern C-major scale. (Remember that these modes were defined on just tuned scales.)

The computer is ideally suited to experimentation with modes and tunings. As always, the ultimate arbiter of these matters is whether the result sounds good.

Appendix 5

Speeding up your programs

Speed is of the essence with many sound programs, so here are the major techniques for each computer to help your programs run faster.

Commodore 64
Integer variables do *not* speed up 64 programs. In fact they slow operations down by up to 30 per cent (only a matter of less than a millisecond, but *every* millisecond counts).

Use variables wherever possible instead of constants (the savings can be considerable). Keep variable names as short as possible (X or X$, for example), and use only as many as absolutely necessary. Arrays should, if possible, be restricted to one dimension.

Avoid repeating assignments (for example, POKEs to the same location). It is often necessary to keep track of a changing value (for example, PEEK(54299)). Repeatedly updating a variable for insertion in a program line is wasteful when the line can include the PEEK directly.

Drop all unnecessary REMs and PRINT statements, especially within the main body of the program. Concatenating lines using a colon saves about half a millisecond over putting two commands on separate lines. GOSUB and RETURN is quicker than two GOTOs, although both work out quicker than FOR ... NEXT loops. Avoid calculations within the main loop of the program, and complicated mathematical functions almost anywhere.

Eliminate spaces in program lines and use the lowest possible line numbers.

If you need more space on a line – say, to add another command line and colon – retype the original line using keyword abbreviations. In general, organize your program so that any time-consuming operations are performed outside of the main play loop.

The BBC model B

Most of the suggestions outlined above are applicable to the BBC. One major difference is that integer variables *do* save time on the BBC. Many integer calculations can be carried out using commands like DIV and MOD, which mean you need never perform any real arithmetic. DIV, for example, gives the integer part of a division, so that A% DIV B% is quicker than A%/B%, which is quicker than A/B if all you require is an integer result.

Concatenation, short variable names and packing lines without spaces also work; concatenation is especially useful on the BBC, since it allows such a considerable logical line length.

It is a good and oft-repeated idea to keep two copies of any program – one in readable form, with long variable names and numerous lines and spaces, and one with everything packed up as tightly and unreadably as possible. This is useful if you need to debug the program or need to remember how it works.

Index

L.L.M.E.
THE MARKLAND LIBRARY
STAND PARK RD., LIVERPOOL, L16 9JD

214

Micro-Music

string variables, 142–3, 151
strings, 68
style, 160
subroutines, 126, 144, 151–2
sustain, 68–70, 73, 187–92, 194,
  200–1
synchronization, 82, 121–2, 183–4; bit,
  129, 200
synthesis, additive, 38; direct, 15–16;
  hybrid, 16; subtractive, 38, 54
synthesizer, 12, 13, 14–5, 124, 125,
  135, 152, 200–1

tape recorder, 12, 151, 155
TBA 82OM, 197, 201
telecommunications, 13
teleharmonium, 12
tempo, 24, 28, 30, 75, 80–2, 93, 120,
  151–2, 169
test bit, 122–3
'TI', 82, 193
timbre, 54, 103, 124–5, 192
tie, 86, 151
time, 17, 28, 79
'TIME', 82
time, compound, 91–2; four-four, 123;
  signature, 91–3; simple, 91–2; waltz,
  91
tone generator, 195
transducer, 17
transistor, 14, 40
transitional phenomena, 95–6
transposition, 30, 57
trautonium, 12
treble clef, 204
tremelo, 71–4, 97, 131; arm, 190
triangle, 115
triplets, 159
trombone, 96
TTL, 195, 198
tuning, 9, 55, 152, 176, 182, 202–5

twelve-bar blues, 91
tympani, 123

UFO, 114
unpitched tones, 51–2, 110
'UNTIL, 135
up beat, 121

variable names, 135, 206
VCA, 14
VCO, 14
vibration, 10, 15, 18, 23, 34–5, 95
vibrato, 14, 21, 30, 71, 97–9, 187
violin, 35
Vocoder, 13
voltage, 14, 15, 24, 46–7
voltage control, 14
volume, 51, 65, 129, 133, 182–90, 198

wah-wah, 38, 129
'WAIT', 193
watt, 11
wave, pulse, 23–6, 29, 99, 104–5,
  192–3; ramp, 25, 105, 200;
  sawtooth, 52, 54, 105, 192–3, 200;
  sine, 23–6, 29, 99, 104–5; sound,
  15–6, 18, 23, 33–4; square, 24, 39,
  52, 54, 71, 111, 192; triangle, 44–5,
  54, 101, 105, 192–3, 200
waveform, 15, 24, 33, 44–6, 49, 51,
  52–4, 70, 99, 104–5, 126, 151–2,
  200–1, 203
wavelength, 33
whole tone, 161, 204
wine-pressing chants, Albanian, 169
wood block, 123
woodwind, 35–6, 68, 105
World War II, 12, 13
write, 198–9

Zinovieff, Peter, 16

215707

C.U.6a

This book is to be returned on or before
the last date stamped below.

2 4 NOV 1992

CANCELLED

-5 DEC 1994

1 0 FEB 1995

CANCELLED

2 3 OCT 1995

CANCELLED

1 2 MAR 1997

3 0 OCT 1997

HERMAN.   9 4 6 9 1

L. I. H. E.
THE BECK LIBRARY
LIVERPOOL L16 8ND